predic

2006 annual – **your guide to the year ahead**

Page 15

Page 186

design by Alexandra Bourdelon
front cover illustration by Annie at www.annierudden.com
world map illustration by Louise Willers

Page 173

contents

4   A TIME OF HARVESTING Forecasts
for society and politics in 2006

11   YOUR NUMBER'S YEAR AHEAD Find
your number and read your year ahead

Page 4

15   YOUR GUIDE TO THE YEAR AHEAD
Your 2006 star sign predictions

173   TAROT PREDICTIONS What the tarot
says about the year ahead

182   CHINESE LOVE SIGNS Do you love a
rat or a dragon? Find out with our guide

187   WORLD'S WEEKLY PREDICTIONS
Astrological forecasts for the nation
week by week

All correspondence to: Prediction Magazine, Leon House,
233 High Street, Croydon CR9 1HZ.
Price £6.99 from all good newsagents and bookshops.
© Copyright IPC Media Limited 2005. All rights reserved.
Distributed by Marketforce, 5th Flr, Low Rise Buildings, King's Reach Tower,
London SE1 9LS (020 7633 3333).

Published by IPC Country and Leisure Media Ltd, part of
IPC Media Group of Companies. Printed by Broglia Press, 52 Holton Road,
Holton Heath Trading Park, Poole, Dorset BH16 6LQ. Origination by CTT, Units
C/D, Sutherland House, Sutherland Road, London E17 6BU.

A time for *harvesting*

Numerology can give us a good indication of what lies ahead in both the political and social sphere. Here we predict what the year ahead holds for us all

By Daniel A. Stafford

*h*arvesting is all about what you have sown in a specific cycle. If you have laid a solid foundation and worked at it over the years, you can expect to collect a big return. However, if no proper foundation was laid and you have not followed through properly then the returns are not going to be as good.

First we need to look at the aspects that will be dominating this year: 2+0+0+6=8. In numerology the Eight is about harvest, money and balance. It is the most materialistic of all numbers and really relates to our lives on this material level. We are here to learn the lessons of the material life in all its forms. So this is going to be a year when we will find out if the last seven years have been lived properly in a karmic sense. It is not what we think we have done, rather whether we have lived up to what the gods expect of us. Within the Eight we have two numbers, the Two and the Six. The Two, the number of the current millennium, is about co-operation, harmony, partnership,

peace and love. People do not like to be alone under this number and seek partnership with others on all levels. If our approach is negative we can experience upset, breakdowns in relationships and partnerships, unhappiness and loneliness and loss. The Number Six is also about partnership, marriage, health, the home and family with some protection. If we are negative we can see the breakdown of relationships, upsets in the home and even bad health.

Astrology and numbers

Those with an interest in astrology will see we have aspects of the Moon (2) and Venus (6) in 2006 ruled by Saturn (8). The Moon-Saturn aspect will make many feel uncomfortable as it can suggest problems in partnerships and losses of all kinds, not forgetting the restrictions that Saturn brings to the lives of so many. Venus with Saturn will help to ease some of the pressure, but it will still be there to some extent. Venus-Moon will bring some nice experiences, especially on the emotional level, but we must remember, it is a minor aspect.

So on the world level 2006 is going to bring some major problems with the world economy, although these are already apparent in 2005. Those who think that things will improve this year need to think again and look at what is already happening. Underlying problems in this area will come to the surface, maybe as shocks, hitting the markets unexpectedly. Those agreements between the nations that have not been dealt with positively will come under severe pressure. The World Trade Organisation, the United Nations, the European Union and other large organisations of this nature will be affected.

Conflict in the Middle East

Areas of the world that are unstable will also receive hits raising the temperature, leaving many people wondering if we are about to face some major problems, the Middle East is the most obvious on this level. Whether we will be able to avoid major conflict will depend on how well our politicians handle these situations and whether they have taken the wrong approach in recent years. Politicians in all countries are going to need to put settlement and peace above their egos and avoid backing what appear to be vested interests. Being hot headed will be a recipe for disaster; give and take by all sides could bring about the kind of peace we all dream of. Settlements where everyone gets something should be the order of the day, but that also means everyone has to give something as well. If some countries dig their heels in over things, agreements are unlikely to be reached and we will all suffer as a consequence.

World money worries

The world economy is not in a sound state. The U.S.A. is still recovering from the recession caused by the bubble bursting in hi-tech in 2000. This recovery is fragile and not as soundly based as many would have us believe. They now have a housing bubble to rival the one we had here in the U.K. in the late 1980s and this can't go on much longer without a problem arising. South America is still struggling from the financial collapse in Argentina a couple of years ago, although this part of the world has suffered from endemic corruption for many years. Africa, you could call it the 'lost continent', is still a basket case and no matter what steps are taken to positively improve the situation it will be at least 20 years before anything really concrete will be seen. That assumes the corruption problem could be wiped out today! Governments around the world have contributed to this African mess by allowing corrupt leaders loans that went straight into Swiss bank accounts, instead of feeding their people and doing something abut the health problems, especially the frightening spread of AIDS.

Russia and Europe

The former Soviet Union countries tend to have work and employment issues, this is why so many of their people are seeking to come to the European Union. Russia seems to have returned to its old ways when the Tsars and their friends had fortunes and the ordinary people had trouble feeding themselves. Today we have reverted to the situation whereby some politicians have untold wealth through oil and other resources while many struggle to put food on the table for their families. No wonder so many look back nostalgically to the Communist era when everyone at least had food to eat.

The European Union is in a deep economic mess. In France and Germany alone there are 20 million people unemployed. The Euro is starting to lose its value in the currency markets, losing 10% of its value already in 2005. This will increase inflation and with it unemployment, leading to more complaints from the citizens as they see their savings disappear before their eyes. History students will see great parallels with the Weimar Republic of the early 1930s and we all know what that produced.

China on the world stage

China is going to become a more dominant player this year on the world stage, although its growing economic strength may be halted temporarily, especially as its currency could be devalued. This move might cause temporary problems but in the long term will increase China's hold over the Far East and eventually lead to world domination, although probably not in the lifetime of most of Prediction's readers. The U.S.A. is likely to hold its own for at least another 50 years, but after that China will dominate the world and if its actions in Tibet are anything to go by it will make the U.S.A. look positively tame! It is unlikely that we will see China playing that big a role on the world stage in 2006 in an obvious fashion but you can be sure that the Chinese will be extremely busy behind the scenes, pulling strings and encouraging those countries around it to see their point of view. After all, who is going to argue with such a powerhouse and its implied threats?

Nationalism on the rise

The problems within the European Union are going to dominate European politics and even world politics to some extent. Writing in June 2005, we see problems over the E.U. constitution coming to a head. The balance of 2005 and most of 2006 will be spent trying to find ways of getting this constitution into law, instead of facing up to the real problems within the Union.

The French electorate will only agree to something that deals with their fears over jobs and immigrants. This means no more expansion and no reform of the restrictive practices that have led to this high unemployment. So nationalism will raise its head as politicians will not get elected otherwise, then there will be the putting up of barriers in trade to save their vested interests. Even if politicians don't want to take this road, they will have little option as the only thing that counts is getting elected.

As already mentioned the Euro is a major problem, not just in the minds of the voters, but in reality as well. It seems extraordinary that already there are calls in Germany, France and Italy for the return of their currencies. The Italians wanting the Lire back leaves you wondering whether to laugh or cry! As the economic situation in Europe deteriorates in 2006 and the markets see the politicians arguing over how to get the constitution passed, they will sell the currency and we can expect to see the Euro devalue by at least another 25% as the year progresses. Yes, European holidays and breaks will become cheaper and more affordable, but more jobs will be lost and more arguments will arise with the blame game taking centre stage. The question is can the European Union be saved? 2006 will give us some very good clues as to the likely outcome. Fence mending and bridge building will have to go into overdrive to get things back

Some Euro countries will want their currency back

Do you want your future revealed – right now?

For a limited time, one of "The World's Most Documented Psychics" will provide you an incredibly-revealing 30-day "Reading" FREE OF CHARGE.

Here it is: Your chance of a lifetime – – and your opportunity to receive an incredible "reading" that could help you to discover eye-opening insights about yourself and what the future may hold for you – right from the mind of the amazingly-gifted psychic, Anthony Carr.

You'll probably be dazzled, spellbound – but mostly grateful – when you read what psychic mastermind Anthony Carr can reveal about you and predict what the future may hold for you -- next week, next month, next year, and beyond.

You see, there is a reason why Anthony Carr is considered by so many as one of "The World's Most Documented Psychics." There is a reason why movie stars, entertainers, TV stars, celebrities and other newsmakers put their trust in Anthony Carr. And the reason is this:

Anthony Carr "reads" the future. His accuracy – his uncanny ability to predict what may happen – is absolutely incredible.

Now, Anthony Carr is ready to use his remarkable powers to help you look into YOUR future – *without it costing you a penny.*

For an eye-opening personal report that may make a major impact upon your life, simply fill out and return the FREE Psychic Form at right. Then get ready to experience the most revealing, remarkably accurate Psychic guidance imaginable.

Imagine, extraordinarily valuable insights about yourself and about what the future may truly hold for you – right from the mind of The World's Most Documented Psychic.

When you return the FREE Psychic Form you will receive a detailed personal report designed to provide you with

extremely important advice – advice you should cherish ... advice that may help you find your way in life.

And this report, direct to you from famed psychic Anthony Carr, is yours absolutely FREE. (This is not a misprint, or gimmick, or "game" of any sort. It is totally FREE if you just respond on time.)

Why is Anthony Carr willing to provide you a FREE personal Psychic Reading?

Because Anthony Carr is held in such high esteem – because he commands so much respect and admiration from celebrities – he has been almost exclusively serving wealthy people. (Charging as much as $500.00 for a single reading.)

However, it has always been Anthony Carr's fondest wish to help as many people as possible. To share his "gift" with virtually anyone who may truly benefit from the unique insights he can offer through his celebrated Psychic talents. (Not just the rich.)

So for a limited time, Anthony Carr is doing something special – allowing people like yourself to obtain guidance from a renowned Psychic totally FREE.

Do this now, *without delay*: Fill out and return the FREE Psychic Form at right. Don't miss out on your chance to receive a personal Psychic Reading from Anthony Carr himself. Considered by so many as an amazingly accurate Psychic, Anthony Carr writes two internationally-syndicated columns...has written a number of noteworthy books on the subject...and his amazingly accurate predictions appear in famed

news-weeklies.

He has "revealed" the fututre of renowned celebrities (Sylvester Stallone, Richard Burton, Douglas Fairbanks, Liv Ullman, Dr. Benjamin Spock, Phyllis Diller, Jack Klugman, etc. out of his own curiosity). Anthony Carr has been hailed as a modern-day Nostradamus. He has predicted with uncanny accuracy countless highly-known events: the 9/11 attack on the World Trade Center, the Columbia disaster, the SARS outbreak, the re-election of George W. Bush, the death of Yassar Arafat, the death of Princess Grace, the crash of the Russian satellite, the $13.5 million lottery win for a Canadian couple, the discovery of the Supernova, the finding of the Titanic, the 1994 Los Angeles earthquake and much, much more.

Now Anthony Carr has taken on a new task: To help as many people as possible *who really need his help.*

This could include you.

Clip this Form and mail to: **Anthony Carr**, c/o J.E.M. House, Cranleigh, Surrey GU6 8TT

on track, but the financial markets will call the shots in the end.

The Middle East is likely to remain a thorny issue and in 2006 hopes of a settlement to problems dating back thousands of years are going to take true statesmanship on the part of world leaders and all the parties involved. If Iran decides to go ahead with reprocessing uranium to produce weapons grade nuclear material, then we are back to 'red alert' again in the Middle East. The U.S.A. may honour its commitment not to bomb Iran. However, with the Israeli government likely to face internal unrest over the removal from Gaza, an Israeli bombing raid on these nuclear facilities in Iran, as they did in Iraq some years ago, would bring the Israeli people together against a common enemy, whilst wrecking any chance of a settlement with the Palestinians and leading to further conflict in the Middle East as a whole. The Iraqis did not react, the Iranians certainly will. This is certainly a doomsday scenario, but one that could come about with the kind of aspects currently dominating our lives.

To avoid this world turmoil and find safety for Israel and Palestine both sides are going to have to make major compromises. The Palestinians are probably going to in order to obtain their own state with borders and safety for their people and the return of refugees. Whether Israel is prepared to give up some of its cherished dreams in order to have the safety they need, only time will tell. This situation can't continue as it is, so something will have to happen by the end of 2006. The thought of peace in the Middle East is a wonderful dream, achieving it is going to be something of a rocky road.

Rough with the smooth

2006 is going to be a very interesting year, some fireworks are going to be experienced both economically and politically. Sudden shocks on the world stock markets will be experienced and those dealing in shares and currencies will need to be extremely cautious. The more unstable the markets the higher the price of oil and gold will rise, with new record highs possibly being achieved as new worries appear. There is also likely to be extremes in the weather with some extraordinary storms and the possibility of another major earthquake or volcanic eruption.

With major disruptions and problems arising as the year progresses, health will hit the headlines. Whether it is things like the hospital bug M.R.S.A. not being dealt with or a major outbreak of something new is hard to say, but we need to be more prepared and eat more sensibly.

Those who act with understanding towards other and avoid allowing the ego to dominate and keep on top of their finances will sail through this year with lots of exciting experiences and progress in their lives. Keep an eye on what's happening in the world, even if it holds no interest for you generally. This information is going to tell us about the future and how bright it will be. ■

What should I do in 2006?

We all need to prepare for an awkward phase and this is best achieved in 2006 by cutting back on spending, reducing debts as much as possible. Finding ways of earning extra money and generally reducing your outgoings so that you can survive the sudden shocks that the year produces.

We need to make an extra effort to get along with the people around us and try to find an understanding with the people we have problems with. To dig one's heels in now will lead to major bust-ups and even the parting of ways, so we need to think carefully before we take up intransigent positions.

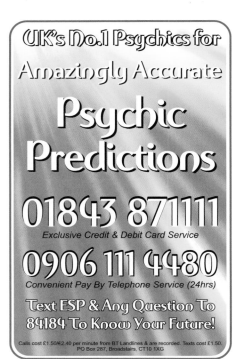

Your *number's* year ahead

Find out what 2006 will hold for your destiny number

Working out your number

Add the digits of your date of birth together until you're left with one digit.
E.g. 1/10/74
1+1+0+1+9+7+4= 23, 2+3= 5, your destiny number would be 5.

2006 as a number

2006 is the number 8. This is because 2+0+0+6=8. The vibration of the number 8 is a steady one with an emphasis on homely comforts and a hint of nostalgia. The year ahead promises to be a lot more stable than previous ones. Read what lies in store for your destiny number this year.

1

Number Ones can be rather driven, self-absorbed, and are natural leaders. This means that in 2006 you'll be forced to step away from the work arena somewhat and will have to begin to seriously think about your home life. Are you spending too much time in the office, looking for world domination? Remember to take time out to relax with your loved ones too.
Perfect love match: 2

2

Number Twos thrive on team work and will love the harmonising effect of 2006. The stability and emphasis on home life will give you much cause for celebration. Weddings may be a strong possibility, either your own or that of a close family member. Just be careful to avoid any stress that this may give rise to, especially in relation to those who know how to push your buttons.
Perfect love match: 1

3

Number Threes are wild and wacky. Your genius is in bringing together different people and you will have ample scope to do so in 2006. Have at least three big parties this year as you will find that you bring together a couple of people who will be so grateful that they'll give you some financial benefit, even if it is just use of their holiday home.

Perfect love match: 3

4

Practical and down to Earth, Number Fours can be relied upon to keep things on an even keel. This year will go down in your personal history as a particularly splendid one. You like things to be steady and predictabe and that's what you'll get. Lest people think that this is boring, you can easily show them the glamorous side of calm and collected!

Perfect love match: 8

5

Number Fives are very chatty and friendly and they can find a number 8 year somewhat boring. This won't be unpleasant by any means but you may find that you get stuck in a bit of a rut. Instead of deciding to make some fireworks by shooting yourself in the foot, you should try using this time to turn inward a bit and have some quiet time to rest and recuperate.

Perfect love match: 6

6

This can be rather an Aquarian number in that Number Sixes like to have justice and equality in the world. A number 8 year might seem a bit too nostalgic for you if you want to get your projects moving forward but don't dismiss this inward-facing trend as completely useless. You can learn a lot from the mistakes and successes of the past.

Perfect love match: 5

7

Hippy and trippy, Number Sevens are the loved-up ethereal pixies of the world. While some numbers may find the solid stability of an 8 year restricting, you are actually a lot more adaptable than you seem at first. As such you'll enjoy the rhythm of this year as much as the last and some of you may very well find that you have a child in 2006!

Perfect love match: 9

8

This is your year so enjoy it as much as you can. Number Eights are the steady, happy, stable members of the number world. There is nothing dull about this but you should be careful that stability doesn't turn into being in a rut! You will find the vibration of the year sits with you perfectly and, if you've been unhappy about your job or relationship, you may well find very pleasing developments in these areas during this year. You will also benefit from traveling this year, even if it is only for your annual two weeks away.

Perfect love match: 4

9

Number Nines are the real mystics of the number world and are highly evolved human beings. As such you won't find an 8 year particularly trying because you tend to take most things in your stride. People will turn to you for advice. Just be sure not to be kept indoors too much solving the problems of your younger siblings or friends — you need a break too!

Perfect love match: 7

Tell Robert Currey three things about you and he'll tell you everything about yourself.

Like you, your **Equinox Horoscope** is unique. And from just three pieces of information—your date, time and place of birth—astrologer Robert Currey gives you unique insight into your life. An **Equinox** astrological birth chart reveals much about you—your ideal career path: how others see you; the key to social, romantic, spiritual and material success, as well as deeper—and often hidden—strengths. Unlock the secrets contained in your **Character Portrait** to discover who you really are. With your new-found self awareness, take a look at the next 12 months. Our **Year Forecast** is individually tailored to your birth chart, and helps you plan your energies for the astrological trends that lie ahead. What if you have children? The **Child Profile** is a horoscope for babies and children up to 14 years. It gives valuable insights into your child's developing personality, talents and prospects.

Robert Currey

When it comes to your love life, our **Compatibility Profile** explores the potential for a loving relationship between you and your partner. Beside the central theme of love and intimacy, it helps you to understand and improve the quality of a close union by comparing both individual horoscopes.

All this from just three pieces of information? Yes! And even if you don't know your time of birth, we can still tell you a surprising amount from just two.

* If you don't know your time of birth, a special though less extensive 'Flat' chart can be drawn up.

www.equinoxastrology.com

Your guide

to the **year ahead** 2006

by Rick Hayward

The following section provides a month-at-a-glance guide to the year ahead for all the Sun signs, starting with Aries and ending with Pisces. So simply find the illustration that marks the beginning of your sign's forecast and read on to discover what 2005 holds in store for you.

symbols key

In the following pages you will see certain symbols to the side of the text, representing various matters that may have an effect on your life. These highlight periods when a particular influence will be felt most strongly and are therefore an additional guide to the prevailing trends in your affairs throughout the year.

THE KEY: Heart- relationships & love affairs. **£-sign**- money & material matters. **Sun**- health. **House**- domestic matters. **Suitcase**- travel & communications.

aries

march 21 to april 20

Planetary Ruler:	Mars		**Flower:**	Nasturtium
Quality & Element:	Cardinal Fire		**Animal:**	Tiger
Colours:	Bright Reds		**Gem:**	Ruby
Metal:	Iron			
Wood:	Mahogany		**Fabric:**	Wool

Your ruling planet Mars combines with a powerful solar energy to get the year off to a positive start. Your forward-looking frame of mind will be focused on matters of a very practical nature and you'll be more determined than ever to upgrade your status and material prosperity in the coming months.

A feeling of increased stability prevails throughout January, making you feel more confident about any restructuring you wish to push ahead with, particularly in regard to career interests, creative activity and everything to do with long range goals. Your sense of purpose will be strengthened as the pattern of events makes you realise more clearly your real strengths. You may decide to scale down in certain areas and to concentrate your energies on a narrower field. But the more realistic you are in regard to your own aims and capabilities, the greater will be your reward.

A combination of Mars and Jupiter make this a decidedly financial month! The main theme is one of tremendous progress, but you may need to curb over-confidence around the 15th when these two planets oppose each other. During the third week you are strongly advised to tread warily in any joint venture or where there is a need to make an up-front financial commitment.

It is also very important to be careful in matters of investment and insurance. Don't be tempted to go overboard if you feel you have a claim to make. The danger is that you'll end up with huge legal costs, along with frayed nerves. Provided you keep your feet firmly on the ground and avoid getting caught up in unrealistic schemes, you can expect to have steady progress.

Later in the month opportunities to travel and your social life will combine to produce a friendly and stimulating atmosphere. This is a prime time to seek out kindred spirits in order to exchange ideas and clarify your aims and objectives. Activities that engage you more closely in immediate community affairs or teamwork will have the gratifying result of enriching and expanding your circle of significant friends - and useful contacts!

At the slightest hint of potential clashes over financial matters, be ready to discuss issues in detail with your partner and work together to get joint priorities sorted out. There is a chance that your opposite number will be considering a moneymaking scheme that you know is a recipe for disaster. Be prepared to confront the issue, because it is material interests that could create tensions in relationships throughout January.

There'll be no miracles for lonely hearts this month, but the breathing space - and the opportunity to regroup it represents - will be more than welcome after a recent emotional assault course. Try not to dwell on the past and to enjoy the simple pleasures of singledom that your attached friends probably miss.

LUCKY DATES 1st, 13th, 18th, 29th.

Two major focal points during the month ahead indicate that tensions surrounding material and financial affairs over the past six months are beginning to ease. On the 17th your ruler, Mars, comes to the end of an unusually lengthy stay in the sign of Taurus. What this has meant to Aries people over the past six months or so is a feeling of running faster just to stay on the same spot. There may have been spurts of progress, but they've been followed by added expenses that put you back to square one.

From mid February you'll begin to feel that you have greater control over the situation, particularly as Venus turns direct earlier in the month, giving more than just a hint of a boost to your status and perhaps a lucky break in regard to career and creative aims.

 Once again the month's main theme centres on the practical side of life, but with an increasing and welcome trend towards a stress-free state of affairs. Efforts you have made over the past six months are now beginning to bear fruit, with changing events giving you greater scope for manoeuvering things in your favour. However, be prepared to bide your time until after the 17th if a major decision is looming over your current employment or career trajectory. What takes place during the second week will help to you get your bearings, but don't be afraid to seek professional advice if you have doubts.

As Jupiter swings retrograde soon, it would be in your interests to seek a settlement if there are any legal matters that need to be dealt with. Aim to get everything on a steady course, especially in regard to jointly held resources, investments, loans and important business ventures.

 Although you can expect the pace of life to gather a hectic and perhaps erratic momentum later in the month, you will probably welcome this trend because it opens up possibilities for variety and experimentation. Prevailing trends favour a change of routine late in the month, and no doubt there will be plenty of scope for travel as well as for developing stimulating dialogue with people you happen to meet.

Earlier in the month you need to be ready to bite your tongue. There is a chance something you say in all innocence may be misconstrued, and suddenly you will find that feelings have been hurt. If something is said to you in confidence, make sure you're careful to keep it that way!

Your energy and vigour will be up to their normal levels for most of the month, but there is a danger of nervous and emotional tensions building up around the 14th and 28th, or you may feel you are becoming a little overwhelmed by petty duties that must be carried out and commitments that must be kept. Do your best to keep things simple, otherwise you'll end up feeling resentful and crabby - and that won't endear you to any of your friends and family!

LUCKY DATES 9th, 13th, 20th, 25th.

The presence of Saturn in a creative area of your solar chart throughout the year ahead inclines you to take more seriously the potential for transforming spare time activities into something more professional. There are indications that you are putting increased effort into the development of creative interests, probably due to the encouraging influence of an experienced person from whom you can learn something valuable.

Saturn represents the presence of a mentor or guru figure in your life - someone that helps you to get in touch with your own deeper potential. If this has not happened yet, there is a greater chance of meeting such a person during March or in the months immediately following. In one way or another it seems that you are in the process of finding a new direction that gives greater depth to your own learning curve.

A marked improvement is a real prospect for the romantically inclined and the tide is at last turning for those who have been feeling emotionally isolated over the past few months. It might sometimes seem insensitive when people tell you that there are plenty more fish in the sea, but the fact is that you would be doing yourself a disservice - and missing opportunities - by clinging onto a relationship when the old flame has lost its glow.

An unusual and dramatic turn of events later in the month casts a decidedly idealistic aura around amorous encounters. Developments will be swift and may take you completely by surprise, but at last you'll begin to feel that the goddess of love is smiling on your cherished hopes and wishes.

There will be times in the coming month when you'll be whizzing about all over the place, keeping appointments, visiting friends and relatives, and generally being on the move. It might be quite strenuous at times, most notably around the 11th when there is in fact a danger of accidents due to hurry, but it does seem that this hectic state of affairs will suit your mood.

Important communications are likely to focus on private and confidential matters, bringing a need for deeper and more sensitive reflection on your own life and attitudes. If you're into therapies and personal growth, it's a time of increasing insight and learning. The same applies for those who take a serious interest in mysticism and the spiritual path. It is a good time to keep a journal, take more notice of dreams and seek out individuals who may be able to offer you guidance and clarification.

A Solar eclipse in your sign at the end of March warns you not to take risks with your health. Your tendency to drive yourself forever onward may bring you much success during these weeks, but be careful of overstretching your energy reserves and risking a state of exhaustion. A brief retreat, even if it only to the comfort of your own home, may well be just what the doctor ordered.

LUCKY DATES 1st, 11th, 16th, 27th.

Something that has been slow-moving or on the back-burner for the past four months or so will begin to gather momentum and occupy a more central place in your life from early April onwards. It's a time when you'll begin to feel the benefits of past efforts and the experience you have gained. Again the main focus is on the need to find a more creative outlet or expression in your life. Opportunities are likely to come via an older person or someone who is in a position of authority.

Until mid-month, try not to spread yourself too thinly, for it will be only too easy to take on more than you can handle or let other people exploit you. Stick to what's important for you, even if this risks the accusation of being selfish. If you're hoping to introduce greater diversity into your life, or perhaps get away from your usual routines for a few days, choose the latter half of April.

 You may not be going far from familiar territory in the first half of the month, but you will probably be clocking up a high mileage. Relatives are liable to lumber you with added duties around the 8th, so be prepared to lay aside your own arrangements, even if it is simply to keep the peace.

The pattern changes from the 16th when Mercury begins a swift flight through your own sign. Not only does this augur well for journeys and for adding the spice of variety to your activities, but it will bring you increased scope for dabbling in new interests, making interesting contacts, and expressing yourself with great effect if you are involved in debate and discussion.

Increased mental clarity will enable you to cut through difficulties, make snap decisions and get your message across. If it's a case of working towards an exam, now is the time to buckle down and get to work.

 Your ruling planet begins to stir up energies closer to home from mid-month onwards. This is good news for those who are aiming to make desirable changes, either a complete change of residence or improvements to your present home. If money has been the main obstacle, chances are that prospects will begin to look more encouraging.

All efforts and initiatives geared towards home and family affairs are more likely to bring the results you hope for. Watch your step, however, when Mars is at odds with Mercury on the 18th. This is when mixed messages could throw a spanner in the works in regard to a property deal. If you're a parent, deal tactfully with youngsters who might be feeling touchy around this time.

♥ Late in the month you need to be prepared to talk over an emotionally sensitive issue with your partner, family, friends or colleagues, rather than continuing to push it into the background. You're usually quite direct so this is a time to actually use that quality and have it all out in the open.

LUCKY DATES 5th, 14th, 20th, 26th.

One of the most powerful cosmic events of the year occurs on May 5th, indicating either a subtle change in your underlying philosophy of life or unexpected transformations focusing on partnerships and shared resources. Jupiter throws a fortunate aspect to Uranus, signalling a new window on the world and a feeling that negative influences hanging over from the past are finally being left behind.

The energies being stirred into life by these planets have their greatest impact at a deeper psychological level. Metaphorically speaking they represent a rebirth or renewal and a breaking free from old limitations. Events that have taken shape or are in the process of taking shape are almost certain to have a beneficial effect, not only on your material circumstances, but more importantly on the way you approach the world. All of this points to personal enrichment at many levels in the coming months.

Having Venus in your own sign for most of the month makes this a special time for romance and lovemaking. Something that showed considerable promise earlier but had not given the appearance of developing into anything significant will probably do a kind of somersault and, before you know where you are, the whole thing will turn into a deep and passionate attachment.

This is only one possible scenario, but whatever transpires you can expect something of the unexpected as far as your love life is concerned. Dates of special significance are the 10th and 26th, when Venus throws a friendly aspect to both Saturn and the mysterious Pluto. Those of more mature years are likely to reap the greatest benefits of these trends, although if a meeting takes place around the latter date it is sure to be something extra special. Don't be surprised if you find yourself strongly attracted to someone from a different cultural background.

A continuing accent on domestic affairs makes this a progressive month for making changes, going ahead with renovation projects, or employing builders, plumbers and other workers around the house. Take advantage of the unusually fortunate trends on the 7th and 8th if you are intent on moving house, buying or selling property, or looking around for somewhere to rent either for business or as a residence.

The emotional climate within the family circle threatens to boil over late this month, but better to risk a few hurt feelings and make progress towards resolution than continue to pretend that problems don't exist.

Mercury moves at full tilt through the money area of your solar chart between the 5th and 19th, giving a stimulating trend to all commercial interests or one-off business projects. But make sure that you watch the legal and official angle around the 12th if a contract is under consideration. There could be hidden concerns that you hadn't thought of within such a legal document.

LUCKY DATES 7th, 8th, 14th, 24th.

The key feature this month is the Jupiter-Saturn aspect on the 22nd, which puts a powerful spotlight on the way you occupy your spare time and how you approach the more serious longer-term interests and goals of your life. There is a possibility of conflict here, this being a time when you may have to come to terms with limitations and the need to make the optimum use of your creative and material resources.

In other words, this is not the time to let things ride, especially if you are aiming to put a part-time activity on a more solid foundation. Be prepared to take seriously the possibility of going solo, or perhaps joining forces with another person in order to further your objectives. Provided you have a realistic attitude to your own level of ability, then a successful new dimension could now be added to your lifestyle.

Although financial affairs are not to be taken lightly in June, there is much to indicate that existing problems will be smoothed over and that you'll have the necessary wherewithal to splash out on leisure, pleasure and luxuries. However, there are two dates when you will need to exercise caution - the 7th and 15th. Things may look tempting, but there is a danger you'll end up lumbering yourself with the proverbial white elephant!

Generally speaking, you can expect to find yourself on an easier path with regard to cashflow and should now have the funds necessary to give yourself and your surroundings a much desired make-over.

A message from - or chance meeting with - an old buddy may throw you into a somewhat nostalgic mood early in the month. This is a time for catching up on news and gaining information which brings clarity to a puzzle, for it seems that a long-standing mystery concerning a certain person will at last be clarified.

The deeper energies of your psyche are stirred into action when Mercury links with Uranus on the 12th. Again there is a harking back to the past, but this time there is an opportunity for you to reach a new level of mental clarity and integration within yourself. A phase of doubt and uncertainty concerning the spiritual or moral facets of your life will finally be resolved, giving you a feeling that you are on the right track. It's an excellent time for seeking out kindred spirits with whom you can discuss these deeper dimensions of your life.

Success in love will depend upon your level of inner maturity and your willingness to admit that no one is perfect. But if you have been running a love affair on the power of wishful thinking, this is a time when reality is likely to kick in with a vengeance! Be careful not to take anything for granted where other people's emotions are concerned. You can't dictate what they should be feeling to them and, while it may not make sense, you have to respect their take on the matter.

LUCKY DATES 3rd, 10th, 19th, 23rd.

There may be times when you find it hard to keep your act together in July, but provided you have a pretty clear idea of where you are going and avoid being sidetracked along the way, you should come through unscathed. The main bugbear is Mercury's retrograde cycle that is in force for most of the month. Be prepared to retrace your steps if a situation seems to be leading into a cul-de-sac. Chances are that you are looking at things from too narrow an angle or letting your prejudices get the better of you. Cultivate openness and be prepared to consider alternatives.

The good news is that Jupiter, the Greater Benefic, comes to the end of a retrograde phase on the 6th. If you've been plagued by legal and official matters over the past few months, or had to fight for your rights in some way, the whole thing will be resolved soon after this date.

The Jupiter factor has a direct and fortunate bearing on personal and especially joint financial interests. Here is where long-standing problems and disagreements will finally be resolved, leaving you with a lighter financial burden and a better chance to accumulate some cash. Someone closely associated with you - perhaps your marriage partner or a person you're in business with - is likely to experience good fortune.

Whatever happens, it looks as if you'll benefit via a close personal link, and there is also a good chance of boosting your resources through investment, rebates, legacies or sheer good luck. Indeed, with Venus throwing a powerful angle to Jupiter late in the month, don't be surprised if a lucky windfall comes your way.

Passions are liable to become intense and all-absorbing during the first half of the month. This may suit you fine, especially if a new amorous attachment has recently emerged. However, there is a danger that these passions will become overwhelming and end up turning into an emotional battlefield.

The Venus-Pluto opposition on the 14th could bring underlying tensions to the surface, but as there are helpful trends in the background it is likely you'll be able to weather the storm and break through to calmer waters. However, do make sure that you are honest with yourself!

A family matter you believed had been brought to a satisfactory conclusion may need further attention during the second week. Don't jump to conclusions, but if you sense that a youngster is having problems be prepared to approach the matter sensitively.

Once Venus moves into the home area of your solar chart on the 19th such tensions will fade into the background and the emotional climate becomes decidedly sweeter. Unexpected developments at the very end of the month may make impromptu celebrations at home essential. The rather wonderful message is that your family fortunes are now on the up-and-up.

LUCKY DATES 9th, 15th, 17th, 29th.

A situation may arise early in the month that makes you realise that perhaps it is time to move on. This is not likely to entail any emotional upheavals, but it will make you feel a tension between the old and the new. You're likely to become very aware of just how easy it is to get stuck in old habits. Attitudes, activities and relationships that were once highly relevant in your life may no longer be appropriate and may be restricting you in some way.

Provided you believe in your own skills and creative potential, this situation will not present any major problems, because it seems that the right doors will be opened to you and your instincts will guide you along the right path. But try to accept the fact that there are times in life when the forces of change and transformation can no longer be ignored.

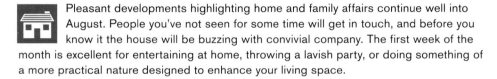 Pleasant developments highlighting home and family affairs continue well into August. People you've not seen for some time will get in touch, and before you know it the house will be buzzing with convivial company. The first week of the month is excellent for entertaining at home, throwing a lavish party, or doing something of a more practical nature designed to enhance your living space.

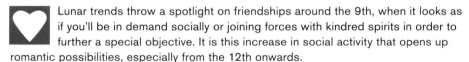 Lunar trends throw a spotlight on friendships around the 9th, when it looks as if you'll be in demand socially or joining forces with kindred spirits in order to further a special objective. It is this increase in social activity that opens up romantic possibilities, especially from the 12th onwards.

Venus, the planet of love, then begins to transit an area of your solar chart especially associated with amorous experiences, making this a promising time of the year for meeting someone with whom you could develop a romantic affinity. The high note occurs around the 22nd, when there is a decidedly fateful trend focusing on love and romance.

This has great significance for those who are taking a vacation or travelling a great distance at this time, because it seems that a change of scenery is closely linked with affairs of the heart. Also, there are indications that a newly established relationship is destined to stand the test of time.

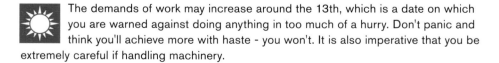 You are on course for a steady improvement in your financial affairs throughout the month, with a promise of something unexpected on the 29th that hints at fortunes changing for the better. With a powerful emphasis on employment throughout the month, this is an excellent time to develop initiatives with a view to improving both your prospects and earning potential.

The demands of work may increase around the 13th, which is a date on which you are warned against doing anything in too much of a hurry. Don't panic and think you'll achieve more with haste - you won't. It is also imperative that you be extremely careful if handling machinery.

LUCKY DATES 2nd, 6th, 22nd, 29th.

Certain contrasting elements may give you a feeling of vertigo at times during the month ahead, but at least this will present you with a sense of fresh challenges and prevent you from languishing in the doldrums. Relationships on all levels are brought into clearer focus, giving you a chance to make needed re-adjustments and set the record straight where there may have been disagreements in the past.

A key feature is the solar eclipse on the 7th, which falls in a rather secretive area of your solar chart. It suggests that certain hidden influences are becoming active at the deeper levels of your mind. Ideas that have been floating around are likely to take on a clearer shape, revealing to you that perhaps you are not making the best of your creative potential. This eclipse also means that any opposing elements in your life are likely to fade into the background over the next few months.

You will be drawn into the company of people who are on your own mental and spiritual wavelength during the latter half of the month. This will give you increased scope for airing your views, clarifying ideas and getting a different perspective on your current aims and objectives. The 15th and 23rd are good dates on which to seek professional advice on matters such as career progression or education, but also those of a more confidential nature.

Travel does not have a high profile, but it's likely you'll be hearing much from, or about, a friend who recently moved away from your immediate vicinity. There may be some talk of an important journey later in the month.

From the 8th the pressures of work begin to ease and your strenuous efforts over the past couple of months will begin to pay dividends. Don't be afraid to stick your neck out if a new job possibility comes up earlier in the month, but it is important not to give into the temptation to go for anything too adventurous around the lunar eclipse on the 22nd.

Avoid any risky ventures when Jupiter is at odds with Neptune around the 24th. Someone may make you an offer that appears rather glamorous and profitable, but don't let this fool you into parting with any up-front cash. There is a real danger of falling foul of confidence tricksters and charlatans at this time.

The lunar eclipse brings health issues to the fore later in the month, although this probably won't mean that you are about to succumb to any debilitating ailments. It is much more likely that you'll feel concern over the antics of a friend or relative who seems to be feeling negative and getting careless about their own well-being.

For yourself, this would be an ideal time to take a break, chill out and do something completely different. The best health tonic for you right now will be some time away from your usual routine.

LUCKY DATES 4th, 10th, 16th, 26th.

Now that the dust has settled you'll begin to feel more confident about pressing ahead with what is important to you. Over the past few months you've probably felt that the demands of other people, and life generally, were depriving you of a certain freedom to choose your own options or do your own thing. But changes are on the way, and before the month is out you'll feel that you have a much firmer handle on your own destiny.

The Mars-Neptune aspect early in the month suggests fresh inspiration due to the helpful influence of a friend. By joining forces with another person, much can be achieved, especially if you are campaigning or are intent on furthering group or community related projects. For the politically inclined and those interested in developing alternative lifestyles, this is your month, so make the best of it!

There are times this month when you'll be in a relatively privileged position when it comes to making money or improving your resources. Beneficial aspects on the 10th and 22nd ensure success in all joint ventures, and perhaps you'll receive encouraging news concerning an investment, legacy or legal settlement.

Delays caused by a long-standing battle with bureaucratic red tape will finally be resolved and funds that have been tied up will be released, all of which will give you a wider margin of freedom and flexibility in the way you organise your budget and forward financial planning.

Having Venus in your House of Partners for most of the month ensures harmony and a deeper understanding between yourself and the one you love. The trends are decidedly enticing for those who wish to take the plunge into matrimony either now or in the very near future. Everything seems to be flowing in your favour as obstacles melt away and existing doubts are blown to the winds.

For the unattached, the prospect brightens considerably, especially when Venus throws a highly romantic aspect to Neptune on the 14th. It's around this date that a chance encounter will turn on the light of love.

There is also a possibility that an affair that has so far been rather half-hearted or sporadic will gather a more positive momentum and revive your flagging hopes. Whatever happens, there is every promise of experiencing deeper satisfaction in this particular area of your life.

Everything takes on a brighter aura due to welcome developments at the financial level. Efforts to create a more congenial lifestyle and living space are more likely to meet with success, and anything to do with home and family affairs will come up to your hopes and expectations. If you're aiming to change residence, don't waste too much time thinking about it if something promising appears on the horizon late in the month. You'd be advised to strike while the iron's hot.

LUCKY DATES 4th, 7th, 10th, 22nd, 31st.

The pattern of events and experiences during this month will have the effect of concentrating your mind, intensifying your desire to change, and to transform things for the better. It is as if you are being given a new option, either to stay on familiar ground or break with the past and push beyond your horizons. This may sound rather dramatic, but in fact if changes do take shape you'll find that the transition from the old to the new will be clearly marked.

You have very helpful influences around you at this time, something you will notice in regard to friendships, and perhaps you'll meet up with someone who acts as a catalyst and steers you towards a course of action that is very much in keeping with your real potential. If you have felt life to be a struggle for some time, this is where you reach a clear road and progress can be made.

 There may be some minor problems to contend with until the 18th, this is likely to be something to do with the legal side of things. However, the underlying trend is progressive and particularly beneficial for those working in partnership. Interesting opportunities are opening up, providing you with greater scope and new incentives to boost your earnings or make better use of existing resources.

Throughout the year the fluctuations of your financial fortunes have been linked with someone closely associated with you - most notably your marriage partner or a significant business associate. There may have been times when your interests have clashed, with one of you wanting to stick to the status quo and the other wishing to explore new areas and take forward new opportunities. In view of the prevailing helpful trends, you can be sure that the whole thing will settle into a highly satisfying and productive channel before the month is over.

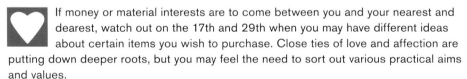 If money or material interests are to come between you and your nearest and dearest, watch out on the 17th and 29th when you may have different ideas about certain items you wish to purchase. Close ties of love and affection are putting down deeper roots, but you may feel the need to sort out various practical aims and values.

On a lighter note, a journey around the 21st may have an aura of romance about it. Someone you happen to meet on your travels introduces an element of glamour and gives you a feeling that you have met before. This may turn out to be quite literally true. Unexpected elements enter into amorous encounters late month, though you are advised to avoid impulsive and casual flirtation.

 At the end of the month your energy levels may take a plunge, obliging you to ease the pace and take seriously any warning signals your body and subconscious are sending you. Aries sometimes has to learn that always driving forward is not necessarily the best policy. Don't be tempted to ignore any requests from your body to slow down.

LUCKY DATES 1st, 8th, 15th, 21st.

Quite suddenly you'll find that wider horizons are beginning to beckon as the year moves to a close, opening up inspiring and exciting prospects for the coming year. Either through long distance travel or educational activity you can expect a tremendous enrichment of your life and personality. It is as if you are being given a chance to add a new dimension to your experience or open a completely new chapter in your life.

Whatever happens, it seems that you are moving towards a more adventurous phase of activity. It will be time to explore fresh options, either in the realm of ideas and the higher mind, or at a more practical level in the field of activity that brings out your entrepreneurial spirit. Altogether, a highly progressive trend kicks in and is likely to carry you far.

Jupiter has now moved into the sign of Sagittarius - another "fire sign" that vibrates strongly with your own. As your ruling planet joins forces in the same sign on the 6th, everything points to an upsurge of activity and a highly optimistic state of affairs. With the festive season approaching you'll be in an extrovert and generous mood, which may incline you to invite just about everyone you know to join you in celebration later in the month.

Travel is high on the agenda, so perhaps you will be suddenly inspired to spend the Christmas festivities away from home. If you do, it is unlikely you'll be disappointed! Even if you're not planning any major journeys this month, it is highly likely that you will find your mind revolving around the theme of distant horizons. The 11th is particularly auspicious for all matters relating to travel or long-range contacts - particularly if this has to do with immediate business concerns.

While it is unlikely you'll be short of funds this month, there is a real need to keep financial matters well organised rather than trusting too much to good fortune. The really positive news is that a fairly long-standing problem will finally ease its grip on your wallet and allow you to feel much more comfortable about splashing out on gifts and goodies.

The Venus-Pluto conjunction on the 8th suggests an unusual twist of events that plunges you into an intense phase of amorous activity. An affair that has taken place at a distance for several months will finally bridge the gap and make you feel that the Fates are on your side. With Pluto there is always a connection with the past, so perhaps someone you knew and were fond of several years ago will gravitate back into your orbit.

The goodwill and generosity of people around you will put you in an optimistic frame of mind. Christmas and the New Year can sometimes be a lonely time if you're feeling isolated from those around you. Luckily, for you, this year will find you in the right mood to welcome in the New Year!

LUCKY DATES 1st, 8th, 11th, 19th, 28th.

taurus

april 20 to may 21

Planetary Ruler:	Venus	**Wood:**	Cherry
Quality & Element:	Fixed Earth	**Flower:**	Carnation
Colours:	Green, Cream,	**Animal:**	Cat
	Madonna blue	**Gem:**	Jade
Metal:	Copper	**Fabric:**	Satin

Since late July 2005 the fiery planet Mars has been tracking backwards and forwards in your own sign and will continue here throughout the first six weeks of 2006. Mars usually takes only six or seven weeks to transit each sign, but sometimes goes into an apparent retrograde phase - which is what has been happening for you. The upshot of this is that you have experienced a progressive trend in your affairs and have been more determined than ever to achieve your aims and goals.

The retrograde phase may have brought difficulties and a need to do some drastic restructuring of the way you approach life, but it now seems that you are emerging from this stressful time and are beginning to feel that you are well and truly on the right track. All of this has been entirely due to your own initiative, courage and of course your proverbial staying power in the face of obstacles. You begin the year therefore with a feeling of well justified confidence.

 There is something decidedly fateful woven into the events of January, with travel likely to be a key feature in the general scheme of things. Dates of particular significance in your life are the 1st, 8th, 13th and 17th, when long distance communications and contacts are likely to focus your attention and stimulate your mind. Also, don't be surprised if you suddenly find yourself making impromptu arrangements for a fairly lengthy journey. These are certainly favourable dates on which to plan a future trip, whether it is for business or simply for the fun of it.

On a more mundane level, you're much more likely to achieve some positive movement and gain a satisfying result if you tackle any legal and official matters on the dates given above. Mentally you'll be on good form, able to see your way ahead clearly and make all the right decisions.

 Established relationships rather than new romances occupy the emotional field throughout the month. Indeed this is where the forces of destiny are likely to take you by surprise. Prospects are good, especially for those who are aiming to enrich their domestic lifestyle in the coming year.

Your partner is due to experience a bout of good fortune, finally bringing an end to the limitations you have been obliged to accept over the past few years, and your efforts to create a more stable base to continue your life together will finally begin to bear well-deserved fruit.

The only date when tensions may be experienced is the 15th, when Mars is at odds with Jupiter. A battle of egos is likely, and your own stubborn streak could well end up getting the better of you.

 It's your own effort and determination that will get you where you want to be financially, but watch your step later in the month when a career opportunity may not be as promising as it appears on the surface. Ask the right questions and probe a little deeper before you sign on the dotted line.

LUCKY DATES 1st, 8th, 13th, 23rd.

Mars finally takes leave of your sign on the 17th, marking the end of an unusually active and perhaps changeable chapter in your life over the past several months. In many ways this suggests an easing of pressures, a steadier pace, and a chance to take a breath and get your bearings.

Another important feature is your ruling planet Venus, which - from the 3rd - will help you to attain a calmer and more harmonious outlook on your life. This is a welcome trend for those who have experienced tensions with relatives or in-laws over the past couple of months, or where there has been a kind of conflict of loyalties in regard to friends, lovers or family affairs. Whatever happens, you'll get the feeling that the tide of events is back to flowing in the right direction.

 As Venus begins to gain a more positive momentum throughout the month there is no doubt that this will be reflected in the sphere of your amorous experiences. After an emotionally uncertain phase, the situation will definitely begin to show more promise.

It could be that you finally decide to break off a relationship that is obviously not going to make it, but this may also have something to do with a more attractive prospect for love appearing on the scene. Interesting times are forecast between the 23rd and 28th, when it looks as if very sympathetic links are being forged.

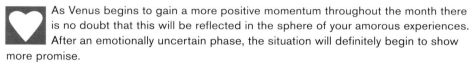 Unexpected developments on or around the 14th enable you to make new friends and influence people. Don't be afraid to take a different direction if you are engaged in group activities or wish to put something on a more up-to-date and streamlined footing. It's a time for considering alternatives and doing a bit of lateral thinking, preferably by developing a helpful dialogue with people who share both your ideas and ideals.

Travel has a decidedly pleasant aura throughout the month, and makes for a tempting proposition. If you're intent on taking a break, choose the final week of February, when the prevailing cosmic trend is good for your soul. Alternatively, this is a great time for browsing the internet for potential holidays and excursions for later in the year. And when it comes to planning pleasure trips, do yourself a favour - be adventurous and do something different!

 As Saturn is well established in the lower sector of your solar chart throughout the year, there is no doubt that home and property interests will be a key factor in your happiness this year. The full moon on February 13th highlights domestic affairs and signals the completion of an important project, bringing a feeling of emotional contentment within the family circle. There will be a nice feeling of having finally achieved a sense of peace and serenity so if you're planning a change, take your time, as there is no need to rush when things are going well.

LUCKY DATES 3rd, 5th, 15th, 25th.

There are lessons to be learned during these weeks and you'll be made very aware of how you often tend to sabotage your own interests by seeing things from too narrow an angle. It's a time to let down your defences, confront your emotional insecurities and - above all - realise that your real value consists in what you are rather than what you have. If you try to bluff it, friends won't be impressed!

Both Mercury and Jupiter turn retrograde early in the month, warning you not to get sidetracked from your main aims and objectives. There is a danger that the situation will fall into a state of confusion and chaos mid-month if you don't keep a firm hold on your priorities. Don't let other people make you feel guilty if you are unable to comply with their requests and demands. The fact is that you simply cannot be in two places at the same time.

The need to keep a firm grasp on things is particularly important in regard to financial affairs throughout the month. You have the dynamic planet Mars pushing through the money area of your solar chart, inspiring you to take a bolder approach in dealing with commercial interests and resource management. However, Mars is often described as the spendthrift planet, which is worth bearing in mind around the 11th when an adverse aspect with Uranus flashes a warning signal.

Although you are a careful person when it comes to money matters, there may be a strong temptation to fork out large amounts of cash on something that could turn out to be a white elephant. Be doubly cautious if you are thinking of buying second-hand vehicles or machinery.

It is also important to bide your time until later in the month if a major financial decision is hanging over you.

Your assessment of certain acquaintances is likely to change and you'll be forced to accept the fact that your original estimate was perhaps a little optimistic. If this means altering or pulling out of a group project, now is the time to lay your cards on the table. Basically, it's a time when personal differences will come to the surface, revealing that various ego trips have been the real motive for action, rather than a genuine desire to work with a team.

Jupiter continues to activate your House of Partners, ensuring emotional and material contentment for those who are married or have an established relationship. Although the retrograde cycle of this benign planet is not in any way negative, it means that over the next few months certain deeper emotional elements need to be clarified.

If you're planning to take the plunge into matrimony, it would be best not to dive in headlong, for this is a time when the waters will need to be tested very thoroughly if regrets are to be avoided.

LUCKY DATES 5th, 16th, 26th, 27th.

Early in the month Saturn becomes increasingly active in the lower sector of your solar chart, indicating a point in your destiny when a new chapter is likely to unfold. This may not be obvious to you immediately, but according to the most reliable astrological rules, Saturn in this area symbolises a new beginning. What happens - or rather what you decide between now and the end of the year - will set the pattern for the main theme of your life for several years ahead.

This is an important time for Taureans, not only because something new is emerging, but more importantly because you are beginning to feel more secure within yourself and have a clearer insight into your real strengths (and weaknesses). Saturn has to do with the laying of foundations upon which a solid structure can be built - a theme that especially appeals to the spirit of Taurus.

The Saturn factor puts a powerful focus on domestic and property interests, indicating a steady improvement in this area during the coming months. From small beginnings, which may seem rather slow, something positive and enduring will finally emerge. For those who are planning to set up home, buy or sell a property, the prospects are entirely favourable. It is also a good time to think about putting down deeper roots.

Venus shines more brightly for love and lovers from the 6th onwards, promising a time when your romantic hopes and wishes are much more likely to come to fruition. Not only this, but you will be surrounded by a decidedly friendly atmosphere, be more in demand socially, and will have plenty of scope for spending more time in congenial company.

Dates of special appeal for the romantically inclined are the 18th, when a Venus-Uranus conjunction introduces an element of the unexpected and sudden attractions; and also the 20th, when a friendship is likely to develop into something more intimate.

Don't take anything for granted, especially if you are involved in business and commercial dealings in the first half of the month. You may need to exercise fairly strict discipline, especially if you are working with colleagues inclined to get carried away by the promise of quick profits.

Wait until Mars leaves the money area of your solar chart on the 14th, after which financial pressures of previous weeks will ease and you'll be in a better position to use your budget wisely.

Information that comes to light later in the month solves a mystery, and advice from an older person helps you to form your own ideas into a clearer shape. Research and deeper studies at this time can be expected to bring you satisfying results.

LUCKY DATES 4th, 18th, 20th, 29th.

The pace of life may become rather jumpy at times, but it is unlikely that you'll lose the thread of your main interests. Mercury's swift flight through your sign between the 5th and 19th brings the kind of experience that keeps you on your toes and firing on all cylinders. There's also a need for greater adaptability and a willingness to improvise more than you are usually inclined to do. Accept the fact that there is more than just one way of reaching the top of the hill.

A key cosmic phenomenon is the tremendous grand trine of Mars, Jupiter and Uranus between the 5th and 8th. This means progress and a chance to make the changes you desire. However, you'll get the best results through teamwork rather than going it alone, and you can count on the energetic and inspiring support of those who are on your wavelength.

 Mercury's lively influence gives you a clear mind and enables you to come up with the right answers if problems arise or there are obstacles to be overcome this month. Make your best efforts in the second and third weeks if you need to get a message across, attend interviews or buckle down to studies. All activities that have anything to do with learning, teaching, publishing or the media will certainly deliver the goods at this time.

Towards the end of the first week, a journey taken at a moment's notice will be an essential element of important developments to come. You may not be going far, but it looks as if a major change in your routine will result from this.

You can also expect intriguing events centring on the activities of relatives or friends - all of which contribute to an unusually rich pattern of experiences during the first half of the month.

 An aura of secrecy surrounds matters of the heart throughout the month and what you hear through the grapevine concerning yourself could prove to be highly flattering.

Dates of special interest are the 8th, when events taking shape in the background may have heartwarming echoes at a later date. Also the 26th, when Venus links with the mysterious Pluto to produce a truly magical effect!

Mercury gives a positive stimulus to commercial activities from the 19th onwards, but you need to be careful not to be pulled too far into unconventional activities around the 26th. If you wish to experiment and try out imaginative ideas, wait until Mercury links with Neptune on the 29th.

There may be good news concerning your career prospects at this time, and it would be worth your while to inquire into the possibilities of upgrading your credentials. More qualifications could very well equal more money in this case.

For fundraising ventures and bargain hunting, you'd be best to focus your best efforts in the final week of May.

LUCKY DATES 6th, 7th, 24th, 26th.

If this turns out to be a challenging month, which is likely, you can take comfort from the presence of Venus in your own sign. A conflict of duties is liable to emerge, creating tensions on the domestic scene, but if it's a case of having to sacrifice immediate arrangements for long term interests, then you will just have to dig in your heels and weather the storm.

Provided that you are not simply being downright stubborn or riding roughshod over other people's feelings, this is a time when you have it in your power to give a much firmer sense of direction to your life. Again there is a suggestion of new beginnings, and if this means breaking up an old pattern in order to give yourself a clear space, don't allow others to persuade you otherwise.

 Venus in your own sign gives much support and will ensure that those who have special regard for you are on your side. A romantic attachment you established earlier in the year is due to take a welcome quantum leap to a new level of stability and fulfilment. You'll begin to appreciate what it means to have found a real kindred spirit, someone with whom you are able to continue to develop and enjoy a truly deep understanding.

Besides the more intimate dimension highlighted by Venus, this planet ensures that friends can be relied on and harmonious relations established on all levels. Also, if you are a lover of the arts and are keen to develop your own creative abilities, this is a time to cultivate contacts with like-minded or sympathetic individuals.

 There will be pressure on you to deal with important property issues during the third week. This may be to do with urgent repair work that cannot be put off any longer. An element of unavoidable disruption is indicated, although this could either be due to the fact that you are employing builders or decorators or that you're tackling major jobs yourself.

Whatever happens, there is much to suggest changes beginning to take shape that will ultimately improve your domestic circumstances. However, it is essential you make sure you are in full accord with your partner before pushing ahead with alterations and refurbishment, as there are indications of disagreements over domestic interests around this time.

There will be wider options for varying your usual routines by getting out and about, and the possibility of devoting more time to those interests you have been forced to neglect a little since the beginning of the year. Invites and messages received on the 9th or 12th will help to pull you out of a rut and find the company of like-minded individuals.

This month is a good time to focus your mind on enriching your circle of significant contacts and widening the scope of your communications. Don't be a shrinking violet when you have the opportunity to be the centre of attention.

LUCKY DATES 3rd, 11th, 13th, 23rd.

Three major planets - Jupiter, Saturn and Neptune - occupy pivotal areas of your solar chart, indicating that powerful forces are at work in the background of your life. Without going into the deeper realms of metaphysics, the main upshot of this is an increasing depth and seriousness in your attitude to life, a feeling that your destiny is somehow being woven into a wider purpose, giving you a greater sense of direction.

As Jupiter begins to gather a more positive momentum in early July, you'll find that someone who occupies a significant place in your life provides you with a sense of increased self respect and a feeling of being appreciated for what you are, rather than for what you have.

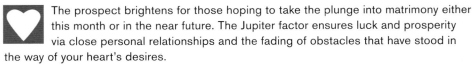 The prospect brightens for those hoping to take the plunge into matrimony either this month or in the near future. The Jupiter factor ensures luck and prosperity via close personal relationships and the fading of obstacles that have stood in the way of your heart's desires.

If your love life has been through a number of zigzags and bumpy patches over the past couple of years, you can expect something that will appeal to your need for a more settled period and less upheaval. However, the quality of personal relationships depends very much on your own inner maturity. There is no doubt that past experience has helped you to achieve a more realistic set of expectations, so thankfully this time it is unlikely you'll repeat past mistakes!

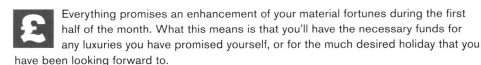 Everything promises an enhancement of your material fortunes during the first half of the month. What this means is that you'll have the necessary funds for any luxuries you have promised yourself, or for the much desired holiday that you have been looking forward to.

Basically, this is a time for self indulgence and perhaps enjoying a spending spree. You may also find that by doing something spontaneously generous you can make a genuine contribution to other people's enjoyment.

The only dodgy date in July is the 14th, when you'll need to be on your guard against shady deals and dishonest attempts at persuasion from those who simply wish to part you from your money.

 You are advised to doublecheck travel arrangements in the latter half of the month. Mixed messages are likely to throw your plans off track and those you rely on may leave you in the lurch. The bottom line is not to take anything for granted and to insist that those you deal with make themselves clear.

Provided you keep everything organised, irritations can be minimised, although probably not completely avoided. There isn't much to worry about as long as your head isn't in the clouds. One thing is for sure: a change of scenery later in the month will be everything you expected it to be in terms of fun - and much more!

LUCKY DATES 3rd, 10th, 27th, 30th.

Having Mars in favourable aspect to your own sign throughout the month puts you in the mood for adventure and brings added scope for expressing yourself via creative and leisure activities. It's a favourable month for those who are actively involved in sports, and you're sure to get a lot of satisfaction from any activity that somehow tests your physical capabilities and staying power. This includes holidays and journeys that contain strenuous activities that put you in touch with the great outdoors.

Powerful aspects involving Uranus at the beginning and end of the month throw your aims and objectives into sharp focus. Changes that have taken place over the past three or four months will now be steering you towards a path that offers you increased independence. With Uranus, there is always an unexpected twist of events that intervenes to alter the situation. If this happens, it is bound to favour your interests.

 This is an ideal month for setting out on a quest of discovery. You may be intent on fun and frolic via journeys and holidays, but you will find that something grabs your attention, pulling you into a more serious frame of mind. You might experience a certain déja vu, or meet someone who has an intense spiritual influence and throws you into a reflective mood. Whatever happens, the journeys you take will in some way alter your perspective on life.

 For those staying on home ground, it looks as if you're going to be busy from the 11th onwards, although this is something you'll welcome. The most likely scenario is that you'll be entertaining a spate of visitors, some of whom have been out of touch for years.

Taurean parents may be obliged to accommodate more kids around the house as a favour to friends who are taking a break. Things may get hectic, but all in all you will find the experience a whole lot of fun!

 This is a time when younger Taureans are likely to become more discriminating in regard to the company they keep. This is no bad thing, because it means that you get wise to time-wasters and hangers-on and begin to appreciate the value of real friendship.

If it's romance you seek, there is much to suggest a decidedly passionate phase of experience. The forces of attraction are greatly increased as Mars transits a very amorous area of your solar chart. But watch out for unexpected problems when this planet is at odds with Uranus on the 13th. This is where sparks could fly and a seemingly ideal romance will dissolve in an epic outburst of hurt pride. Watch out, too, for elements of jealousy and possessiveness that threaten to spoil an otherwise promising affair late in the month. You'd be well advised to avoid suffocating a romance before it's even properly begun with your desire to 'own' your partner.

LUCKY DATES 2nd, 12th, 15th, 22nd.

Being born under the sign of Taurus means that you are characteristically well attuned to the material world, but this does not necessarily mean that you are totally materialistic. As Venus is your ruling planet, there is also a strong artistic element in your personality. This is something that is strongly accentuated during September, when you'll have greater scope and incentive for enhancing and expressing your creative energies.

You do like the good things in life and what you always strive to achieve is comfort and stability. You are a good provider, and this is why people tend to depend on you for support. It seems that your greatest potential and best qualities are being brought to the fore at present, so it is likely you'll end the month feeling that you are loved and appreciated.

Not only does Venus enhance your creative abilities and enable you to enjoy life to the full during September, it also has the potential to work wonders for your love life. Whether you are seeking your ideal partner or simply wish to enhance the quality of an existing relationship, the influence of Venus will help you on the path to realising your wishes.

There are just two dates, notably the 16th and 25th, when the path of love may not be entirely smooth. A sudden break in a relationship is indicated, probably due to a clear realisation that it is not going to make the grade. Basically this is a time of truth, but it certainly won't be a bad thing if it frees you from an affair that's been causing stress.

Generally speaking, it does seem that your love life is moving into a more satisfying phase from this month onwards, so if there is a break it will be a blessing in disguise.

Occupational and career interests come under a forward-looking trend from the second week onwards, so if you feel it's time to make changes and haul yourself out of a rut, your efforts are likely to bring positive results. Granted, you are not the sort of person who relishes the prospect of change, but there may be opportunities heading in your direction that you would be foolish to refuse.

You may feel that your current work situation and career path does not allow you to make full use of your skills or is not allowing you to reach towards your full potential, something that has probably been making you feel restless over the past few months. So don't be afraid to take a few calculated risks should something interesting crop up in the latter half of the month.

The transit of Mars shows that you are tapping into a deeper source of energy and will be inclined to pay more attention to getting yourself into better shape physically. The efforts you make in this direction - including changes to your diet or exercise regime - will not only have excellent results but will also do wonders for your self esteem. Your ideal of beauty will be within your reach and you'll enjoy the compliments you receive as a result of this.

LUCKY DATES 4th, 11th, 21st, 26th.

Relationships on all levels are highlighted increasingly during the coming month. Several planets are activating your opposite sign, signifying a time when other people are likely to play an interesting and perhaps central role in your life. As Jupiter continues to be the dominant feature in this area, you stand to benefit through the good fortune and generosity of others.

It is not only at a purely material level that such benefits will accrue, but more importantly there will be subtle influences getting through to you at a deeper psychological level. What this means is that the ideas of certain people will exert a strong influence, inclining you to alter your views, take up new interests and develop a broader outlook on life.

 The presence of Mercury in your opposite sign throughout the month brings experiences that stimulate you mentally and gives you a chance to develop useful dialogue with persons on your own wavelength. Those interested in healing, mystical practices and experimental lifestyles are particularly favoured by the aspects of this planet on the 10th, 15th and 22nd.

On a more mundane level, October is a good month for tackling those pesky legal and official matters or seeking professional advice on areas of a technical nature. However, make sure you get all your loose ends tied up by the 28th, otherwise you'll be inviting further hassles.

 The energising planet Mars throws helpful aspects to Neptune and Saturn in the first half of the month, signalling constructive developments in regard to your main aims and ambitions. Once again, there is a progressive accent on matters of employment and career, with every indication of a quantum leap forward and a fruition of past efforts.

However, this is not a time when you can afford to underestimate your own capabilities, for success depends on you using your own initiative and utilising your fertile imagination at this time.

 Although your energy levels will be high and you'll be on good form physically, you may be feeling emotionally sensitive around the 7th. It could be one of those unaccountable irrational moods that most of us suffer from occasionally, but it might be in your interests to look into the why and wherefore of it. Be honest. If someone is getting on your nerves, admit it and don't bottle up your feelings.

 Surprising! Sudden! Dramatic! This sums up the pattern of events at the very end of the month. If you have despaired over the non-eventfulness of your love life in recent months, the situation is due for a radical turnaround as Mars and Venus meet in your opposite sign on the 25th. There will be some amazingly unexpected encounters that lead to pleasant romantic thoughts from that date.

LUCKY DATES 10th, 14th, 22nd, 23rd.

There is a continuing accent on significant others throughout the month, but with special reference to relationships of a more intimate nature. This does not imply that everything is going to be plain sailing, but it does mean that you are being given a chance to sort out underlying emotional tensions, hang-ups, or old bones of contention.

Much of your attention will be taken up with the affairs of other people, which means that your own immediate interests may need to be given a lower profile or put on the back burner for a while. There will be times when you feel put upon, but it would be better for all concerned if you comply with the wishes and demands of others during these weeks. You may not end up in total accord with certain people or situations, but at least you'll have a clearer picture of where you stand.

The presence of both Venus and Mars in your House of Partners for most of the month makes this a highpoint of the year for affairs of the heart. At best it means that your existing ties of love and affection will be strengthened and obstacles to your heart's desires will be overcome. The passionate and dramatic trends that emerged late last month continue into the early days of November, leading to unexpected developments and the possibility that there are yet further surprises heading swiftly in your direction!

However, there are a couple of very emotionally tricky dates this month, when Venus then Mars are at odds with Neptune. These are the 7th and 17th, when appearances could prove deceptive and your intentions towards someone could end up being totally misunderstood. If an existing amorous attachment is in need of honest and open discussion to keep it healthy and maintain good lines of communication, now is the time to face up to reality and clear the air.

Messages will be flying back and forth at a dizzying rate during the first half of the month, but this will probably be for an excellent reason. Whether it is business, your educational interests, community affairs or some other important project that is causing the lines to crackle, there is no doubt that much ground will be covered and issues discussed.

This hectic pace of communication will slow considerably after the 18th. Indeed, you will need to be more flexible in your arrangements because you'll find other people are more likely to be unreliable, forgetful and hard to pin down.

Jupiter's shift into Sagittarius later in the month points to an expansive and positive trend in both personal and joint financial interests over the following 12 months. What happens around the 24th will give you a good hint of what is yet to come, but be careful you don't let this lull you into a false sense of security - there could still be hitches on the road to success. As such, remember to save as well as spend in the coming weeks.

LUCKY DATES 1st, 10th, 15th, 21st.

Once again the main focus is on other people and how you relate to them. However, there is a shift from an emotional to a more material theme in these matters. What this means is that the influence of certain people will have a significant and perhaps highly fortunate impact on your fortunes. It looks as if you'll be joining forces with another person, either now or in the coming year, in order to get a money-making venture off the ground.

Whatever happens, the events of December will put you firmly in your natural element and give you a chance to prove your worth as an eminently practical person. Whether it is finance, business, property or longer term investment that occupies your attention at this time, your sense of proportion and realistic approach will stand you in good stead.

There is a decidedly progressive trend in financial matters as the year draws to a close. Not only will a fairly long-standing problem be resolved, but you stand to benefit through the good fortune, initiative and generosity of other people. If you feel that a project can be put on a more profitable basis by pooling resources or going into partnership, now is the time to take this possibility more seriously and sound out potential parters. Chances are that someone will make you an offer or come up with a bright idea that will enable you to put your skills and material resources to more constructive use.

Don't be surprised, either, if your finances are given a welcome boost via a large bonus, rebate, windfall or surprise gift before the month is out!

An intensification of mental activity is indicated as Mercury pushes through your Eighth Solar House between the 8th and 27th. This is excellent news for those seeking inspiration by taking part in deeper studies, carrying out research projects or embarking on quests for occult knowledge. An element of serendipity will enter into the situation, enabling you to make all the right connections and come up with the right answers.

Over the festive season you can expect to be entertaining friends who have travelled far to spend time with you. Alternatively, if you are planning to travel at this time, the experience will prove delightful.

There is definitely an intimate link between travel and romance later in the month, although it could also mean that you find yourself strongly attracted to someone from a glamorous or exotic background.

Interesting transformations are taking shape, and what you might dismiss as a friendly flirtation may end up as an ideal relationship. Whatever happens, it looks as if you'll be highly popular on the very last day of the year, surrounded by a warm aura of friendship and affection. You can look forward to ending the year on a wonderful high, with positive vibes radiating out from you.

LUCKY DATES 1st, 10th, 21st, 31st.

gemini

may 21 to june 22

Planetary Ruler:	Mercury		**Wood:**	Beech
Quality & Element:	Mutable Air		**Flower:**	Larkspur
Colours:	Sharp Yellow, Black & White Combined		**Animal:**	Monkey
			Gem:	Tiger's Eye
Metal:	Platinum, Aluminium		**Fabric:**	Cotton

Events that are as yet only indirectly connected with you are nevertheless destined to bring changes during 2006. You start the year with a relatively quiet personal situation and a feeling that not much is happening. But appearances will be deceptive, because it seems that there are energies building up in the background like a rising force, steering you towards what is potentially a highly productive year ahead.

An area of dissatisfaction has probably been looming larger since the middle of last year, making you feel restless and with a need to break free of something that no longer engages your creative energy. Basically, you will find that the early stages of the year will be a time for re-adjustment and restructuring. You may be urged to break with certain facets of the past as new possibilities begin to emerge and promise an enhancement of the quality of your life.

There is no cause for panic, but you may have to accept that it is a necessity you slow the pace during the third week. Mars is at odds with both Jupiter and Neptune, giving you the message that overwork may suddenly take its toll. Admit that not even the versatile Gemini can do everything, and this is precisely what you may have been trying to do lately.

The best way to keep your mind occupied in the first half of the month is to concentrate on issues you have been neglecting and make an effort to tie up loose ends. Projects that you began then laid aside half finished several months ago may be nagging at the back of your mind and something you have been constantly putting off will need urgent attention if you are not to fall into a state of chaos. Take advantage of the quieter trends to get your life in order!

Later in the month something that had seemed a remote possibility will become much more credible. While a journey may be a key ingredient in the situation, it could also be that you will finally see your way towards taking up a course of study with a view to further enhancing your career prospects.

Romance may have a rather low profile in January's astrological agenda, but what takes place around the 23rd may give a hint of coming attractions. Developments will move slowly, and there will perhaps be an element of disappointment or promises may be broken. Nevertheless there is something hovering around the fringes of your life that is sure to lift your spirits before too long, so don't fall into despair.

Choose to take action in the second week if you need to sort out a financial problem, discuss a possible joint venture or upgrade in areas such as insurance, investments and other long-term interests. This will be a time that you can take a clear-headed decision that will serve your interests for some time.

LUCKY DATES 9th, 13th, 17th, 29th.

It is the slower moving planets that give an indication of major trends, focusing on areas that are likely to have special significance as life unfolds from year to year. During 2006 the benign planet Jupiter occupies a sector of your solar chart relating to very practical matters such as employment. Here is where you are more likely to experience an element of luck and opportunity, greater job satisfaction, and scope for improving your credentials.

Generally speaking you will take a more pragmatic attitude to life, concentrating on essentials rather than attempting the impossible. What this may mean is a certain narrowing of your range of activity, but this will be an option you choose rather than something forced upon you. And as Jupiter is the key factor, it is this attitude that will be your main formula for success.

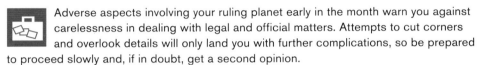

Adverse aspects involving your ruling planet early in the month warn you against carelessness in dealing with legal and official matters. Attempts to cut corners and overlook details will only land you with further complications, so be prepared to proceed slowly and, if in doubt, get a second opinion.

Travel is highlighted in the first week, but there are a number of provisos attached to this. Something urgent may crop up which obliges you to make last minute arrangements for a journey, and it is here that your characteristic flexibility will be put to the test. Later in the month a message you receive will have a positive bearing on career interests.

You may well have found it hard not to over-stretch your funds lately, but once Venus regains a positive momentum in early February any shortages should be made good. Progress may be slow at first, but an improvement to both your personal and joint financial affairs is forecast around the 14th and towards the end of the month. The effect of Venus will be an easing of financial pressures and greater scope for improving your resources and earning abilities.

You can also look forward to a significant development with regard to your career prospects and employment later in the month, which should also shine a more encouraging light on your financial affairs.

Venus is of course the planet of love, so here too the prospect begins to look more promising. Subtle transformations in your attitude to romantic entanglements and relationships have been going forward over the past months, maybe due to a difficult emotional experience.

You may now realise that it is not always the other person that is to blame if things go wrong or your relationships always seem to progress through a similar pattern or path that ends in grief. Love will always end up wrecked on the rocks if it is based on an ego trip!

The 25th will prove to be a date of special significance for lonely hearts this month. You may well meet someone that makes your heart go a-flutter so be sure not to let those negative patterns put a dampener on a pleasant situation.

LUCKY DATES 8th, 14th, 20th, 23rd.

The presence of Mars in your sign throughout the month brings an extremely dynamic element to all your endeavours and indicates a fast-moving time in your life. Events are likely to demand a high energy output, but you'll be feeling extra confident and will be able to call all the shots. This dynamic planet gives you tremendous support if fresh initiatives need to be taken or where there is a need to take the lead.

However, as Mercury moves retrograde for most of the month, any temptation to spread your energies too widely will work against you. Therefore make up your mind what is of greatest priority early in the month and stick to it!

 There may be a decision concerning employment and career hanging over you during the coming weeks. This is unlikely to throw you completely off course, but it does mean that you'll need to reconsider certain targets and ask yourself whether you are perhaps going beyond your level of competence. Be sceptical of those who promise you the Earth and a quick buck.

The tense aspect between Jupiter and Neptune mid-month warns you to stick to what you know and to keep things on a modest scale. Wishful thinking in regard to money-making schemes is bound to be a loser.

 After a slow and uneventful couple of months on the relationship front, it looks as if all nature of matters that appeal to your romantic instincts will begin to gather momentum from the 5th onwards. Venus then moves into favourable angle to your own sign, promising to work the right kind of magic and draw both love and friendship into your orbit.

This magical element is given a powerful boost when Venus joins Neptune on the 26th. A journey or perhaps contact with someone overseas may end up playing a fateful role in the development of love. It's an unusual twist of events that brings cherished hopes and dreams to fulfilment at this time, so be prepared for pleasant surprises!

 Apart from the amorous implications, travel is almost certain to be a source of delight, particularly during the final week when you'd be doing yourself a favour to get away for a short break. If you have not already done so, this is a special time to plan a future excursion or exotic vacation.

Take note of any suggestions that come from friends and keep an open mind for alternatives to your usual choices. Something that you had not thought of previously may prove to be a genuine inspiration.

 Slow down and chill out when Mars and Uranus are at odds on the 11th. You also need to heed the warning signals and don't let yourself be bullied into taking rash action that could end up leading to accidents. Keep your eyes and ears open and take extra care of your health.

LUCKY DATES 1st, 5th, 17th, 25th, 27th.

A key feature in your current planetary pattern is the transit of Saturn through a sector of your solar chart, focusing on the way you think and express yourself at an ordinary everyday level. Although Saturn shifted into this area last July, it is only now that you will begin to notice the effects. This trend will continue for another year or so and will mean that you will develop a more serious-minded attitude to life.

At best Saturn is a great structuring influence, helping you to bring a sense of order and purpose into your dealings with the world at large. It strengthens your ability to concentrate (which is always a good thing for Geminis, who are often accused of being scatterbrained). What takes shape in April will have the effect of focusing your thoughts, and making you reflect more deeply on the fact that perhaps there are things in your life that are really nothing more than a drain on your time and energy.

For those engaged in serious studies, the Saturn factor helps considerably. You'll begin to appreciate that nothing truly worthwhile and lasting can be achieved without a certain limitation of your interests.

You need to accept the fact that you cannot do everything. However, there are certain items on your agenda that could be improved considerably by narrowing your field of vision - at least for the time being.

During the latter half of the month, Mercury (your ruler) signals an enrichment of social activities and offers you a chance to play a more purposeful role in group activities or community affairs. It's a time when new friends will gravitate into your orbit and stimulate your mind. Whatever your main area of interest, this will be greatly helped by cultivating contact with individuals or groups who are on your wavelength.

The Mars-Pluto opposition on April 8th signals a danger of ending up at loggerheads with your partner. Issues with the potential to cause conflict - but that have been pushed out of sight - will begin to generate tensions and you may need to come to terms with something that happened long ago. At best, this presents you with an ideal opportunity to establish a much deeper and meaningful understanding with your nearest and dearest.

New romantic encounters are likely to take shape in a rather unromantic setting later in the month. A likely scenario is that your place of work will be where it all begins to happen!

Towards the end of the month you are likely to get the lucky break you have been hoping for in regard to your career prospects or advancement within your current job. A splendid combination of Venus and Jupiter will smooth your path to success and enable you to exert a positive influence on those in a position to further your aims and ambitions. You'll find it easy to impress, so take the opportunity to speak to those higher-ups that are usually out of your sphere of influence.

LUCKY DATES 4th, 8th, 20th, 26th.

Events will incline you to increase the amount of energy given to the improvement of your material resources during these weeks. The onus is very much on you to make the most of current opportunities, and this is where your inborn quickness of wit and ingenuity will enable you to steal a march on any competitors.

It is towards the end of the first week that something unexpected is likely to present you with a major decision, with the main focus on current occupational or career interests. Uranus, the planet of inspiration and originality, is the ruling factor in the prevailing cosmic picture, signalling a need to change direction and to strike out in a more independent manner.

In view of the powerful accent on practical and material affairs, there is no doubt that financial matters will be the main focus of your attention this month – particularly around the 7th. If you have been working towards a certain goal in recent years but have not been feeling confident about raising your aims with a view to seeing it through to a conclusion, now is the time when you are likely to get the break you've been hoping for.

This is one of the best times in the year for making important purchases, particularly of machinery, technical equipment and automobiles. If you're intent on streamlining and updating a business project, now is the time to take the initiative.

If work and other practical demands have been getting in the way of your love life recently, a more inviting prospect begins to beckon as the month progresses. And it is not only romantic hopes and wishes that lay under a benign sky. It's a time when your social spectrum presents a more varied picture, when friends gravitate into your circle and you begin to feel that other people genuinely appreciate you for what you are and not only for what you know.

Dates of special significance for romantic encounters are the 8th, 24th and 26th. As Pluto and Saturn are much in evidence, you will get the feeling that the Fates are taking a hand in these matters and moving in mysterious ways!

The speedy flight of your ruling planet throughout the month helps to give a sharper focus to your thoughts and should allow you a clearer view of what could be a rather changeable phase in your life. Matters of a private and confidential nature will occupy your attention between the 12th and 16th, and if something has been causing you worry and uneasiness, a sympathetic friend is likely to be a saving grace around this time.

Once Mercury enters your own sign on the 19th, you can expect the pace of life to gain a satisfyingly brisk momentum, allowing you ample scope for expressing your diverse range of talents. This is a terrific time for getting out and about, as your famous gift of the gab will be much in evidence.

LUCKY DATES 5th, 12th, 18th, 29th.

Early June is when your past is liable to catch up with you! However, don't panic, because it could be that efforts you made long ago will find an ideal outlet for expression, giving you the feeling that you have not wasted your time after all. There may also be an element of unfinished business to contend with during the first week, but it would be unwise to jump to conclusions or let yourself be drawn into a situation that, to you, is over and done with.

Events are likely to concentrate around the third week, when certain duties are likely to heaped upon your shoulders. Be prepared to make some sacrifices if relatives or others demand your assistance. Also, don't simply dismiss what an older person tells you as being old hat and out of date. This apparent criticism will turn out to be words of wisdom.

You might not be going too far from home, but you'll be clocking up a high mileage in many local excursions throughout the month. Things could get hectic at times, but this is the kind of scenario that usually appeals to the Gemini temperament. The only time when things could become onerous is in the third week, when you will be obliged to shelve your own immediate arrangements for something urgent that crops up in connection with a relative or neighbour.

There is in fact a health warning when Mars and Saturn form a conjunction on the 18th, but you can minimise the potential for accidents and injuries by taking the time not to hurry. It will be only too easy to strain your nerves or your muscles, which could have a negative effect on what you had planned to do later on in the month. You should be prepared to help out if someone is having difficulties due to poor health during the third week.

Mercury, your ruling planet, brings a lively trend to financial affairs for most of the month. Generally speaking this is good news, particularly if you are aiming to diversify your earning capacities. It's an excellent time to organise a fundraising venture, attend car boot sales, or get a good deal on a part-exchange or something you wish to sell privately.

Dates of special significance are the 9th, when good news can be expected regarding your work situation; the 12th, when something unexpected enables you to boost your funds; and the 27th, which is simply a good date for shopping around.

A secret admirer is likely to come out into the open when Venus moves into your sign later in the month. This could be a delicious surprise in that the interest may come from someone you are keen on. Either way, there is bound to be something taking shape that flatters your ego and makes you feel good, and what you had long hoped for will at last become a reality.

LUCKY DATES 8th, 9th, 12th, 27th.

The presence of Venus in your sign helps you to relax and take things in your stride. In view of the fact that the pace of your life will threaten to go into overdrive at times, this calming influence will help you to keep you from going off the rails. It won't be until after the 22nd that the pace begins to ease, giving you a necessary breathing space and a chance to pick up where you left off several weeks earlier.

The good news is that Jupiter turns direct on the 6th, signalling the end of a difficult transition in regard to your work or career trajectory. Not only will you begin to feel more confident about making an important decision, but it is more likely that events will contrive to favour your interests and steer you in the right direction.

Be prepared to rethink various angles of your current financial strategies after the 10th. Just when you thought everything was on course for success, something is likely to put an obstacle in your path. But don't panic, as this is only a temporary blip and will probably be sorted out later in the month.

Favourable aspects to Venus in the final days of July signal something unexpected in the way of extra cash on the way. There's a chance that your financial situation will receive a boost via a bonus, rebate or lucky win. The indications are that you'll be in the mood for spending, but in the meantime it's best to stick to what you know rather than attempting any clever stuff.

For those travelling far and wide early in the month, there is a small warning about possible delays and confusions. Mars and Neptune are in stressful aspect, so don't take anything for granted in regard to schedules and itinerary. Don't be surprised if you have to make a rather convoluted detour in order to get to your desired final destination.

The latter half of the month gives a brighter prospect for globetrotters and holiday makers. But with Mercury throwing an uncertain note on finances, be on your guard against theft, and don't be surprised if expenses are higher than anticipated.

So far this year domestic affairs have been very much in the background, and maybe there has been a tendency to overlook or neglect this aspect of your life. However, when Mars pushes into the lower sector of your solar chart on the 22nd, your attention will be focused more on the things that give you a feeling of security.

You'll be more strongly motivated to upgrade your living space and more inclined to tackle jobs that have seemed a little too daunting in the past. If you're not a DIY buff, this is an excellent time to employ workers within the home. Improvements made at this time will go well and add value to your home.

If you're thinking of pulling up roots altogether and moving to a more congenial abode, now is a great opportunity to get the ball rolling.

LUCKY DATES 3rd, 13th, 23rd, 29th.

The lunation at the beginning of the month strongly activates Jupiter, giving you the green light for fresh initiatives that have to do with employment and the need for greater job satisfaction. This is the area of your life that is most likely to make you feel optimistic, for this is a time of increased opportunity and greater incentive to expand your range of rewarding activities.

Psychologically, this beneficial trend gives you a greater sense of self value and ensures that underlying anxieties bring a sense of increased mental and physical fitness. The highpoint comes when Jupiter throws a powerful aspect to Uranus later in the month. You can expect the unexpected, and what occurs could solve several problems in one fell swoop!

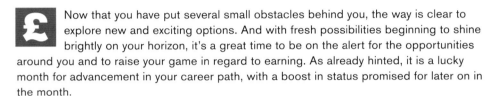 Now that you have put several small obstacles behind you, the way is clear to explore new and exciting options. And with fresh possibilities beginning to shine brightly on your horizon, it's a great time to be on the alert for the opportunities around you and to raise your game in regard to earning. As already hinted, it is a lucky month for advancement in your career path, with a boost in status promised for later on in the month.

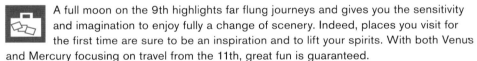 A full moon on the 9th highlights far flung journeys and gives you the sensitivity and imagination to enjoy fully a change of scenery. Indeed, places you visit for the first time are sure to be an inspiration and to lift your spirits. With both Venus and Mercury focusing on travel from the 11th, great fun is guaranteed.

If your reasons for travel have a more serious intention, for instance a quest for knowledge or a voyage of discovery, then you cannot fail to find what you are seeking. Also there does appear to be an element of serendipity connected with a journey. You may meet an old friend or someone who quite by chance shifts your mind onto a new and different wavelength.

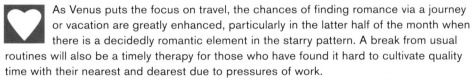 As Venus puts the focus on travel, the chances of finding romance via a journey or vacation are greatly enhanced, particularly in the latter half of the month when there is a decidedly romantic element in the starry pattern. A break from usual routines will also be a timely therapy for those who have found it hard to cultivate quality time with their nearest and dearest due to pressures of work.

There's a fateful trend in force between the 22nd and 26th when prevailing trends favour those of more mature years who are in search of love and friendship. Again, it is a change of scenery that could work the appropriate magic!

 When it comes to your health this month, you don't have too much to worry about. However, with travel on the menu, be sure to exercise caution if you are intent on tasting the exotic culinary delights on offer on your journeys! You don't have to be unadventurous, just a little careful.

LUCKY DATES 3rd, 12th, 22nd, 24th.

A strongly activated Pluto early in the month marks the beginning of a transformation in the sphere of relationships. This does not only apply to intimate ties of affection, but more generally to the way you relate to any significant persons in your life. Your attitude is undergoing a subtle shift of emphasis over the next few months, probably due to the powerful influence of another person.

There is always something fateful and mysterious about the workings of this outer planet, but what it usually brings is an emergence of new energies and new directions. Being in your opposite sign it is likely that someone you meet will change your life and enable you to break free of old habits and routines that other people may have imposed upon you in the past.

 It is significant that Venus forms a favourable angle with Pluto at the start of the month, so there is no doubt that intriguing romantic developments can be expected. Pluto can be rather drastic in action, signalling a meeting with someone you find instantaneously attractive. Passions are liable to run deep and intense, but in view of the pattern of planets this is unlikely to take you out of your depth.

Dates when you may experience tensions in your love life are the 15th and 23rd. Here is where you need to tread tactfully, curb flirtatious impulses, and be careful not to dabble with an emotional situation that you know you can't handle.

 The eclipses on the 7th and 22nd point towards a level of restructuring in your domestic affairs between now and the end of the year. This is likely to link in with new developments regarding your work and career. The possibility of working in a different part of the country or abroad will loom large, which might entail careful thought and a certain uprooting.

However, the prospects are good and the time is ripe, so if you're looking for this kind of change and are feeling adventurous, you can go ahead knowing you have everything going for you astrologically.

 Your creative energies are being stirred into greater activity during these weeks, as spare time interests begin to occupy more of your time and attention. The social life elements of your life become interesting too, bringing you in touch with people who are likely to stimulate your mind and encourage you to get more seriously involved in various extra-curricular activities. You may well take an interest and turn it into a passion through greater involvement in a club or social scene.

Those with a passion for taking part in sports have a good month ahead, but make your best efforts when Mars begins to transit a helpful area of your solar chart from the 8th onwards. Key dates are the 15th, 23rd and 24th, when those involved at a fairly competitive level are likely to score a decisive triumph. All interests that engage your creative ability - in the arts, entertainment, and media - will bring you satisfaction as well as popularity at this time.

LUCKY DATES 3rd, 12th, 23rd, 24th.

A powerful combination of Mars, the Sun and Neptune during the first half of the month make this a truly inspiring time for those born under Gemini. The key focus is on your creative energies, your will to express yourself and your desire to find a direction in which your true potential can be realised. Venus, too, comes under the inspiring influence of Neptune, promising an unusually satisfying state of affairs for those involved in the arts and the more glamourous professions.

Neptune is again highlighted at the very end of the month, generating a dreamy and mystical aura around you. At the very best, Neptune always puts a strong focus on our cherished dreams, ideals and the deeper spiritual elements of the psyche. What it means is that the events of October will help you to transform those dreams and ideals into realities.

 This month's unusual combination of planets has special significance for romantic and intimate relationships. Although there is a danger you may end up getting carried away by fantasies while Neptune is dominating the field, it looks as if you will experience the better side of this planet during October.

It is as if a completely new window of the world is about to open, due to the arrival of someone who is destined to play an important part in your life.

You will find yourself becoming increasingly sensitive to the effect you have on other people's emotions, and perhaps you will begin to see much more clearly why a previous love affair didn't work out to your satisfaction. This increasing self awareness will enable you to understand and break through emotional habit patterns that have sabotaged your love life in the past. And the more open you are to self-change, the happier you will be in the long run.

 Apart from some confusion over a work assignment mid-month, you can expect to make good progress in anything that directly or indirectly affects your financial situation in the coming month. However, if you really are intent on making changes or striking out in a more independent direction, you'd be best to make your efforts after the 24th.

In the meantime, do your homework and make sure you have weighed all the pros and cons very carefully before making a definite commitment.

No one will be able to accuse you of being a typical scatterbrained Gemini in October. A helpful transit of Mercury (your ruler) ensures excellent focus and concentration, along with a more orderly and methodical approach to dealing with practical affairs. If some disagreement arises at work on the 15th, it could be that either you or a close colleague is not being entirely honest and may be indulging in a bit of wishful thinking. Try to get clear about what are facts and what are opinions. It will be easier to resolve the problem once you get that straight.

LUCKY DATES 10th, 11th, 22nd, 31st.

Life will make heavier demands on your time and energy throughout the month, but this is unlikely to prove particularly daunting. You're more likely to thrive on a fresh sense of challenge, particularly if the pivotal interest in your life at present concerns the need to improve your credentials and perfect your skills. Potentially this is one of the most progressive months of the year, when the prize goes to those who take the initiative and are not afraid to break out of a confining circle.

The most important cosmic event is the movement of Jupiter into your opposite sign on the 24th. The efforts you have made over the past year or so are now coming to fruition, giving you a feeling of increased self confidence. Hopefully you will also find others demonstrating a greater recognition of your abilities and talents.

 Work may threaten to fill every available moment during the coming weeks, but this is not something that will worry you. There will be a sense of urgency at times, but you're unlikely to be fazed by this. Indeed this high energy scenario is packed with opportunities for those who are in an enterprising frame of mind and wish to break into a more lucrative field of activity.

A potential bugbear is Mercury's retrograde movement, which signifies minor hassles and possible delays until the 18th. If there are major decisions looming concerning current employment or a business deal, be prepared to wait until after this date before making any big moves.

 Increased pressures and a high energy output does of course put you under a certain strain. Although Mars helps to keep up your stamina, you are advised to watch out for warning signals around the 17th, when this fiery planet is at odds with Neptune. Being a Gemini, it is hard for you to accept that you cannot always do everything at once. But be careful, because this is a time when trying to do everything is liable to trip you up!

 What was promised in the previous month, or perhaps earlier in the year, will finally materialise in the latter half of November. For those who have not had much luck in love recently, the situation will do a pleasing somersault and the whole thing will turn around. There will certainly not be anything run of the mill about new attachments formed later in the month. Suddenly everything looks rosy, especially for those hoping to enter into a marriage in the near future.

 Soon after the 18th a message will arrive, putting an end to something that has been causing you some sleepless nights lately. Recent uncertainty and worry will finally be laid to rest. If this concerns a job or career change, it could very well be a cause for celebration!

LUCKY DATES 2nd, 18th, 22nd, 29th.

Now that Jupiter occupies your opposite sign, you are on course for expansion and personal enrichment through the influence of significant others in your life. Close partnerships, most notably marriage or business, are particularly favoured under this helpful trend. Indeed, the astrological pattern for December paints a bright picture for those who work in partnership or who have close dealings with the public at large.

In some ways, this important planetary shift will call for some readjustments in your lifestyle either now or in the near future. There will be no heavy pressure on you to make changes, but it is more likely that you will come to realise that the time is ripe to realign your ideas about what is and isn't of real value and importance in your life.

With just about everything in the zodiac zooming into your House of Partners, this is certainly going to be month of significant developments for those seeking a meaningful relationship. If you're already married or have a close partner, there is more than just a hint of a rise in fortunes and a much improved outlook for those who have been struggling over the past year or two in regard to such mundane matters as money, housing and family affairs.

If you are hopeful of meeting your affinity before the end of the year, there is everything to suggest that something special is about to crash in on your life. Whatever happens, it looks as if new amorous attachments will come with an element of surprise!

Dates of special interest are the 1st, 8th and 31st.

It is unlikely that funds will run short in the run up to the festive season, but you are advised to organise spending schedules if you are not to end up lumbered with a load of inappropriate gifts. What strikes you immediately as a wonderful idea may be a complete disaster, so think twice before splashing out.

Mercury also joins the party in your opposite sign between the 8th and 27th, giving further emphasis to the significance of other people in your life. During these weeks your natural urge to get out there and make contact, and to be in touch with a wide circle, will have plenty of scope for expression. The people you happen to meet or make contact with at this time are likely to play an important part in your destiny in the year to come.

Interestingly, Mercury throws aspects to both Pluto and Saturn on the 24th and 25th. A reunion with an old friend is indicated, and elements from the dim and distant past will have an uncanny tendency to attract your attention. Whatever happens, there does appear to be an aura of nostalgia around you as the year draws to a close. There is no sadness implied here, but rather a chance to catch up on news and fill in the gaps in your knowledge of others' activities. You'll enjoy taking a leisurely stroll down memory lane, and catching up with old friends, as the year draws to a close.

LUCKY DATES 8th, 14th, 19th, 24th.

cancer
june 22 to july 23

Planetary Ruler:	The Moon	**Flower:**	Convulvulus
Quality & Element:	Cardinal Water	**Animal:**	Crab
Colours:	Silver, Pastels		
Metal:	Silver	**Gem:**	Moonstone
Wood:	Birch	**Fabric:**	Voile

You begin the year on a note of optimism and with a distinct feeling that everything is on course to meeting your hopes and expectations. Jupiter is strongly activated in a lucky area of your solar chart, pointing to a phase of increasing opportunity and greater scope for developing and expressing your best potential. The accent is on the need to get more out of life, to have more faith in your capabilities, and to put behind you the rather inhibited state of affairs that prevailed over the past two or three years.

Mars continues to steer a steady course through your Eleventh Solar House, giving greater impetus to all endeavours that engage your need to co-operate with others in order to achieve your main aims and objectives. From the middle of last year you have probably been noticing that certain persons gravitating into your life have given you a stronger sense of purpose, to the extent that you are now beginning to feel very much in control of your destiny and in touch with your creative energies.

A tremendous increase of activity through January will focus very much on your dealings with other people. At times you'll find that lines of communication are really buzzing, but you'll enjoy the satisfaction of feeling that others are responding to what you have to say. This is a good month for seeking advice, increasing your knowledge, and establishing contact with those who are in a position to help and inspire you. Teamwork will also go well this month and if you're in a position to take a group project in a new direction you'll find everyone is one your side.

At a more mundane level, it is a time when you'll get speedy results in all to do with legal and official business. Don't be tempted to put off something that you know will only create more hassles in the long term if neglected.

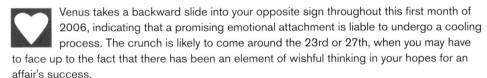

Venus takes a backward slide into your opposite sign throughout this first month of 2006, indicating that a promising emotional attachment is liable to undergo a cooling process. The crunch is likely to come around the 23rd or 27th, when you may have to face up to the fact that there has been an element of wishful thinking in your hopes for an affair's success.

Being a Cancerian, you are inclined to hold on, even when it is obvious that things are not going to work out. This can cause a great deal of stress, but once you make the break you usually realise what a backwater you were allowing yourself to be stranded in. There are better times to come, so don't allow yourself to get bogged down in something you know is second best.

Jointly held assets and resources come into the picture later in the month. Financial prospects are good, but it would be in your best interests to overhaul your existing investments and to get clear about pensions, mortgages and legal arrangements.

LUCKY DATES 4th, 13th, 23rd, 29th.

Mars finally comes to the end of an unusually lengthy sojourn in the sign of Taurus, which means that the focus of your energies is likely to undergo a shift of emphasis during the coming month. The efforts you made over the past six months or so will begin to give a clearer shape to certain key objectives, and by the end of the month it looks as if you'll be feeling more secure about any changes you wish to make.

One valuable lesson you have learned over the past few months is that you cannot expect always to achieve your goals by going it alone. During this phase you have probably made some good friends and made significant links with persons who have the effect of increasing your energy and enthusiasm. The added confidence this has given you will stand you in good stead for what you plan to do in the future.

A rather disappointing or stagnant phase in your love life is due to give way to something more exciting from early February onwards. Venus, the planet of love, comes to the end of a retrograde cycle on the 3rd, which is definitely good news for those who plan to marry in the near future. If you have not yet met up with your ideal partner, the prospect begins to look more inviting, especially when Venus is strongly activated towards the end of the month.

It is not only close and intimate ties of affection that are strengthened, but you will find that all relations on all levels become more harmonious and take a more reciprocal path. You'll make friends more easily and win over those who have been inclined to disagree with you in the past. Basically, it is a good time for to attempt reconciliations and missions of diplomacy!

An unexpected message around the middle of the month could see you making impromptu travel arrangements and perhaps taking off to a far destination. In view of this, it would be a good idea to keep your plans on a fairly flexible basis, otherwise you'll be forced to leave people in the lurch. If a journey has to do with your current work situation or a business deal, the outcome will also have something unexpected - and highly encouraging.

Lunar trends on the 13th indicate a quick turnaround in financial affairs. This could mean that cash will come in and immediately go back out again. Expenses could be heavier than expected, and just when you felt things were getting under control you will be obliged to do some reshuffling and rethinking.

However, this is not going to amount to a disaster, and you could do much to deflect potential problems by taking immediate action rather than putting things off or trying to do things on the cheap. Give yourself plenty of time if you are considering an important purchase or a new investment. You might feel very strongly about something you want to buy and then quickly lose interest after the purchase.

LUCKY DATES 1st, 3rd, 9th, 23rd.

You'll get the feeling that everything is going into a lower gear from early March onwards, but there may be a good reason for this. Both Jupiter and Mercury turn retrograde - this does not mean that actually going backwards, but simply appear to, due to our orbit overtaking them for a while. This usually correlates with a certain change of pace or a need to slow down and take stock.

The Jupiter factor is certainly no negative influence, but it does mean that circumstances will oblige you to put certain spare time interests on the back burner for a couple of months. Those involved in creative activity may find themselves suffering from a kind of writer's block, but this is more likely to be a warning signal that you have been trying to push ahead too quickly, or have been expecting too much too soon.

 Mercury's apparent back pedalling until the 25th suggests a delay or two in regard to travel arrangements and a need to rethink certain areas of your life. The two may or may not be linked, but something will happen that has the effect of stopping you in your tracks and making you consider a range of things from a different point of view.

Matters of a legal and official nature will need careful attention during these weeks. You may be tempted to cut corners and overlook the finer details, but this is a foolish policy and will only lead to you facing further hassles. Often with this backward Mercury transit you end up in a situation where you have to go over the same ground twice due to impatience or a misinterpretation of information. Forewarned is forearmed, so you will have no excuse.

 The theme of slowing down is nothing to get anxious about, for this is a time when it will be in your best interests to cultivate a greater space in your life in which you can simply chill out. Any attempt to force issues or push the idea that you need to be going forward will backfire on you this month, particularly in regard to potential health hazards.

Watch out when Mars is at odds with Uranus on the 11th, when there is a danger of accidents and injuries. This is where you'll get the major warning signals if you have been driving yourself too hard lately. Take heed!

Intriguing developments in your love life are forecast for the end of the month, as an aura of secrecy descends over romantic affairs and you find your mood changing completely. A relationship you thought a non-starter or a thing of the past is likely to transform itself into a deeply passionate liasion. It might not be destined to last, but in one way or another the experience will be worthwhile and may teach you something about your own deeper emotional longings - as well as your less realistic fantasies. You might be slightly disappointed to discover that the imaginary idea you had of a particular person will be preferable to the real version.

LUCKY DATES 9th, 16th, 19th, 27th.

At the end of March a solar eclipse in the topmost sector of your solar chart marked a potential turning point in your career. Over the next month or so you may be faced with a changing situation that obliges you to get very clear about the direction you wish to take in the future. Don't panic though, because this is not going to be totally traumatic. It's more likely that you need to adopt greater flexibility in how you approach your aims and ambitions.

The energising planet Mars pushes into your sign mid-month, helping you to regain your usual level of vitality and tenacity. If something happened to discourage you or throw you into a state of gloom over the past six weeks or so, what happens soon after the 14th will enable you to get back on track and move towards the resolution of yours plans.

 Everything becomes clearer to you in regard to certain legal matters that may have caused problems in the previous month. If you have played you cards right and refused to be fobbed off by comforting clichés, you should be back on course by the second week of April. Obstacles that have held up a business arrangement or a journey will then be out of the way.

What happens in the latter half of the month will concentrate your mind on the need to assert yourself more strongly when it comes to furthering your worldly aims. This is a time to take the initiative, to get stuck into where the action is and perhaps be a bit more upfront when it comes to promoting your personal interests. The presence of Mars in your sign suggests that you ahould be able to get ahead of the competition, so look at doing what you can to raising your game.

 The full Moon on April 13th is particularly apt for those born under the sign of Cancer. Not only is this your ruling orb but it falls in the 'home area' of your chart, and domestic affairs do have a strong affinity with your sign. At best, this lunation brings a feeling of increased emotional harmony within the family circle and particularly favours those who have very young children.

The only thing you need to watch here is that Mercury and Pluto are in adverse aspect on this date, which could mean that a minor crisis in the home will interrupt your work schedules or oblige you to ask favours of relatives and in-laws in order to keep things moving. This won't amount to a major crisis, but it will simply be inconvenient by coming at an inopportune moment.

 The unpredictable elements that have caused some perplexity on the path of love over the past few months are due to give way to something more satisfying and more realistic during April. It looks as if a reconciliation process will end up going forward, due to a sudden realisation that either you or the other person has been under a misapprehension or seeing things through rose-tinted spectacles. It might be a little daunting to look at your relationship in the cold light of day but it will help in the long run.

LUCKY DATES 5th, 14th, 15th, 24th.

Between the 5th and 10th of this month one of the most powerful planetary alignments of the year, involving Mars, Jupiter and Uranus, occurs. What makes this so special to you is that Mars occupies your own sign, while the other two planets are forming a 'grand trine' aspect. The upshot of this will be a noticeable upsurge of energy and activity, coupled with a feeling of increased self confidence. Events taking shape at this time will be the main cause of this sudden upsurge.

Whatever transpires, you can expect to make tremendous progress in your current aims and interests. Obstacles that you have been up against since the middle of last year or longer are at last fading out of sight. New doors open, giving you a greater incentive to explore fresh possibilities and find a broader field of self-expression.

Saturn picks up a more positive momentum throughout the month, signalling the end of certain restrictions that have obliged you to be a fairly strict about your budget over the past six months. Although you cannot hope to make a quick fortune under the sway of this planet, you can definitely do much to make your material interests more secure in the longer term.

You can best use the stabilising energy of Saturn by going for the safer option rather than speculating and investing in areas that might prove to be rather risky. Telling a Cancerian this is perhaps rather unnecessary, because you are by nature careful in financial matters. However, if you do experience a sense of frustration at times, it may be because you're either aiming too high or being unrealistic. Saturn demands a very down-to-earth and realistic approach to finance, so be prepared to work with this planet to get the best results.

The powerful planetary aspect already mentioned suggest that long distance travel will be a major theme in the second and third week. As Uranus is highlighted, there may be an element of the unexpected woven into the picture, but this will be connected with some unusual opportunities for expanding your horizons - not only through travel, but also in areas such as education, creative activity and spiritual interests. Keeping an open mind will help you see things clearly.

You're likely to be involved in a broader range of social contacts and activity at this time, making new friends and deriving a great deal of mental stimulation from the people you meet. Group activities and anything that engages you in affairs of the community will make swift progress, enabling you to widen your objectives and aims, and add useful new strings to your bow.

In such a high-energy month there is a danger of overstretching your inner resources, so be prepared to ease the pace when adverse aspects are in force on the 15th and 31st.

LUCKY DATES 7th, 8th, 21st, 27th.

After a hectic couple of months, you'll feel justified in easing the pace through June. There'll be more time to spend on cultivating personal interests and developing a greater margin of quality time in which to devote to things closest to your heart. You're likely to be in a sociable mood, inclined to call up neglected friends or arrange a special get-together if you're celebrating your birthday later in the month.

Any disruption caused by changes in the past month or two will give place to a more settled state of affairs. Also, if you have felt doubt and misgivings about certain decisions you made recently, the situation will show you clearly that you have taken the right road and are now moving towards a more fulfilling chapter in your life.

Friendships as well as intimate attachments are highlighted by a favourable trend most of the month. Unusual developments are forecast for the romantically inclined, though there are times when you may be chasing rainbows. The tricky date is the 15th, when Venus and Neptune will be stirring up some emotional dust and creating a mirage effect. This is where you naturally romantic nature is liable to land you in a mess, so be warned and keep the lines of communication as open as possible. Someone you have romantic feelings for might try to manipulate you in a subtle way. On the other hand you may find yourself in a position where you can help a friend who is experiencing distress due to an unwise love affair. Be prepared to lend a sympathetic ear, but don't allow false sentimentality to make matters worse.

Just when you believed financial affairs were settling down to a steadier course, things could go awry when Mars is adversely activated on the 18th and 19th. It looks as if you'll be faced with heavier expenses around this time, probably due to car breakdowns or you'll be busy with some sudden urgent repairs that need to be carried out around your house or flat.

Tread cautiously if you are considering a new project in which you need to put in money up front or invest in special machinery and technical equipment.

Information that comes to light early in the month will shed light on an ongoing mystery, putting an end to subliminal anxieties concerning the affairs of a younger person n your life. With Mercury moving into your own sign on the 3rd, your mind will move into a higher gear, ideas will fall into place, and you'll find the right words if you need to give a talk or find yourself in a situation where there's a need to clarify issues.

Travel is highlighted on the 9th and 12th, this being the best time of the month if you fancy a break from your usual routines and need a breathing space. Later in the month a message from a friend or relative who lives overseas is likely to throw your immediate plans into a new perspective. What's more, this is sure to be something you'll welcome.

LUCKY DATES 8th, 9th, 11th, 18th, 25th.

Don't get over-anxious if your life appears to go into a state of limbo early in July. A mixed bag of astrological trends gives a rather ambiguous message and warns you not to panic or jump to conclusions, especially if there is a question mark hanging over certain material interests. The good news is that Jupiter turns direct on the 6th, giving rise to a powerful undercurrent of good fortune. What this means is that soon a lucky twist of events will pull you out of the doldrums and allow you to move ahead more creatively.

This benign planet occupies a congenial area of your solar chart, indicating a phase of increasing opportunity and scope for expressing your true self. If you do experience a certain amount of stress early month, you may find that this turns out to be a blessing in disguise.

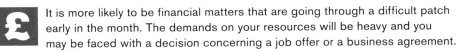

It is more likely to be financial matters that are going through a difficult patch early in the month. The demands on your resources will be heavy and you may be faced with a decision concerning a job offer or a business agreement. Whatever happens, don't allow yourself to be bullied into making commitments that you really are not clear about or feel in any way uncomfortable getting involved with. You could land yourself in some hot water if you don't keep a close eye on your financial dealings. For those involved in commercial activities and fundraising, it is a month to take careful stock of your situation, to do some serious rethinking if things seems to be heading towards a dead end. Once Mars takes leave of the money area of your solar chart on the 22nd the stress factor begins to ease and you should have a firmer handle of the situation before the month is out.

If material affairs are going through a difficult transition, the same cannot be said for those things that are of importance to you emotionally and personally. With Venus gracing your sign from the 19th onwards, your existing ties of love and intimacy will be strengthened and romance will beckon more enticingly for those of you seeking to meet a kindred spirit.

Dramatic and perhaps very unexpected developments are forecast later in the month, when Venus links up with several powerful planets, including lucky Jupiter and magical Uranus. This gives a decidedly glamorous aura to all amorous encounters, and a feeling that at last the goddess of love is smiling on you.

It's a good month to think more deeply and carefully about what you truly value and what is simply cluttering up your life. Being a Cancerian, you are inclined to cling onto things. If this gets out of hand, you tend to end up overloaded and suffocated. In view of prevailing trends, you would be doing yourself a big favour by focusing on your material needs and possessions. Ask yourself if certain items really do contribute to the genuine quality and richness of your life. Give yourself some space - you'll be surprised at how good it feels.

LUCKY DATES 6th, 14th, 23rd, 27th, 29th.

Now that the dust is settling, you can expect a steadier situation regarding material interests during August. A Solar-Saturn combination early in the month suggests that you are regaining control over a situation that threatened to veer out of your control recently. If the source of difficulties was related to finance, property or a joint enterprise, it looks as if everything takes a quite surprising turn for the better. This may be due to your own change of attitude, or a realisation that perhaps you were becoming too entrenched in ideas and methods that are old hat.

Whatever happens, the general feeling is that you a regaining a more constructive momentum, feeling more secure within yourself and in the direction your life is beginning to take.

£ Any problems that have been hanging over you from the previous month will fade into the background from the second week onwards when both Venus and Mercury activate the money sector of your solar chart. Not only does this augur well for the commercially minded and those who are planning to launch a new venture, but it promises a boost to your finances via a bonus, gift, or lucky win.

By the third week of August you'll be feeling more relaxed, with a surfeit of spare cash in your pocket to spend on fun and self indulgence. Just when you were concerned that a shortage of funds would spoil a holiday, the situation will turn around and enable you to relax and enjoy!

Venus continues to cast a rosy glow around affairs of the heart during the first half of the month. This will no doubt be the result of unusual developments in the previous month. If you didn't believe in miracles before, then you probably do now, and those who didn't believe in love at first sight may have been forced by events to change their minds.

Psychologically you'll be feeling more harmonious within yourself, more relaxed in your attitude to life, and more inclined to come out of your shell and be more sociable. Not only will this have a positive effect on your level of self esteem, but it will make you realise that no one else is to blame except yourself if love and friendship seem to have left you out in the cold recently. You're a sensitive soul and often afraid of making yourself emotionally vulnerable, but this can have its downside.

 Having Mercury in your sign until the 11th ensures a speedy response if you're seeking specialist advice or wish to establish useful contacts. After a phase of indecision, issues will become clearer, ideas fall into place, and there is scope for developing creative dialogue with those who share your views.

Distant horizons beckon later in the month, and luck attends those who are feeling adventurous and in the mood for a change of scenery. The more daring you feel the better - adventure hoidays are particularly well-starred this month.

LUCKY DATES 3rd, 12th, 19th, 29th.

Any month that contains eclipses of the Sun and Moon usually marks something of a turning point, according how they fall in your own solar chart. Although eclipses are often looked upon with some foreboding, this is largely a superstition, and in fact these celestial phenomena can mark important and often highly beneficial events in a person's life.

In September the Lunar eclipse on the 7th puts the focus on longer-term plans and will also have significance in regard to your deeper beliefs and philosophy of life. The solar eclipse on September 22nd has a similar theme, with the main accent on mental activity and the way you approach life at an ordinary everyday level.

What this all means is that over the next few months you're likely to be strongly influenced by certain ideas or views and these, in turn, will motivate you to break out of the old routines and bad habits that are blocking your creative energy.

The eclipses throw an interesting light on travel throughout the month. It could be that a place you happen to visit while taking a vacation makes a powerful impression or gives you a feeling of déja vu. You might even begin to consider the possibilities of moving abroad in the near future. Whether this becomes a reality or remains purely a dream remains to be seen.

It has to be said that with Uranus in the 'travel area' of your solar chart, such unexpected events can happen. In other words, long range travel or contact with foreign countries could suddenly change your life. The events of September could give you pause for thought!

Matters close to home are brought into sharper focus in the latter half of the month. Both Mars and Mercury stir up a lively and stimulating trend in this area, so it might be a good policy to prepare for a whole deluge of visitors, especially around the 15th and 24th. Provided you don't leave anything to chance in the coming weeks, stress can be avoided or at least minimised. In fact you are likely to end up relishing the extra company - the more the merrier!

Keep a weather eye of the adverse Jupiter-Neptune aspect on the 24th if you wish to keep investments and jointly held resources on a sound footing. Your partner or someone close to you may be tempted to take financial risks, and perhaps you yourself will be inclined to put too much faith in wonderful sounding promises. Make caution your watchword at this time and stick to what you know best when it comes to investment and other financial matters.

Apart from such quirks, the underlying trend is towards stability and steady expansion in your material affairs. If you have made any whole-hearted attempts to stick to a budget recently you'll discover you will be rewarded quite handsomely for your efforts.

LUCKY DATES 7th, 16th, 21st, 26th.

Several planets are converging on a highly creative area of your solar chart in October, promising a productive and satisfying month ahead. Through the encouraging influence of a friend you may find that a interest that has been taking up your spare time moves more into the centre of your life and occupies your time and energy more intensively.

This stimulating planetary pattern represents an upswing in your learning ability, which is good news for those involved in educational activity, either as student or teacher. It's also a time when new ideas and interests will appear on the horizon of your life and become a major focus of attention in the coming months.

If you are actively engaged in the arts, sports, or entertainment, this could turn out to be a month when you'll get the right breaks and feel that you are making real progress towards success in your field.

For most of the month Venus casts a harmonious aura around the domestic scene, with much promise of pleasant events centring on your own home. Developments within the family circle are sure to please, particularly if you are a parent, the chances are that one of your offspring will have cheering news, perhaps the announcement of an engagement or wedding.

Whatever happens, there is sure to be something to celebrate within the family before the month is out. Altogether, it is a month which offers opportunities for you to do a great deal to establish greater harmony and understanding with those closest to you, so don't be afraid to confront issues that may have been causing underlying tensions over the past few months. A heated debate or discussion will only further your convictions on a particular issue that you feel strongly about.

This is a prime month for buckling down to educational tasks and making an effort to improve your professional skills and creative abilities. By broadening the ways you express yourself artistically, you'll have the added bonus of enriching your social life and meeting up with people who are on your wavelength. Indeed, it is by making contact with like-minded individuals that your own special interests could be put on a more professional and productive basis.

Travel continues to be a key factor in your life successes, and you are likely to set out on significant journeys around the 10th and 22nd, both of which are very much geared to the broadening of your experiences and wisdom. Any special contact and communication with one or more people overseas at these times will broaden your horizons in more ways than one.

An encounter that took place two or three months previously, perhaps something you didn't take much notice of at the time, may have interesting repercussions later in the October. With Venus and Mars forming a conjunction in Scorpio on the 25th, the only word to describe the situation is sexy!

LUCKY DATES 5th, 14th, 22nd, 23rd.

Uranus, the planet of the unexpected, is poised to have some truly magical and miraculous effects on your life early in the month. There are events taking shape that will have a significant impact on your deeper emotional nature, making you realise that there is much more to life than what you can glimpse on the surface. For those of you who are mystically and spiritually inclined, it's a time of fresh insight and true inspiration - a genuine breakthrough to intuitive knowledge.

There are certain influences coming into your life that will steer you towards greater self awareness, giving you a higher sense of purpose, and perhaps putting you in a position in which you can act as a guide or counsellor to others. Being a Cancerian, you are something of a born therapist, having an intuitive understanding of human emotion. If you're interested in the healing arts and therapies, you're likely to be taking these matters much more seriously.

This has all the makings of a spectacularly eventful month for those hoping to find their ideal mate. Things are likely to happen at breathtaking speed, but be all the more satisfying for that. Generally speaking, you are fairly cautious when it comes to entering into emotional relationships, but there is much to suggest that you'll be throwing caution to the winds at this time.

This won't be a bad thing, either! Very often you are so cautious that opportunities pass you by. But something that happens during the coming month will convince you that it is now or never. Take the bull by the horns and go flat out for something that you know will make a big difference in your life. This is not the month to be timid.

Fortune smiles on those who are willing to take a more adventurous and enterprising approach to moneymaking throughout the month. Dates on which would be particularly favourable for launching fresh initiatives will be the 3rd, 8th, 15th and 24th, particularly if you are intent on expanding or promoting a existing business venture or applying for a more lucrative job.

As there is such an unusual accent on creative energy, you have it in your power to cut out a more productive niche for yourself. Efforts made towards establishing your work on a more independent basis or towards ending up in a situation where you can express yourself more creatively are certain to meet with success over the next twelve months. November is definitely not a time to underestimate your capabilities or hide your light under a cloak of false modesty.

Luck attends far-flung journeys in the first half of the month. Whether your travel is for business, in quest of knowledge, or simply for the sheer fun of it, the outcome is likely to be decidedly liberating. It will be an inspiring month for those involved in higher education, particularly if you are intent on making up for lost time and filling in the gaps of your knowledge.

LUCKY DATES 1st, 2nd, 15th, 20th.

There will be times when you'll feel that it's all work and no play in the run up to the festive season. It's very much a case of pacing things out, getting organised and refusing to allow yourself to be emotionally blackmailed into doing chores and favours for all comers. A firm stand is called for if you are not to end up a nervous wreck!

The good news is that your energy and stamina are extremely resilient under the prevailing dynamic trends. Great progress will be made in your special field of work, and this is where extra efforts are sure to pay dividends and bring much satisfaction. All activity geared towards greater productivity and efficiency will get the right results, but make sure you have the full approval of colleagues before pushing ahead with any major changes in your current work schedules.

£ With such an overwhelming accent on practical matters, there is no doubt that financial interests will be a major focus of attention. There are indeed changes forecast in the area of employment and business affairs, but if you play your cards right you'll be able to pull strings in your favour and manoeuvre yourself into a more leading position. The prevailing cosmic pattern is particularly helpful for those who work in a managerial capacity or are self-employed.

Dates when your cashflow situation is likely to become a bit more of a problem than usual are the 10th, 11th and 22nd. A tight rein will need to be kept on your budget at these times, because the demands on your resources are likely to be heavier than expected. You'll probably not be short of the necessary funds for gifts and goodies and having a good time later in the month, but your usual caution may slip and the temptation to slip into extravagance will be great.

♥ Minor disagreements with your nearest and dearest are likely to create some awkward vibes earlier in the month, but once Venus moves into your opposite sign on the 11th, you'll find it much easier to establish harmony and understanding. As long as you cultivate a high degree of openness and honesty at the emotional level, problems will be avoided. But keep your feelings bottled up and you're asking for trouble!

Generally speaking, Venus helps to generate smooth relations on all levels, so if there is a need to offer the olive branch, conciliate opposing factions or call a truce, now is the time to make the right gestures.

The high energy level of December could have the effect of lowering your resistance to any seasonal ailments that might be kicking around. Care is needed when adverse aspects are in force on the 10th, 11th, and around the new Moon on the 20th. You need to avoid doing anything in too much of a hurry, as the main danger is from accidents and mishaps. Thankfully, a more relaxed trend prevails during the final week of the month!

LUCKY DATES 1st, 10th, 18th, 21st, 31st.

leo

july 23 to august 24

Planetary Ruler:	The Sun	**Wood:**	Walnut
Quality & Element:	Fixed Fire	**Flower:**	Marigold
Colours:	Orange, Warm Yellows, Gold	**Animal:**	Lion
		Gem:	Citrine
Metal:	Gold	**Fabric:**	Brocade

2006 has the makings of a very special year for those born under the sign of Leo. Changes in the structure of your lifestyle are forecast, and in many ways you are likely to feel that the forces of Destiny are definitely taking a firmer hand in your affairs.

This is shown by the presence of Saturn in your own sign throughout the year, which gives a note of seriousness and inclines you to be more determined than ever before to achieve your main aims and objectives.

Saturn is described as the "planet of limitations". While this may sound rather discouraging, in fact all it means is that it is time to focus more intensively on what is of greatest importance in your life.

It means that you need to get your act together. This may mean cutting out certain unnecessary or frivolous distractions, but this is something that you are likely to do without prompting.

 The position of Jupiter in the lower sector of your solar chart acts as a helpful complement to Saturn and puts tremendous emphasis on the need to give your home base a greater level of stability. Jupiter represents an expansive trend, which is good news for those who are aiming to enhance and enrich their domestic lifestyle in the coming months.

Property interests are certainly going to be a key issue, so if you plan to pull up stumps and move to a new address, the outlook is decidedly encouraging.

 An emotional change of heart may cast an element of gloom over a romantic attachment in the first half of January and a crisis may be looming around the 22nd when Venus and Mars make a connection. This is not exactly a negative feature, but it does mean that you need to confront any ambiguities and tensions within your relationship. It is important that you have the sensitivity to realise that often you do expect rather a lot from a romantic partner, and it is later in the month when this will be brought home to you in no uncertain terms.

Be prepared to swallow a little bit of your pride and try to see that it is a real person you are dealing with and not just a product of your own fantasies.

 For the ambitious and enterprising, things are likely to move ahead quickly. However, you need to be careful you don't overreach yourself and end up in a position that is beyond your level of real competence at this stage. The Mars-Jupiter opposition mid-month indicates great self confidence, but also a danger you could make mistakes through being over-optimistic or attempting to bluff your way to greater power and prestige.

You are strongly advised to cultivate a sense of realism during the third week, when there is a possibility of deceiving yourself or being led astray by misplaced promises. A realistic sense of the time it takes to do things will also be useful at this time.

LUCKY DATES 1st, 4th, 17th, 19th.

A dramatic combination of Solar and planetary energies around the 6th suggests an increase in popularity and perhaps even a surge of publicity for those whose work has to do with the media. Whatever engages your imagination and brings you in touch with a wider circle of social connections will have a potentially creative and highly satisfying effect in your current work and personal life.

This trend is given further emphasis by the full Moon in your sign on February 13th, when you are likely to find yourself very much at the centre of attention. The only proviso is that an element of deception or illusion could enter into the situation, so it is essential that you keep your critical faculties alert. Although it is a time when opportunities are likely to arise, it would be unwise to let yourself be carried away by the glossy and glamorous at the expense of a more practical reality.

 For those seeking greater job satisfaction as well as something more remunerative, the prospect begins to brighten from early in the month. Venus then turns direct in a very practical area of your solar chart, indicating a smoother path to success in all matters to do with employment.

Being stuck in a situation in which you feel unappreciated and unable to give of your best can be depressing for those born under Leo. So, if you wish to pull yourself out of this kind of rut, don't be afraid to stick your neck out and look for something more to your liking. From a purely financial point of view, messages you receive later in the month are likely to be important, and maybe this will be a time when you hear good news concerning a recent job application.

 A certain amount of discretion will be needed if you are involved in discussion and debate on the 5th. Arguments are liable to become overheated and you may feel the need to charge to the defence of someone you perceive as being taken for a ride. Better to steer clear of anything particularly controversial or sensitive at this time, because it appears that others will be inclined to be both inflexible and dogmatic in their viewpoints.

The latter half of the month is an excellent time to delve into research projects and do some detective work. It's a time when secrets are revealed and a quest for knowledge you have been pursuing for a long time will yield inspiring insights.

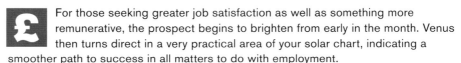 New romantic possibilities don't have a high profile this month, but for those considering marriage later in the year the outlook becomes more encouraging. Certain obstacles, probably of a financial nature, begin to show signs of fading. Likewise there is a more favourable trend in regard to property and housing. Altogether it is as if the Fates are smiling more brightly on established ties of affection. This will be something of a relief to previously beleaguered Leo.

LUCKY DATES 6th, 13th, 21st, 25th.

The pattern of events this month will pull you into situations in which co-operation and teamwork play a vital part in furthering special objectives. Whatever targets you have set yourself, you can expect to make better progress by working in concert with others rather than attempting to go it alone. It's a time when your sense of purpose will be given a boost of energy, thanks to the enthusiastic influence of various people you become associated with during the coming weeks.

Tremendous progress can be made now in all activities that are geared towards social and community affairs. It's a good month for drumming up support if you are campaigning for a special cause or wish to bring about change and reform in key areas of life. In whatever direction you are pursuing your special hopes and ideals, now is the time to take the initiative and listen to those who are on your wavelength.

 Be prepared to take immediate action if a financial problem crops up early in the month. With both Mercury and Jupiter turning retrograde, you are likely to experience a blip in your finances and will be obliged to rethink and reorganise. A good date for seeking professional guidance on money matters is the 14th, but if you're in doubt it might be better to wait until after the 25th before committing yourself to anything new.

Provided you avoid risks and gambling in any form, traumas are unlikely to arise. Your best policy is to keep things on a steady course and stick to what you are familiar with, rather than go for options that might promise a better return. Don't worry if a small source of income dries up. It won't be long before funds will pick up, and in the meantime you'll have plenty of time to do some serious thinking.

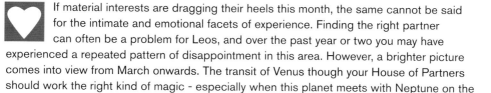 If material interests are dragging their heels this month, the same cannot be said for the intimate and emotional facets of experience. Finding the right partner can often be a problem for Leos, and over the past year or two you may have experienced a repeated pattern of disappointment in this area. However, a brighter picture comes into view from March onwards. The transit of Venus though your House of Partners should work the right kind of magic - especially when this planet meets with Neptune on the 26th. Symbolically, this indicates the ideal match, the lover of your dreams!

 Although Jupiter continues to throw a fortunate light on domestic and family matters, you may find that something has to be postponed. This probably has to do with a hoped-for property deal or a change of residence that you had been planning since the start of the year.

This is not at all bad news, because it could be that favourable changes taking shape are beginning to throw a new light on your plans. The extra time you get to think things through could set you off on a completely new direction.

LUCKY DATES 9th, 21st, 25th, 30th.

By far the most significant planet in your astrological pattern this month is Saturn which, from early April, begins to gather force. Since last November you may have noticed a slower pace in the overall pace of your life, often with an underlying feeling of being held back or frustrated in your efforts. There is always a lesson to be learned under Saturn – you need to see that if anything worthwhile is to be achieved, simply hoping for quick results just won't deliver the goods.

However, if you have made the necessary adjustments to this trend in recent months you are now in a position to make constructive use of the experience you have gained. The pattern of events early in the month will clarify your sense of direction and make you more aware of what is and isn't essential to your future well-being and success.

 Your usual vitality may take a plunge around mid April, the result of a rather hectic schedule over the past few weeks. Generally speaking, it does seem that there is a need for you to adopt a steadier pace and try to focus on your real priorities rather than allowing yourself to get caught up in extraneous activities that just end up leaving you feeling exhausted. If you manage to find that space to take a short break later in the month, it would definitely be the right kind of therapy if you need to recharge your batteries.

 Jointly held resources and soundly based financial interests are likely to occupy your attention, particularly in the third week. A welcome boost to your fortunes earlier in the month could throw a fresh light on these matters, opening up greater potential for investment and fundraising ventures.

Be prepared to give serious consideration to an offer or suggestion that's put to you around the 20th or 24th. You may realise that perhaps a spare time interest could be put on a more profitable basis. It is certainly worth exploring sidelines, especially if this involves working in close partnership with another person.

 There are advantages to be gained from a change of scenery in the latter half of the month. What you experience by way of travel or through cultivating a wider circle of contacts will stimulate your mind and bring you the necessary inspiration that could enable you to change your life.

Arranging things so that you can afford to allow yourself a breathing space would be a good policy, because there does seem to be a need to free up certain energies that may have become blocked or rather stagnant over the previous few months. If you are interested in seeking out the help of a guide or therapist, now is the time to make an appointment. If it's a case of business as usual, then a journey late month will prove helpful and profitable. The change of scenery will also do you the world of good as you have been feeling somewhat trapped of late.

LUCKY DATES 5th, 7th, 17th, 27th.

An unusual intensification of planetary energies comes into force during the first half of May, making this potentially the most eventful time of the year for those born under Leo. Although such a powerful configuration will have some level of impact on just about everyone, it will have a different emphasis according to where the planets fall in any particular chart. For Leo people it is of most importance because the primary focus is on the "angles" of your solar horoscope.

What this means is that changes that were set in motion up to a year ago will finally come to fruition, giving you a new sense of purpose and direction, particularly in regard to your professional and intellectual aims. There is also an indication that your home life is due to undergo a shift of emphasis, opening up potential for enhancing the quality of both your personal lifestyle and your status in the world.

The benign planet Jupiter is at the centre of all this zodiacal activity, giving a generally optimistic feel to what is taking shape in your life at this time. All matters that have to do with property, home and family interests are likely to have an element of something that lifts your spirits and puts you in a position to make a more definite plan for the future.

Jupiter occupies an area of your solar chart that indicates a new beginning. You might not see much evidence of this now or during next month, but there are indications that events which are only having an indirect bearing on your own life as yet, will ultimately open up a new chapter. The upshot of this will be a great enrichment of your lifestyle, with special highlight on matters close to home.

Venus casts a pleasant light on far-flung journeys throughout the month, bringing with it a hint of adventure and romance into the picture. A link with times gone by is likely to be established around the 8th, when an old friend - or perhaps an old flame - gets in touch. It's a time when people you believed to have gone from your life, never to return, are likely to put in a surprise appearance. Perhaps this will be what takes you travelling.

Another key date for travel and long-distance contacts is the 26th. Here too there is a theme of renewing old links, or visiting a place that played an important part in your life many years ago. If you have cause to feel nostalgic around this time, this certainly would not be surprising.

Don't be surprised if romance blossoms as a direct result of a long journey taken on or around the above dates. It also looks as if friendships will become unusually important late in the month when kindred spirits are likely to be drawn into your orbit, giving an added dimension to your social life. This delightful trend will give you much cause for celebration this month.

LUCKY DATES 4th, 5th, 14th, 24th, 26th.

At last you will be regaining your natural energy flow after what seemed to be an uphill struggle over the previous few weeks. This does not imply that you have been totally inactive, but rather that events have had the effect of confining you in some way and restricting you from your usual, more exhuberant, methods of expression.

What has been a bit frustrating is the feeling that you have been missing out in some way, or wasting valuable time. But once Mars pushes into your own sign early in June you will find yourself getting back on course and making huge progress before the month is out.

Indeed this is going to be a month when you will need to adopt a more energetic and assertive approach to life if your aims and objectives are to remain on course. But don't be afraid to alter your strategies if you see any obstacles up ahead. If a certain line of action no longer seems to be producing the expected results, now is the time for fresh initiatives.

The energising impact of Mars obviously helps if you have been feeling under the weather recently. A speedy recovery is guaranteed, and by the second week you'll be back into the swing of things.

Take advantage of this positive trend if you are aiming to get yourself in better physical shape, especially if you are interested in sports and athletics and are aiming to test your physical prowess later in the month.

Mars also stimulates your spirit of adventure and stirs up a need to conquer further horizons, either through travel, within your social life or through a quest for knowledge. Mercury gives further weight to this theme, bringing events and meetings that stir up your curiosity and pull you away from familiar territory. Whether it is through travel or deeper studies, it's a month of exciting discoveries, but it is up to you to take the lead if you wish to break new ground, for it seems that opportunity and initiative are closely linked during these weeks.

This is sure to be a time of progress for those who are intent on furthering their career and or special ambitions. Again it is the dynamic influence of Mars that puts you at an advantage and helps you to access the necessary energy and confidence within you.

Provided you don't step on other people's toes by acting selfishly or by becoming a control freak, success is at your command. Watch your step on the 18th and 22nd, otherwise you could jeopardise your financial prospects and even damage your good fiscal reputation.

Be prepared to put a financial commitment on hold if you run into disagreement around these dates. You will do well to examine all angles of the agreement before you sign anything so don't feel guilty about causing the process to stall.

LUCKY DATES 10th, 19th, 25th, 30th.

Something that has been in the planning stage for several months is likely to be get the green light early in July. Jupiter begins to pick up momentum, throwing a beneficial light on everything that gives you a feeling of inner equilibrium and emotional contentment, while the presence of Mars in your sign until the 22nd ensures progress in activities of high priority.

The feedback you receive from other people at this time will help you to clarify your own aims and objectives. At times you'll feel that you are being criticised for some of your ideas or attitudes, but you'd be doing yourself a disservice by reacting in a defensive manner. it's best for you to be open to suggestions and reflect on the fact that you are the kind of person who can sometimes become a bit fixed in your ways.

The only drawback is Mercury's retrograde movement from the 4th onwards. Unforeseen events will oblige you to do some quick rethinking, probably in regard to social arrangements or group activities. People you were relying on are likely to back out at the last minute, forcing you to postpone something you had hoped to push ahead with.

Events that take shape between the 10th and 29th will have the effect of making you feel more thoughtful and reflective. A confidential talk with a friend will prove very helpful and enlightening if you are in a quandary about a decision that needs to be taken before the end of the month.

Basically, it's a time when your ideas and views are undergoing a subtle shift, giving you a feeling of uncertainty in some areas. It's best not to make any definite commitments till late month if you're unsure about long term issues.

A friendly aura surrounds you most of the month, and until the 19th it looks as if you'll be moving in a wide circle as far as your social life is concerned. You can expect new friends to gravitate into your orbit, probably as a direct result of your greater involvement with groups, clubs and community affairs.

At a more intimate level, there may be unexpected emotional tensions early in the month, but this will at least give you a chance to confront certain underlying differences and achieve a better understanding with the one you love. As for new romance, the prospect is bright, and it is likely that someone you've been on nodding terms with for several months will begin to have closer appeal.

Cashflow will begin to ease later in the month. However, expenses may be heavier than expected. But at the same time, it looks as if your income is due for a welcome boost. There will be greater scope for initiatives in regard to fundraising and commercial activity. Look out for opportunities from unexpected quarters at this time.

LUCKY DATES 6th, 9th, 17th, 25th.

The conjunction of your ruling orb with Saturn in your own sign on the 7th suggests a time when the Fates are liable to take a hand in your affairs. If you celebrate your birthday on or around this date, you can expect important and far-reaching developments over the next 12 months. Granted, Saturn does have a rather sombre reputation, but in this case it looks as if you'll experience the more constructive effects of this planet.

To explain this important feature in a little more detail, you can expect to reap the benefits of past efforts and this, in turn, will enable you to manoeuvre your own lifestyle on a more definite and secure foundation. Psychologically this means that you are in the process of achieving a much more mature level of inner growth.

 Although the Saturn factor will incline you to focus on very practical issues or indulge in a bout of serious thinking, it certainly won't be a dull month. On the contrary, there is increased scope for leisure activity, dabbling with new interests and pursuing the fun side of life.

This makes this an ideal month for taking a break from your usual surroundings by arranging a change of scenery and generally doing your own thing. Having both Venus and Mercury in your sign during the second half of the month suggests that travel will be a real delight, with a very gratifying spin-off in terms of an enriched social life and new friendships to be made.

 If you prefer to go along with Saturn's constructive influence, this is an excellent month for dealing with property interests and considering the possibilities of a change of residence in the future. With Jupiter becoming increasingly active in the "home area" of your solar chart, major developments between now and the end of the year are likely to enrich your domestic lifestyle and open a wider margin for movement if you feel the need for a change.

Incidentally, the astrological pattern is particularly favourable towards those who wish to set up home for the first time or start a family.

 The presence of Venus in your sign from the 12th obviously makes this a prime time for romantic developments. As travel is a key feature in your life during these few weeks, chances are that you'll encounter someone highly attractive while away from familiar territory. The proverbial holiday romance stands a good chance of developing into something more enduring!

 The tense aspect between Saturn and Neptune at the end of the month warns you to take care if sampling exotic foods while travelling and to get immediate medical attention if you feel unwell. Don't ignore symptoms as simply being the effects of over-eating or over-drinking.

LUCKY DATES 4th, 16th, 22nd, 23rd.

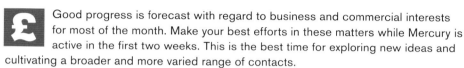

The prevailing astrological trends suggest that the energies of transformation are beginning to become active. It is as if various threads in your life are being pulled together and some of your interests are taking on a more intense appeal. With the mysterious Pluto turning direct early month and linking up with Venus in your sign, it could be that you are due for a burst of creative activity.

The bottom line here appears to take the form of a break with the past or something that liberates your soul and enables you to make use of your potential more fully. If you find yourself taking an interest in something that you had not previously considered, this would not be at all surprising. For many Leo individuals, it will be a month of self-discovery.

Good progress is forecast with regard to business and commercial interests for most of the month. Make your best efforts in these matters while Mercury is active in the first two weeks. This is the best time for exploring new ideas and cultivating a broader and more varied range of contacts.

Venus is in the money area of your chart for most of the month, ensuring that any problems are easily solved and potential disasters can be averted with a little common sense. However, the going could get tough around the eclipses on the 7th and 22nd, when a sense of urgency prevails. Care needs to be taken when it comes to investments, stocks and shares, and also anything to do with insurance claims and tax affairs. In simple terms, avoid taking risks or pushing your luck!

The Venus-Pluto link early this month augurs well for those who are hoping to find their genuine soulmate. There is always something uncannily compulsive about Pluto, which can often mean the beginning of an irresistible infatuation. However, as Venus is well placed and in your own sign, you are more likely to experience something calmer and destined to stand the test of time.

Pluto favours those who have been through the relationship mill and survived, then gone on to take to heart lessons concerning their deeper emotions and desires that they've needed to learn. You may now find that a difficult transition is coming to an end, giving you a feeling of greater confidence and a more enlightened approach to intimate relationships.

Suddenly you are likely to find yourself making impromptu arrangements for a journey around the middle of the month. Relatives will be very much in evidence, and there will be an element of urgency in the situation. Be prepared to alter your plans at a moment's notice if necessary, for someone important to you may need your immediate assistance.

The 23rd brings a more relaxed trend for those who are planning to take a special holiday or honeymoon at this time. You'll find yourself feeling very congenial and ready to enjoy yourself.

LUCKY DATES 1st, 2nd, 18th, 28th.

The Jupiter-Saturn aspect later in the month shows that important developments over the past six months are now reaching a major turning point. Since the beginning of the year there have been indications that a new chapter in your life is about to begin. It may well be the case that this relates to something that makes it necessary to pull up roots and even make a major change of residence.

If not this, then there is certainly an indication that some of your interests are beginning to move in a firmer direction and that you have been working hard to establish your professional credentials.

What takes shape during the coming month will do much to set the scene for several months or years to come. The main theme is that you are finally becoming established in an area that allows you to express your greatest potential. Life may demand a more mature level of response from you, and you may need to consider taking on heavier responsibilities, but this appears to fit nicely into your current aims and objectives.

Travel receives an unusual highlight early in the month and may have a connection with the affairs of relatives. Even if you are not going far, journeys are likely to prove beneficial and perhaps unusual in some way. If you have been parted temporarily from a loved one, this is a time when a reunion is likely to take place. Perhaps it's the case that a meeting with an old buddy is to be arranged, which could mean a longer excursion later in the month.

Mentally, you'll be in the mood for in-depth thinking as Mercury stirs up the deeper energies of your psyche. Those interested in occult and mystical themes will be on the right wavelength at this time, gaining fresh insights and realising that apparently disconnected ideas are in fact closely linked. It is an excellent month for attending talks or discussions on these subjects, or developing a more meaningful dialogue with those who share your interests.

Any important changes taking shape in your life will probably have their main focus in domestic affairs. Jupiter continues to cast a beneficial light on this area, but with several other planets muscling in on the action, this is a good month to push ahead with desirable changes. If a change of residence is going forward, you can expect everything to go according to schedule and with minimum fuss.

It could be that family links are beginning to undergo a period of change, perhaps because one of your own offspring is feeling restless and wishes to make a bid for greater independence. Younger Leos who may have been at loggerheads with their parents recently now have a better chance of stating their case and reaching a better understanding. The maturing influence of Saturn in your sign makes you realise the difference between pure egoism and self respect. This realisation will reap benefits for both you and those around you.

LUCKY DATES 7th, 10th, 14th, 23rd.

There are times in life when it is a good idea to take a serious look at the baggage you have accumulated both materially and emotionally. What you come to realise is that you hardly have space to breathe - it's as if the walls are closing in and all you want to do is cut and run. While this is not really a viable option in November, it would nevertheless be in your best interests to take stock of the situation and see where you can make constructive improvements.

With everything centring on the lower angle of your solar chart, the forces of destiny and the inclinations of your own deeper self are steering you towards change. If this means that you need to throw your excess baggage overboard, then now is the time to act!

You owe it to yourself to create the kind of lifestyle that is in keeping with your current level of need and development. Simply face the fact that it is no longer useful to cling onto things that are past their sell-by date.

 Significantly enough, Uranus - the planet of change - is powerfully activated by your own ruling orb early in the month. This coincides with several other planetary aspects to bring about the kind of events that open new doors.

Trust your deeper instincts if you feel that it is time for radical change, particularly in regard to home affairs. The message of Uranus is in the urge to greater freedom, independence, and more room to move. If you have been feeling cramped by circumstance, you are now given the opportunity and the incentive to do something positive about it!

 Whatever happens, it would be unwise to write off a love affair that appears to be heading for a crash. It could just be a case of misunderstanding, due to your own ego making unreasonable demands. Be prepared to confront issues that have been a source of tension.

Once Venus shifts into a more congenial area of your solar chart on the 17th, everything should begin to fall into place and you'll be able to close the door on past mistakes. The latter half of the month brings a brighter prospect to those who have been feeling neglected, rejected and dejected in recent months.

It could be a chance social invitation around the 21st that provides you with a key to your heart's desires.

 Be prepared for some delays if you need to deal with officialdom in the first half of the month. Matters concerning property or business affairs may suffer a minor crisis around the 11th. But hang in there, because soon after the 18th it looks as if a seemingly insoluble problem or disagreement will find an unexpected solution. It is all a matter of looking at things from a broader angle of vision, and perhaps swallowing a bit of your pride. Don't worry, it won't be too traumatic to do so and you'll be feeling relieved at the ability to move ahead.

LUCKY DATES 3rd, 5th, 22nd, 30th.

Jupiter, the planet of opportunity and expansion, moves into a highly creative sector of your solar chart, marking the start of a highly satisfying chapter in your life. You are by nature a very expressive person, outgoing and extrovert in the way you approach life. Over the past year or so these qualities may not been as much in evidence as usual, probably because you have been seriously involved in very practical affairs, studies or other matters that have forced you to limit your activities in some way.

From this month onwards this is all going to change rapidly. Not only will you be helped along by a number of lucky opportunities, but it is the work you have done - and experienced gained - in recent years that will enable you to make the best of these opportunities.

Generally speaking, you will feel much more confident, more adventurous and more enterprising under this benign trend. In fact you have the power in your hands to create your own luck by taking the initiative and going for what you really want.

It could be said that December is the most important month of the whole year for those born under Leo. It's not only the Jupiter factor that points to a more expressive and creative phase in your life, but now that Saturn is moving towards the end of a lengthy transit of your sign, you'll experience a sense of increasing freedom during the coming months.

Interests that you were obliged to shelve two or three years ago will begin to occupy you once more, for it seems that certain restrictions and responsibilities are easing, allowing you more scope for pursuing creative and recreational activities. One thing is for sure, and that is a vast enrichment of your social life in the weeks up to and including the festive season.

There is more than just a hint of dramatic romantic encounters to come in the weeks ahead. Here, too, you will experience the beneficial influence of Jupiter, which indicates a combination of luck and love. It is likely to be something of bumper month for new love affairs, engagements and weddings. The general scenario is that you are at last in sight of realising your cherished wishes.

Dates of special importance for affairs of the heart are the 1st, 8th, 11th and 31st. This does not imply that you can take everything for granted, especially around the 22nd, when an adverse aspect between Mars and Uranus could spark off an epic emotional storm over something quite trivial.

After a rather disruptive phase in recent times, you'll be pleased to find that the domestic part of your life attains an atmosphere of peace and harmony as the year draws to a close. You'll be feeling rather pleased and contented at the way family and home life shapes up at this time.

LUCKY DATES 5th, 6th, 8th, 18th, 19th.

virgo

august 24 to september 23

Planetary Ruler:	Mercury	**Wood:**	Ash
Quality & Element:	Mutable Earth	**Flower:**	Clover
Colours:	Soft Brown & Green, Dusky Hues	**Animal:**	Magpie
Metal:	Platinum/ Aluminium	**Gem:**	Agate
		Fabric:	Linen

You're likely to be in a forward-looking frame of mind as the New Year arrives, impatient to push ahead with projects that you were obliged to put aside over the previous two or three weeks due to the Christmas rush. Your energy levels will be up to the mark, too, which is all to the good in what looks like being a month of intense activity.

Having the energising planet Mars in favourable angle to your own sign throughout the month ensures that a satisfying momentum will be achieved in all activities that require your excellent organising skills and conscientious approach to practical matters. And although you are reputed to be a creature of routine, there is much to suggest that you will be breaking a familiar pattern and branching out in a new direction. Initiatives that are geared to your long range goals are under a progressive trend, so don't be afraid to take a more adventurous approach to life, you'll be surprised at the results!

The retrograde cycle of Venus throughout the month calls for certain readjustments at the emotional level if a relationship is to be kept on a smooth course. You will be made very aware of underlying disharmonies and tensions that may have been building up subliminally for several months.

However, this potentially negative Venus trend offers you a chance to reach a deeper level of integration within yourself and to realise that perhaps you have fallen into the bad habit of taking the other person too much for granted. If a recent romantic attachment seems to be going nowhere, you may have to admit defeat later in the month.

The prevailing trends are particularly helpful to those intent on improving their knowledge and skills with a view to upgrading earning potential or creative expression. Whether you are a student or a teacher, or simply curious to delve into something that has begun to grab your interest, it is sure to be a rewarding month.

What takes place between the 9th and 13th points to an important journey in the near future and the opening up of a broader horizon of activity that engages your higher mental energies. Contact and communication with a person overseas will play a decisive role in your plans at this time, and the whole thing begins to look decidedly exciting and inspiring later in the month.

Relatives and in-laws are liable to make heavier demands on your time and energy around the middle of, and towards the end of, the month. This may be due to someone being under the weather or in need of your practical assistance. Be prepared to shoulder some extra chores, that might also involve looking after other people's kids for a day or two. However, if you're a typical Virgoan, you should be able to rise to the challenge very well. In fact you'll find that you relish the opportunity to prove that you really can do it all. At least the demands from those around you means that you definitely won't have any cause to complain that life is dull during this first month of 2006!

LUCKY DATES 4th, 9th, 13th, 17th.

The demands of life continue to call for a high energy input, but the progressive trend continues and you'll be at your best when dealing with a fresh sense of challenges to be overcome. For those feeling adventurous and ambitious, the best time for taking a more assertive approach is after the 17th, when the dynamic planet Mars pushes into the topmost sector of your solar chart. There will be no stopping you then!

Creative interests come under a more helpful sky from early in the month onwards, when people you happen to meet socially will turn out to be on your own wavelength and may be in a position to help you to achieve a more professional approach. For the ambitious who are intent on making a splash in the arts, media or entertainment, look out for potential opportunities later in the month.

 After a phase of being in the doldrums there is every indication that romance is beginning to beckon more enticingly. Due to a previous disappointment or emotional trauma, you are probably feeling rather cautious about getting too deeply involved in a new affair. However, this is not such a bad thing, because the transit of Venus through Capricorn favours those who are willing to take time and apply the gentle art of allowing things to happen.

The promise of finding a kindred spirit is at its optimum during the final days of the month, when the message will be very clear that someone thinks very fondly of you.

 Anything that calls for careful negotiation and dialogue will bring the desired results while Mercury activates your opposite sign from the 9th onwards. This is a time to follow up information, so be sure to get in touch with people who are able to advise and offer helpful suggestions.

Take advantage of this trend if you are seeking a definite decision on a legal matter or agreement, but it is important to be sceptical of anyone who attempts to blind you with science on the 14th.

 Career interests come under the dynamic influence of Mars during the third week of February. This marks a transition to a more progressive and challenging phase of activity - a chance to prove to the world what you are really capable of. There will be a need to act quickly if opportunities arise, so don't hang about if an offer comes your way or you see an ideal job opportunity.

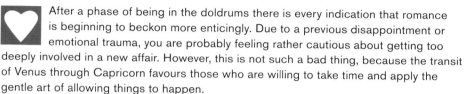 You probably won't be lacking in energy and vitality during February, but you may be feeling emotionally touchy around the full Moon on the 13th. You are likely to say things you immediately regret, and then have to put up other people's moods. This can quickly descend into a vicious circle. If it is at all possible steer away from people you know are likely to irritate you.

LUCKY DATES 3rd, 5th, 15th, 25th.

You may be struggling to keep to planned schedules throughout the coming month due to the unreliability of certain persons or because all kind of extraneous demands distract you from your main interests. This is something that will call for greater flexibility and a willingness to alter arrangements at a moment's notice.

The underlying trend continues on a progressive note, but you cannot expect to keep to a straight course. In theory your well organised plans might be perfect, but in practice it will be a different story. It's all a case of being realistic in your expectations, particularly in dealing with other people on an everyday level. Remind yourself that most of us mortals are not quite as methodically minded as those born under Virgo.

Provided you can adopt a relatively flexible approach, career interests and employment will continue to move forward. Indeed it is your willingness to make changes or to look on your work situation from different angles that will stand you in good stead. The only date when problems are likely to arise is the 11th, when you may have to be less insistent that you alone know what is best when it comes to policymaking and method.

A transit of Venus through a very practical area of your solar chart brings an easing of certain pressures, particularly for those who are seeking suitable employment. If you're not totally satisfied with your current work situation, efforts to improve this situation will meet with better success in the latter half of the month.

It's the practical rather than the emotional facets of personal relationships that come into sharper focus during these weeks. It could mean intense discussions with your partner concerning possible changes in domestic affairs or career interests. You might also decide to postpone a wedding date, or even change your mind about this altogether.

The message here is that it would be unwise to rush into making commitments that you don't feel completely ready for. It's a time for reflection, for straightening out feelings that may have got bogged down in fantasy and wishful thinking. With a lunar eclipse in your sign on the 14th, your feelings are liable to undergo a change over the coming months, so take your time in all matters that engage you at an emotional level.

It is not until after the 25th that you can expect to be clear of the hassles that have held you back or deflected you from your well-planned course of action. Until this date, don't put all your eggs in one basket and be especially wary of verbal promises and agreements. Misinformation is liable to create problems and misunderstandings, and if you're are involved in discussions and negotiations you may need to backtrack if people are getting the wrong messages. Be sure to repeat yourself very carefully to ensure you're all on the same page.

LUCKY DATES 1st, 9th, 24th, 31st.

After last month's muddling through, it looks as if you will be getting back into the right groove through April. People who have been elusive and unreliable will be more co-operative, and indeed from mid-month onwards it is team spirit that is likely to play a highly productive part in your activities.

As work pressures begin to ease their grip, you'll find yourself with more time on your hands, either to cultivate your social life or to give serious thought to potential changes that you have in mind regarding career or business interests. Towards the end of the month you will gravitate into a wider circle of activity, perhaps to do with your local community or a club you belong to. Any new friendships struck up at this time will have the effect of boosting your enthusiasm and leading you into a wider social circle with all the benefits that brings to your personal growth.

Now that you have disentangled yourself from an awkward emotional situation, the prospect begins to brighten considerably as Venus voyages through your House of Partners. This helps greatly if you have been at odds with someone close to you recently, or where misunderstandings have caused ructions. A more harmonious influence prevails, enabling you to pour oil on troubled waters and reach a deeper understanding with your nearest and dearest.

A special date for those seeking new romance is the 20th, when an unexpected twist of events could throw you together with someone special. Even if the effects are not immediate, there is much to suggest that sympathetic links are being formed around this time.

An agreement or business project that you have been finding difficult to get off the ground is likely to get the go-ahead soon after the 16th. As you are something of a born worrier, the situation in recent weeks may have left you feeling nervously exhausted, but what takes shape later on in the month will make you realise that much of your anxiety was entirely misplaced. Whatever happens, you can expect both personal and joint financial interests to become much more settled as the month progresses.

Take advantage of favourable trends on the 19th and 26th if you need to deal with tax affairs, insurance, investments or legal payments.

Now that Saturn is beginning to move forward, worries concerning the health of other people in your life will fade into the background. You will also find that lingering seasonal ailments will finally disappear, leaving you feeling brighter mentally and physically.

For those who work in the health services or who take an interest in alternative therapies, developments late in the month will be very welcome by enabling you to put things on a more professional basis. Look into insurance and training for alternative therapies at this time if you are keen to turn an interest into a career.

LUCKY DATES 4th, 19th, 24th, 27th.

The alignment of several major planets during the first half of the month suggests that you are becoming increasingly active at a social level, perhaps more interested in aims and purposes geared towards the improvement of services and the solving of world problems. For those who are politically inclined or who have a well-developed social conscience, the prevailing trend is particularly helpful.

Even if your aims and objectives are of a more modest and personal nature, there is no doubt that you'll make tremendous progress, thanks largely to links with influential friends or groups who share your ideals. The underlying message is that best progress will be achieved by joining forces with others rather than attempting to go it alone.

If you work for yourself or are considering the possibilities of taking a more independent line, you have a great deal of support in the cosmic background. Not only will you be greatly assisted by friends and colleagues but also, now that a number of financial hurdles have been overcome, you'll feel easier about taking fresh initiatives and upgrading your targets.

From a different angle, it looks as if the fortunes of your partner are due for a boost later in the month. You also stand to gain via a bonus, rebate, legal payment or perhaps a small legacy. Whatever happens, you can expect to feel easier about finances before the month is out.

The attractive force of Venus becomes more intense throughout the month, which is good news for those who have experienced a certain cooling effect in their love life recently. Existing romantic ties will undergo a transformation, taking a quantum leap onto a more satisfying level, which may be largely due to a subtle change of attitude that brings down some of your emotional defences.

Don't be surprised, either, if a relatively casual acquaintance develops into something more amorous at this time. And if married life has fallen a bit flat in recent months, a break from usual routines will be the best therapy!

It's a successful month ahead for those whose work has to do with travel, overseas contacts, or science and technology. You'll find that your learning curve takes a sharp upward swing, thanks to dialogue with people who inspire you with new ideas and open up wider horizons for expressing both your creative skills and technical ability.

It's an excellent month in which to pursue educational interests. You'll be on good form mentally, having little difficulty assimilating new information and making all the right connections. Evening courses won't be too demanding and will, in fact, be rather stimulating for you at this time. If you're seeking to gain knowledge of a more mystical nature, the 29th could prove decisive.

LUCKY DATES 6th, 18th, 27th, 29th.

Your energies are taking an inward turn during these weeks, making this a psychologically significant phase when certain of your life priorities are undergoing a shift of emphasis. If you feel fairly well-established in your lifestyle and your career at present, it would be unwise to push for further change or achievement. Take time to appreciate what you have already accomplished over the past few years, and devote your energies to improving the quality of your private life.

The fact is that if you attempt to forge ahead with worldly aims and activities, you'll run up against obstacles and end up feeling that your energy and time have been wasted. Efforts devoted to inner personal growth are more in line with prevailing cosmic trends.

 Persons born under Virgo are very health-conscious and often end up working in areas that have to do with diet, health and the caring professions. These matters are likely to take on added significance during May, which is an excellent month for developing and perfecting your knowledge and skill in these matters.

As far as your own health is concerned, there is a potentially negative phase during the third week, when a series of stressful planetary aspects may combine to send you a warning signal. Tough work schedules and other pressures are likely to take their toll at this time, so be prepared to drop into a lower gear and, if possible, take a break from your usual routines.

 Venus sailing through a harmonious area of your solar chart throws a pleasant light on far-flung journeys. All the more reason to escape from the usual daily grind, even if it is only for a couple of days. Again there is a decidedly therapeutic element linked with travel, and by taking a break you will realise that perhaps you have neglected your deeper emotional needs by allowing yourself to be taken over by mechanical routines.

 There is a close link between travel and romance during the second and third weeks. It could be that a relationship that has been conducted via email for several months transforms itself into something much closer. Lovers' meetings are sure to be blissful around the 23rd.

Lunar trends on the 11th bring a promising message for those planning to take the plunge into matrimony. An unexpected turn of events will enable you to overcome a problem connected with domestic issues, making you feel more optimistic about the future. If you have an established relationship or are married, you'll have good reason to feel easier about going ahead with changes geared towards enhancing your lifestyle. This may just be a spot of home improvements but anything you do that improves your shared time together will be welcome at this time. Altogether it seems that a phase of increasing emotional contentment is beginning to make itself felt.

LUCKY DATES 2nd, 9th, 13th, 22nd.

july ♍ virgo

Matters relating to your current work situation may be thrown into a state of turmoil early in the month. Your inborn sense of order and tendency to be methodical will be put to the test, as people look to you to keep the whole act together and prevent things from falling into total chaos. This will be only a temporary blip, but be prepared to take quick action if a sudden problem needs urgent attention.

The good news is that Jupiter turns direct on the 6th, putting a more positive accent on your daily routines and allowing you to get a firmer grip on essential practical affairs in the coming months. An element of uncertainty - of being in a state of suspense - has perhaps caused some tension over the past few months. But from this month onwards you will feel that your feet are more firmly planted on the ground.

It would pay to get all your travel arrangements and special meetings clear and finalised in the early days of the month. Leaving things to chance is definitely out of the question. From the 10th onwards you will find that group activities are disrupted due to the absence of colleagues or because other duties call. While this may not be totally disastrous, it will certainly mean that you are obliged to put things on hold until later in the month.

Jupiter throws a positive light on mental activity form early July onwards, signalling a phase of progress for all those involved in educational activity and study. It is certainly good news if you are taking an exam either now or in the near future (which includes such things as the driving test).

Even if you had not previously thought of it, chances are that between now and the end of the year you will become increasingly focused on the need to widen your mental horizons and develop new skills.

For the amorously inclined, the outlook is looking decidedly promising from the 19th onwards. You'll be in popular demand socially after this date and feeling more gregarious than might usually be the case. Not only will this help greatly if you are hoping to find a kindred spirit, but it will also draw new friends into your orbit. Alternatively, it could be that a friendship undergoes a surprise transformation into a fully-fledged romance.

It would be unwise to make any moves that might affect your income, even though there may be an exciting offer heading your way in the first half of the month. Be extremely wary if something crops up on the 5th or around mid-month. There may be a conflict of loyalties, but if in doubt stick to familiar ground.

Favourable trends late in the month enhance the potential for boosting your resources by developing extra-curricular fundraising ventures. It is better to wait for these opportunities rather than commit to anything early in the month.

LUCKY DATES 3rd, 11th, 19th, 29th.

The Fates are moving in mysterious ways early in the month, bringing a feeling of change together with a link with the past. Saturn, planet of time and destiny, is powerfully activated at this time, giving more than just a hint that a new chapter in your life is about to begin. There are events taking shape in the background that are sure to have a profound influence on your personal circumstances in the near future.

This is nothing to feel unduly alarmed about, because the upshot of this unusual trend is to strengthen your sense of purpose and to give a more definite and constructive direction to your life. Something unexpected is likely to be woven into this intriguing picture, with the main accent on significant relationships and meetings with remarkable people.

 The energising planet Mars beats a path through your own sign, giving a progressive and at times rather hectic feel to the events of August. Both physically and psychologically this dynamic planet will have the effect of raising your level of self confidence and inclining you to adopt a more assertive and competitive approach to life.

Mars will greatly enhance the qualities that enable you to always deal in a highly efficient manner with the practical affairs of life. It is likely that other people will be looking to you to provide a sense of direction and initiative, and you will certainly thrive on the added sense of challenge this gives you. It's a time to push yourself into the lead and to get where the action is.

If it's adventure you want, or a chance to prove your prowess in some sporting field, then this is the month when you will be in your element. Your energy levels will be high and your skills will be much improved.

 Romantic affairs have an aura of secrecy in the latter half of the month, when you will prefer to cultivate a greater space in your life that you can devote to intimacies. Provided you steer clear of clandestine attachments, you can expect to feel more deeply in tune with the one you love at this time.

The temptation to venture onto dangerous ground is strongest during the final days of the month, when Neptune could weave you into something of a blissful illusion.

A potentially tricky date for personal relationships is the 13th, when sudden disagreements and arguments are likely to flare up. If you're married or have an established relationship, this is a time when a certain number of underlying tensions will need to be confronted.

 A tendency to become over-fastidious about diet may have a negative effect on your health at the end of the month. This is an excellent time to reorganise your eating habits for the better, especially if you have become hooked on fashionable food fads recently.

LUCKY DATES 6th, 14th, 23rd, 24th.

A month when eclipses fall in your own and your opposite sign, plus several major planetary shifts, is almost certain to contain events that could change your life. Such changes may not necessarily be instantaneous or dramatic, but it does seem that between now and the middle of 2007 your objectives will undergo some kind of modification as your attitudes alter and new influences enter into your life.

The tremendous planetary activity in the sign of Virgo promises a stimulating month ahead, bringing you plenty of scope to widen your sphere of influence and activity. Mars continues to bring events that demand a high energy level during the first week, while Mercury ensures mental alertness and the ability to make on the spot decisions.

 Venus, too, moves through your sign from the 6th, promising heartwarming encounters for the romantically inclined. Something that has been under wraps for a while will emerge into the light and perhaps a secret admirer will come forward with an ardent declaration of love!

The chances of establishing an intimate link with a genuine soulmate are greatly increased at this time, but it is essential that you tread lightly and don't attempt to force what could begin as a rather tender bloom.

Two emotionally tricky dates are the 16th, when married Virgos are liable to clash with their partner; also the 25th, when a friend may come to you for tea and sympathy. But be careful how you dole out advice, and accept the fact that your acute critique is not likely to have much impact. Some people do need to learn the hard way!

 The company you keep during the first two weeks will keep you mentally active, for it looks as if some heated debate is grabbing your attention around the 3rd and 9th. This is where your excellent logical and critical faculties will stand you in good stead. If issues need clarification, this is where you will be at your best.

 The forces of transformation are likely to focus on matters a little closer to home from early in the month, onwards. Pluto becomes more active and points strongly to a possible change in your residence over the next 12 months. This trend is then given further weight by Jupiter, which moves towards the lower angle of your solar chart. This means any initiatives towards change taken this month are likely to have a fortunate outcome.

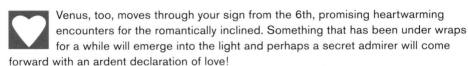 Be prepared to meet with heavier outgoings around the middle of the month, when you may be faced with bills for urgent repair jobs or need to update equipment that is important to your work. This may be an expensive nuisance. Apart from this, you can expect a progressive phase in all to do with business and financial activity.

LUCKY DATES 4th, 11th, 12th, 21st, 23rd.

Matters of a practical nature are very much the focus of attention for most of the month, bringing you plenty of scope for exercising your good sense and conscientious approach. There may be extra chores to deal with and, at times, a sense of urgency, but this is unlikely to faze you. Indeed you'll find that certain persons are extremely grateful to you for helping to turn an awkward situation around.

It's a time when much depends on your own enterprise and initiative, particularly if you are aiming to improve your credentials and earn yourself a great amount of kudos. The Jupiter-Saturn aspect later in the month suggests a need for you to consolidate a range of interests and pull your ideas together. It is the experience you have gathered in the past that will come in very useful at this time.

 A tremendous accent on the money area of your chart for most of the month makes this an exciting time for developing new projects, particularly if you are commercially minded and looking around for fresh outlets and initiatives where you can expand your business.

Existing business and fundraising activities will gather momentum and all efforts to improve your earning potential will meet with success. What's more, you can rely on other people to co-operate with you, and it would certainly be in your interests to give serious consideration to any new or unusual ideas that are suggested to you - particularly around the 10th of the month.

The presence of Venus in this area shows that you are in the mood for spending on the good things of life. You are more likely to have the necessary funds currently, so if you feel like treating yourself or your loved one, now is the time to be generous.

 It looks as if you'll be on the move for most of the month, not necessarily travelling far from familiar territory, but nevertheless clocking up a high mileage. Relatives are likely to be the cause of all this whizzing to and fro, and it is likely that most of your journeys will be more of a duty than a pleasure. However, certain people you chance to encounter on your travels will prove highly congenial and mentally stimulating. An element of serendipity could land you with a new friend or two.

The Mercury-Jupiter conjunction on the 22nd hints at a fortunate message heading in your direction, perhaps good news concerning your career or a job you recently applied for. If you have studies to complete, make your best efforts before the 28th, after which you may find it hard to concentrate.

 This is an excellent time for you to embark on a fitness campaign and work towards getting yourself into optimum shape. However, it won't all be about sweating it out in the gym. You're feeling more relaxed about life now that certain stresses and strains have eased, so do yourself a favour, pamper yourself!

LUCKY DATES 1st, 10th, 18th, 22nd.

Between the 8th and 18th Neptune receives stressful aspects from Mercury, Venus and Mars, flashing a warning that appearances will prove deceptive and the messages you receive will be ambiguous. This is where you need to keep your legendary critical faculties well honed, because it will be only too easy to be led around in circles and end in a state of complete chaos.

You may also find that you are left to clear up various messes caused by the carelessness of other people, but if this involves interfering with emotional affairs that are no real concern of yours, then steer clear! The prospect does brighten and the mists clear once Mercury switches to direct motion on the 18th, but until then keep your wits about you.

Cultivate a detached attitude in your dealings with relatives and those with whom you come in regular contact on a day-to-day basis. This rule is in force until the third week, after which you can breathe more easily. The fact is that other people's traumas are liable to impinge on you and put you in a state of worry or nervous tension - never a happy state for the Virgo temperament!

If possible, choose a date after the 18th if you are planning to arrange a special meeting or attend an interview or discussion. Mixed messages will put you in a dilemma during the second week, when you are advised to keep things simple and stick to well-worn routines.

Now that things are beginning to take a steadier course financially, you will be in a better position to re-organise your budget and consolidate certain matters that have been swaying in the balance lately. Business affairs will take a smoother course and any depletion of your resources due to recent heavy expenses will make a steady recovery as the month progresses. Worries about money will finally start to take a back seat later in the month.

The stressful Mars-Neptune aspect on the 17th warns you against taking risks in regard to health, especially where diet and eating habits are concerned. Once again there is a warning not to get hooked on anything too faddish; this can lead to obsession with the 'right' and 'wrong' foods to eat. While it is fine to be concerned about your diet, neurotic fussing will only serve to turn you into an emotional wreck and that is not to be encouraged at all.

With the two beneficial planets Venus and Jupiter moving into the lower sector of your solar chart towards the end of November, you can expect a tremendous improvement in your domestic circumstances, both at an emotional and a material level. If you have been feeling restricted with regards to your living situation, this will help ease your troubles. This expansive and enriching trend continues throughout 2007, and what happens late month will give you a preview of what is to come.

LUCKY DATES 5th, 15th, 18th, 22nd.

Matters of a very personal nature are a major preoccupation as the year draws to a close. This is definitely not bad news, because it looks as if there are very positive developments taking shape that will ultimately enhance your lifestyle. An intense grouping of planets in the lower angle of your solar chart suggest a time of endings and new beginnings. But what this implies is that you are finally breaking with restrictions you've allowed to exist in the past, and beginning to get a very clear idea of desirable changes you wish to bring about over the next twelve months.

An element of luck woven into this positive tapestry of planetary influences is bound to make your life more colourful and creative than usual. Indeed, you can expect events to arrange themselves in such a way that you will suddenly find yourself in the perfect position to push ahead with plans much sooner than anticipated.

 Everything appears to focus on domestic affairs as the festive season approaches. You're likely to find yourself with a full house even before the festivities get into full swing, so it would be in your interests to get in an abundance of provisions.

At a practical level, this is an excellent time to put effort into upgrading and refurbishing your living space. It is likely that you'll be feeling restless and perhaps with an increasing sense of dissatisfaction with the present set-up. This might not be the most convenient month to push ahead with major renovations or a change of residence, but there will certainly be no harm in getting the ball rolling if you have such major changes in mind for the coming year.

 If your experience in previous months has been something of an emotional wasteland, things are about to change. Once Venus moves into a congenial area of your solar chart on the 11th, romantic possibilities begin to emerge very clearly. This will be helped greatly by your increasing social popularity during the latter half of the month, which should also ensure that the company you keep is delightful.

From a different angle, those interests that are closest to your heart will be enhanced through the encouragement of certain friends. You may find that an activity pursued on a relatively amateur level can be shifted onto a more professional basis by joining forces with someone on your wavelength.

A short journey early in the month will bring out your proverbial sense of duty. Be prepared to play the good angel if an elderly relative or neighbour needs a helping hand. You'll actually enjoy being useful to them and your good samaritan behaviour will leave you feeling full of Christmas cheer. Later in the month it is more likely that people will be coming from far and wide to pay you a visit. There will be much intriguing news to catch up on, ending the year on a very lively note.

LUCKY DATES 10th, 18th, 21st, 29th.

libra

september 23 to october 24

Planetary Ruler:	Venus	**Wood:**	Sycamore
Quality & Element:	Cardinal Air	**Flower:**	Orchid
Colours:	Pale Green,	**Animal:**	Dove
	Pink, Blue	**Gem:**	Opal
Metal:	Copper	**Fabric:**	Silk

You might be the airiest of air signs, but the events taking shape early in 2006 will oblige you to keep your feet firmly on the ground! Matters of a decidedly practical nature are very much in focus, with the main accents falling on financial and domestic affairs. The underlying trend is forward-looking, but you might not see much evidence of this while your ruling planet backtracks into the lower angle of your solar chart.

There will be a need to display patience this month, and much will depend on your ability to keep things in equilibrium. Be prepared to meet with a minor emergency during the third week, when you may need to call on technical experts to put something in order. Alternatively, don't trust too much to luck if you are hoping for advancement in your career or wanting an overnight success in business.

This is definitely where the action is during this first month of the year! The situation may get tense around mid-month, when you'll experience a see-saw effect in money matters. Cashflow will be vigorous, but money is likely to come in and go out at an alarming rate. Added expense will be due to mechanical things going on the blink or several bills descending on you at the same time.

Care will need to be taken with regard to jointly-held assets and investments - again around the middle of the month. Steer clear of anything of a risky nature and be extremely wary of those who come to you with seemingly risk-free offers. However, as long as you keep a sense of realism and stick to the safe option, you'll come through the month with your bank balance intact.

Just when you were feeling that a new romantic link was heading in the right direction, something will put the kibosh on the whole show - at least temporarily. It could be that mundane pressures pull your attention away from intimate affairs for most of the month, but perhaps you should not allow yourself to become too despondent about this.

If you do experience something of a lull in a romance after what seemed a wonderful beginning, this will at least will give you a chance to catch your breath and see things in clearer perspective. What you are likely to realise is that the path of true love needs time and cannot be forced.

At various times during the month you can safely expect to receive a spate of visitors, some welcome, others something of a trial. Dates on which to entertain choice company in your own home are the 9th, 13th, 17th and 23rd. These are also good dates to think seriously about upgrading your living space, but don't be tempted to splash out unless your partner or family members are in agreement with your ideas and colour schemes. You could end up having to re-do the lot if those that share your house are not consulted and hate the end result.

LUCKY DATES 1st, 17th, 23rd, 29th.

You'll be relieved to see that a household problem will be resolved soon after the 3rd and a feeling of increased emotional contentment will descend over the situation. Something you were obliged to put on the back-burner around mid-December now gets the green light, thanks to the kindly suggestions or encouragement of a friend or older relative.

The underlying theme this month is that you are feeling more in control of a situation that was threatening to both perplex and confuse. A broader view of the cosmic pattern indicates that you are emerging from a transition phase, beginning to see your way ahead more clearly, and feeling stronger within your own deeper self.

 Business and financial matters continue to have a relatively high profile in your current scheme of things. The good news is that Mars finally shifts from the sign of Taurus, signalling the end of various pressures and a better return on efforts you have made in the past. For those of you who are married or otherwise in a partnership, there is promise of a boost in your fortunes via the determined effort - or luck - of your partner.

Any long-standing difficulties you've been facing of late that relate to investments, mortgages, tax and insurance are heading for a satisfactory solution soon after the 17th. But don't attempt to rush through a deal or sign anything that commits you without first weighing up all the pros and cons.

 Your ruling planet Venus begins to throw a positive and pleasant light on all things domestic from early this month onwards. At a practical level, you'll get the go-ahead for a project that has been held up since early December. If this has to do with refurbishment, renovation and a change of décor, you may find that your tastes have changed in a subtle way over the past few months. What you previously had in mind may now appear to be either rather outmoded or decidedly naff!

Emotionally, you can expect greater harmony within the family circle, and a great atmosphere later in the month when a very welcome visitor is due to arrive.

If you have been feeling cooped up and tied to dreary routines over the past few months, the situation is heading for a change once Mars kicks into your Ninth Solar House on the 17th. Not only does this release an easier energy flow within you; it also promises greater scope for broadening your horizons, either through travel or social contacts.

A helpful transit of Mercury enables you to look at things clearly and objectively, allowing you to cover a lot of ground if you are involved in intensive mental work during the month ahead. Your tolerance for work will also be increased and you'll forge ahead with any projects you'd previously put on the back-burner. It is also certainly a good time for exploring new ideas and overhauling your philosophy of life.

LUCKY DATES 3rd, 8th, 14th, 24th.

If changes are taking shape in your employment situation, try to hang in there. Decisions are looming large, but if you play your cards right and are willing to shoulder some added responsibilities for a short while, an apparent crisis will turn out to be blessing in disguise. However, if you are being driven to the end of your tether or feel that you are simply being exploited, now is the time to take radical action!

You'll need to adopt a flexible strategy for most of the month, as your usual routines will be disrupted and various extraneous demands constantly divert you from more important tasks. Here too there are hidden and unsuspected opportunities woven into what seems like total chaos. By keeping your eyes open, you may find that strings can be pulled in your favour, so try to oblige if favours are asked of you.

 The above-mentioned changes in work patterns may throw your finances into a state of affairs that leaves you rather anxious. If you're in a quandary about a current job offer, or are strongly inclined to look for alternative employment, it would be unwise to do anything on impulse and be panicked into hasty decisions. If possible, bide your time until the 25th, when a confusing situation will be clarified and an unexpected twist of events should conspire to give you a better sense of the right direction to take.

The underlying astrological pattern is supportive, endowing you with energy and enhancing your intuitive and creative power. So if things appear difficult, do your very best to take it easy, and remain confident that something will turn up.

 If material affairs are threatening to go into meltdown, the same cannot be said for your amorous interests. Between the 16th and 27th events are likely to move ahead at breathtaking speed, making you feel that you have at last come in from the cold.

For too long you may have been attempting to prop up an affair that has been rather sporadic, half-hearted and downright exasperating at times. But from this month onwards the situation shows signs of changing quite radically. It could be that certain obstacles are removed, or you meet someone with whom you feel an instant affinity. Altogether a highly promising outlook!

You may find it hard to get other people, especially work colleagues, to accept your ideas, but maybe you are being a bit premature and need to realign your thoughts. Accept the fact that not everyone is keen to break familiar patterns overnight.

A long range journey later in the month is sure to lift your spirits and bring you in touch with the kind of people who are very much on your own spiritual wavelength. New friends you make at this time are sure to be part of your circle for some time to come. The final week is excellent if you can see your way to taking a break.

LUCKY DATES 16th, 19th, 26th, 27th.

After a rather stressful transition, you should find that things begin to fall into place during the coming month. This doesn't mean you can afford to take anything too much for granted, but at least you'll have a clearer idea of what takes priority and what can be safely cast aside.

If your confidence has suffered a blow recently and you have become disheartened by the dubious motives of certain people around you, the situation is likely to turn around and you will begin to feel your faith in human nature being restored. On the 5th the planet Saturn takes a more positive direction and points to the development of a greater sense of purpose in regard to your special aims and ideals.

Experience gained and lessons learned in the past will stand you in good stead, especially in areas that depend on co-operation and teamwork.

You can expect a speedy and helpful response from other people during the latter half of the month, which is the best time for seeking professional advice or sorting out a legal matter. A lively exchange of ideas seems to be moving forward during the third week, which is good news for those involved in vital discussions and debates. However, you may need to exercise discretion on the 18th when differences of opinion could get overheated.

There is an adventurous feel to journeys in the first half of the month, with special highlights on the 1st and 8th. Symbolically, the prevailing pattern shows that treasures will be discovered via travel. OK, this might not mean that you dig up gold on a remote island, but it could mean that you meet someone interesting or visit a place that is destined to play an important part in your future destiny.

The stress factor that you experienced recently will fade into the background during April, but be warned that around the full Moon on the 13th you may be feeling hypersensitive emotionally and therefore liable to overreact if you feel someone is criticising you.

Towards the end of the month you may be obliged to alter your own arrangements due to someone feeling under the weather. It might be in your interests to keep a close eye on any pets that you keep and take quick action if you suspect that something may be wrong with one of them.

Although you cannot expect to make a fortune overnight at present, there are positive indications of advancement in career and worldly status during the latter half of the month. With Mars pushing into the topmost sector of your solar chart, and Venus casting a kindly light on work interests, you can't fail to take steps forward at this time. Don't be impatient and know that what you do now will not go to waste. Events taking shape towards the end of the month will smooth your path to success and enable you to take strategic initiatives.

LUCKY DATES 4th, 13th, 20th, 29th.

An expansive and progressive trend comes into force during the first half of the month, making this a prime time for pushing ahead with your central aims and ambitions. For those of an enterprising nature, or who work in high-powered jobs, the cosmic pattern is very much in tune with your interests and almost guarantees a substantial advancement in the coming weeks.

Even if your aims are of a relatively modest nature, events will somehow contrive to guide you into a more dynamic path where you can develop and make optimum use of your greatest potential. Basically, this is a time when your personal initiatives, combined with a certain element of luck, will lead to an enhancement of your status and reputation, so you'd be foolish to underestimate your capabilities.

 With such an unusually dynamic accent on practical interests, there can be little doubt that what happens during May will have a pleasing impact on your financial prospects. New doors are likely to swing open, bringing opportunities to the career-minded and greater incentives to those involved in business and commerce.

Take advantage of the stimulating influence of Mercury between the 5th and 19th if you are joining forces with another person to promote a fundraising venture. This is also the best time to overhaul your investment portfolio and to discuss the various options that allow you to make best use of your existing assets. The only date to be wary of is the 15th, when appearances will be deceptive and misinformation could cause problems in business affairs.

 To those considering marriage either this month or in the near future, the message is clear: go for it! The presence of Venus in your opposite sign guarantees a more vibrant and intimate rapport between you and your loved one. All close ties of love and affection will be strengthened, and for those still hoping to meet the ideal partner, the prospect is decidedly enticing - especially when Venus is strongly activated on the 24th and 26th.

And it is not only intimate ties that feel the beneficial influence of Venus. If frictions and underlying differences are causing bad vibes, now is the time to offer the olive branch, confront issues, and establish a better understanding with those people you have been out of sync with lately.

Life gets interesting soon after the 19th, when travel comes into the picture and you get the go-ahead for certain project that you were forced to shelve earlier in the year. It is not only travel that broadens your horizons, for this is a time when you are likely to be exploring new ideas and establishing a wider network of contacts in order to increase your knowledge and enhance your range of creative expression. Losing yourself in interesting artistic endeavours will have many pleasing results. There is bound to be something that grabs your imagination around the 29th.

LUCKY DATES 8th, 13th, 19th, 24th.

The going may get rather tough during the third week of June, but you can rely on others to pull their weight and you are unlikely to be lacking in energy. If a sense of urgency does prevail at times, it will be for a good reason and will tie in nicely with the tremendous progress you can make in the coming weeks. If you have been working hard to establish your credentials and further either career or professional aims, you'll begin to see positive results stemming from your efforts from this month onwards.

Saturn continues to steady your course, helping you to guide your destiny via contact and co-operation with people of maturity and wisdom. Long term aims and objectives are very much at centrestage throughout the month, and it is here that you will benefit by taking heed of timely advice and making sure that you are keeping to a realistic course of action.

Personal and joint financial interests are under the beneficial sway of your ruling planet for most of the month. The trend is towards greater stability, so it is likely that you'll be giving much attention to matters relating to future security, insurance schemes and perhaps legacies.

Your partner, or someone closely associated with you, is likely to experience a boost in their fortunes, much to your delight. Generally speaking, the steadier course that money matters are taking at this time will allow you to feel easier about splashing out on things that enhance and add to the quality of your life. However, a good motto to adopt around mid month is "let the buyer beware" - particularly if you are tempted to purchase something of an artistic nature.

Feelings are likely to be gaining in intensity in the first half of the month, and there is just a chance that a friend or third party will be feeling a bit miffed in regard to a recent romantic development in your own life. Tread tactfully, or be prepared to allow a respectable interval of time if someone happens to be on the rebound, so to speak.

Apart from this possible discrepancy, the prospects continue to be bright for those hoping to find a meaningful relationship. Late this month is an excellent time if you are hoping to spend some time away from your usual surroundings with the special person in your life.

The Mercury-Pluto opposition at the start of the month warns you to doublecheck the small print if a contract or legal agreement is under consideration. Something from the past may have to be confronted and cleared up once and for all. The closure you get from this will reap many emotional and practical benefits.

Your mental energies will best be focused on matters of a very practical nature throughout the month, particularly career interests and the need to gain qualifications.

LUCKY DATES 7th, 11th, 13th, 23rd.

With Jupiter resuming forward momentum from early in the month you can expect a steady improvement in your material fortunes and the end of a fairly long-standing financial problem. Generally speaking, there is a more optimistic feel in regard to your worldly aims and interests. This may be because you are beginning to feel that you are at last getting ahead of your game and reaping the benefits of past efforts.

This does not mean that you can take things for granted where career interests are concerned. The retrograde cycle of Mercury indicates a need to go over the same ground again and to clarify any issues that may be generating obstacles. You can use your time to best effect by doing your homework and sorting out your priorities, for you may find that you are seeing a situation from too narrow a perspective and therefore sabotaging your own interests.

 Even if certain glitches affecting your career or employment need ironing out, this is not likely to have any negative effects on financial affairs. Everything points to a phase of expansion and enrichment, with something of a lucky break heading in your direction towards the end of the month.

Don't be afraid to stick your neck out if an opportunity to increase your earning powers comes your way. By taking a more imaginative and unconventional approach, you may find that fortunes can be improved and obstacles overcome. Jupiter indicates a supportive trend, which will be extremely helpful for those who are launching a new business venture or wish to embark on a fundraising scheme.

 Venus, your ruler, casts a pleasant light on far-flung journeys for most of the month, making this a prime time for taking a vacation and escaping from your usual routines. A change of scenery will not only be excellent therapy if you have been under stress lately, but it will have unexpected benefits in terms of your social life and friendships. Around the middle of the month it looks as if a journey will entail revisiting the past in some way - there is a sense of nostalgia, perhaps because you will rendezvous with an old friend or lover.

On a more mundane level, you may find that communications go on the blink between the 10th and 29th, with the main problems liable to be focused on your current work schedules. An important project will be held up and some quick rethinking may be needed if things are to be kept on a steady course. By late month the dust should settle, but in the meantime you need to keep a critical eye on what others have in mind.

 Lunar trends around the 11th signal that there will be a sensitive atmosphere within the family circle, something you need to take into account. However, the cause of this is probably something quite trivial, so don't panic. Keep the lines of communication open and all should be well.

LUCKY DATES 3rd, 10th, 27th, 30th.

A fortunate trend continues to benefit your material interests, and something begun in the previous month will flourish beyond your expectations. Don't be afraid to take a bold approach if you are aiming to make desirable changes in your lifestyle. Now that various problems and uncertainties are behind you, the way is clear to explore the possibilities and realise your cherished hopes and wishes.

There's a friendly and co-operative aura around you throughout the month, with much to suggest that someone, perhaps a person quite influential and authoritative, will help you to further your objectives. Your social life promises to swiftly gather momentum, as new friends are pulled into your orbit and your own personal interests are extended to include a wider circle of significant and useful contacts.

The 12th marks a turning point for those who may have been languishing in the doldrums over the past months. This is when you'll begin to experience a more active social life and are likely to encounter someone attractive. However, don't expect that tender passions will crash into your life. Developments will take a slow course, but you can be sure that this is a good sign and promises a more enduring relationship.

As already hinted, friends are due to play a more significant part in your life at the moment, especially in the latter half of the month. Pleasant events are connected with a friend around the 22nd, when you may find yourself celebrating an engagement or some other good news.

Whatever involves you in group activities and teamwork will give you tremendous scope for expressing your creativity and imagination, and if you're interested in alternative lifestyles and environmental concerns, you can expect tremendous support from kindred spirits.

It looks as if you will begin to take a more serious interest in social and world affairs in the latter half of the month. Those interested in political issues, social reforms and humanitarian concerns are likely to have plenty of grist to their mill at this time. Again it will be through wider contact and communication with like-minded individuals that your sense of purpose will be strengthened in these areas.

A splendid aspect between Jupiter and Uranus late in the month signals a sudden upturn in your fortunes, perhaps financial luck or an ideal job offer. If you have any unusual moneymaking ideas floating around in the back of your mind, perhaps you should bring them forward. This is a particularly helpful trend for those aiming to strike out in a more independent or unconventional direction in regard to earning a living. It is important to remain open to interesting suggestions from friends and don't be afraid to experiment. You may find that a long-held dream of lucrative self-employment is finally on the cards.

LUCKY DATES 3rd, 12th, 22nd, 29th.

Information that's revealed to you in the earlier part of the month will throw light on the behaviour of a friend who may have been going through a rather secretive phase recently. Indeed, the theme of discovery is very much to the fore and will take the form of insight into the deeper motivations of some of the people who are closely associated with you. Instead of jumping to conclusions and seeing things in the worst possible light, you may realise just how much you are driven by your own prejudices.

The pace of life is due to gather an energetic momentum soon after the 8th. Apart from mid-month when there's a danger of ending up at odds with others due to a sudden lapse of your usual tactful ways, you can expect that events will bring you increased motivation and the incentive to press ahead with your important aims and objectives.

 Not only will events demand a greater energy output on your part, but once Mercury begins to activate your sign on the 12th it looks as if you'll be dashing about all over the place. Provided your schedules remain well organised, this increase of activity and movement will prove to be rewarding and mentally stimulating.

Although your general attitude is fairly laidback, this is not going to be much in evidence in the latter half of the month. It may be necessary at times to assert yourself very forcefully in order to tackle certain tasks or head off a problem before it grows out of proportion. By the end of the month you will have reason to congratulate yourself on the amount of ground that you have covered!

 Eclipses on the 7th and 22nd have a direct bearing on your health. This is nothing to get anxious about, but it does mean that you need to be alert to warning signals. In a month when events demand energy and stamina, there is a danger that you push yourself too fast and too far. Take extra care therefore on the eclipse dates.

 Jupiter continues to cast a benign influence on your financial affairs, so don't dither if an opportunity to increase your funds arises. It's your own initiative and willingness to explore broader avenues that will bring positive results at this time, though you may need to restrain a tendency to let confidence run away with you later in the month.

A certain panache may be needed if you are aiming to make a profit out of your creative abilities or through organising a large-scale entertainment late month. But be on the alert for those who are out to exploit your good intentions.

 Your intimate affairs will remain decidedly secretive and extremely low key this month. However, this is not because something shady is going on, but simply because you prefer it that way. Your friends will not suspect a thing and that's the way you'll like it this month.

LUCKY DATES 1st, 13th, 23rd, 24th.

Events that are taking shape will stimulate your imagination and creative energy during the first half of the month, and all of a sudden your social life will take on an added dimension. Don't be surprised to find yourself becoming popular and the centre of attention at this time! This is very good news for those who are aiming to make a splash, to get into the limelight and to get where the action is.

It could be said that you have it in your power to forge your own destiny by tuning into a deeper level of creativity within you. The prevailing invigorating and inspiring trends will certainly benefit those who are eager to gain publicity and promote their own or others' talents. Altogether it seems you have an unusual month ahead, with unexpected twists of events opening new dimensions of experience – plus a touch of glamour!

This glamorous element will be most in evidence to those who find themselves woven into new romantic developments. In many ways this is an unusually eventful month in regard to affairs of the heart, most notably because of several powerful aspects involving the mystical and magical Neptune on the 4th, 10th and 14th. Love is likely to have a fairytale quality, but this does not mean that you are looking at things through rose-tinted spectacles (which is usually the case with Neptune).

And it doesn't end there! This intriguing pattern of planets does of course fall in your birthday month, which shows that the following 12 months will bring surprising and highly satisfying developments as far as intimate ties are concerned.

On a more practical theme, you can expect business and commercial interests to move in a profitable direction throughout the month. The presence of Mercury in the money sector of your solar chart brings the incentive to diversify your interests; explore and try out new ideas; and establish useful contacts. If you are hoping to improve your credentials and boost your earning potential, now is the time for action!

Fundraising ventures, one-off business deals, or simply shopping around for bargains are favoured under the positive influence of Mercury. But watch out when this planet is in trickster mode on the 15th, when there is a danger of loss through deception, theft or sheer carelessness.

Towards the end of the month you may need to take a closer look at property matters, for instance mortgage schedules or an insurance claim. If you are considering going shares with a friend in purchasing or renting property, make doubly sure that you get sound legal advice, and be prepared to back down if the other interested parties are not totally committed.

Generally speaking, this is a time when it would be worthwhile to take a more serious attitude to security issues. Check your property to see if it could benefit from an alarm or better locks.

LUCKY DATES 4th, 10th, 14th, 24th.

There is a kind of full circle effect going on this month. It seems that what took shape earlier in the year will have important repercussions around now, giving you the feeling that a cycle of activity is reaching completion. Matters of a very practical nature are brought into sharp focus throughout November and, while there may be some hassles and delays to contend with until the 18th, the underlying trend continues to bring expanding fortunes.

It is likely that the winds of change will be felt most strongly in areas such as employment and business interests. This is unlikely to throw any major problems across your path, though it might be necessary to overhaul and update certain methods and targets. Jupiter's sign switch later in the month indicates an urge to broaden your mental horizons and break free from routines that you now feel to be a restriction. In this way you will prepare yourself for the opportunities that will come your way in the near future.

 Having such a powerful planetary grouping in the money area of your solar chart makes this a potentially eventful month in regard to your material fortunes. The trend is helpful, except that the retrograde motion of Mercury until mid-month warns you to stick to familiar ground rather than allowing yourself to get sidetracked by people whose ideas and promises are likely to be unrealistic.

Cashflow will be vigorous and expenses rather heavy around the 17th, but what begins to take shape soon after this date will enable you to get a firmer handle on the money situation. Towards the end of the month caution is called for if you are thinking of dealing in second-hand mechanical equipment or vehicles.

 Journeys, especially the shorter variety, will be source of delight during the latter half of the month. Events taking place in the affairs of relatives will call for visits to and from, and perhaps a close friend or ex-lover will invite you to share in a celebration. Be prepared for an element of the unexpected on the 25th, which necessitates impromptu travel arrangements. What seems like an inconvenience will turn out to be surprisingly pleasant!

 The delights of travel may be connected with romantic developments around the 21st - a date when you are also likely to hear welcome news concerning a friend or relative - or someone who has at last emerged from an emotionally difficult experience.

Librans have a good understanding of human relationships and can give helpful advice, but you are advised against offering guidance on the 25th.

 If you're a practitioner in some field of therapy, the changing cosmic agenda later in the month will bring you a feeling of increasing confidence in your abilities, and this will be reflected in your success. There will be a perpetuating cycle of more satisfied clients feeding your confidence - and your client list.

LUCKY DATES 3rd, 10th, 20th, 21st.

As the festive season approaches and the year draws to an end it looks as if you'll be caught up in a tremendous spate of activity. If you believe that variety is the spice of life, then the events of December will certainly prove the point! The pace will verge on the frenetic at times and you'll find it hard to keep track of what's going on, but nevertheless it seems that you'll be getting much enjoyment from this lively state of affairs.

Long-established and all-too-familiar routines are likely to loosen their hold, giving you a sense of increased freedom and you may find an incentive to revive interests and activities that you were forced to lay aside earlier in the year due to more pressing duties. Whatever ends up happening, this is definitely not going to be a dull month!

Be prepared to give serious attention to money matters early in the month, particularly if an old problem cannot be ignored any longer. What you have achieved in the previous months will no doubt be cause for self-congratulation, but don't forget that there comes a time when you need to take stock, reorganise your budget and consider where you go from here.

The good news is that the heavy demands on your resources of previous weeks gives way to an easier trend, allowing you to consolidate your assets and make good a temporary shortage of funds.

Journeys either for business or pleasure (or a mixture of both) will meet your expectations, bringing an added bonus in the shape of interesting social contacts and genuine friendships. You'll be drawn into a lively exchange of ideas and opinions around the 10th, so if you wish to get your views across forcefully this is the time to speak up!

Unexpected developments in the affairs of relatives may mean a quick change of plan for the festivities. It would be in your best interests to adopt a flexible agenda later in the month, for it seems that through no fault of their own people will be unable pay you a promised visit.

Even if things don't go entirely to plan, the presence of Venus in the lower angle of your solar chart in the latter half of December ensures peace and good will within the family circle and beyond. On the very last day of the month the Moon throws a benign aspect to your ruling planet, promising a friendly and affectionate welcome to the New Year.

Many Librans will be able to look back on 2006 as being an unusually fortunate year, not only from a purely material angle, but more importantly because you are now feeling more secure within yourself and confident about the direction in which your life is heading. A number of issues that have been unresolved for some time will have found a resolution during 2006.

LUCKY DATES 1st, 10th, 19th, 31st.

scorpio

october 24 to november 23

Planetary Ruler:	Pluto	**Wood:**	Redwoods
Quality & Element:	Fixed Water	**Flower:**	Anemone
Colours:	Dark Red,	**Animal:**	Falcon
	Brown, Black	**Gem:**	Jasper
Metal:	Iron, Steel	**Fabric:**	Tweed

Your sense of purpose is becoming increasingly focused in the early stages of 2006, bringing with it tremendous determination to stay on course and to get a very clear definition of what you wish to achieve in the coming months. Having three powerful planets in the strongest angles of your solar chart makes this very much a year when past efforts come to fruition and new possibilities appear on your horizon.

Being a naturally strong-willed person, your tolerance threshold for those who threaten to distract you and waste your time tends to be low, which may often give rise to tensions and feelings of resentment. This is something you're likely to experience around mid January, when you may be accused of being ruthless or on a power trip.

The unusually intense pattern of planets could incline you to be somewhat obsessive in pursuing your aims, and indeed this will get you where you want to be, but remember that not everyone is endowed with your kind of intense psychological stamina.

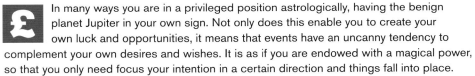

In many ways you are in a privileged position astrologically, having the benign planet Jupiter in your own sign. Not only does this enable you to create your own luck and opportunities, it means that events have an uncanny tendency to complement your own desires and wishes. It is as if you are endowed with a magical power, so that you only need focus your intention in a certain direction and things fall into place.

Don't get too complacent though, because although Jupiter can bring tremendous luck and expansion, it is only too easy to undermine your good fortune through over-confidence or attempting to lord it over other people. However, if you wish to strike it rich, this is certainly a time to make special efforts.

The fiery planet Mars continues an unusually lengthy transit of your opposite sign and throws a tense aspect to Jupiter mid-month. If a crisis has been looming in recent months, this could mean a showdown. It could be a case of make or break, but it would be best to confront those emotional undercurrents that have been generating tensions in personal relationships.

There is a danger of sabotaging your own best interests by attempting to impose your will on other people, but if this involves an intimate partner you'll only have yourself to blame if suppressed feelings erupt and bring an ultimatum. It's not exactly the easiest month for intimate attachments, but problems can be minimised by reflecting on your own behaviour and the effect this has on others.

Whether you like it or not, you will be obliged to give greater attention to home and family affairs later in the month. Be prepared to forfeit a social engagement if a relative needs your help, or if an old friend pays you a visit at short notice. You will have plenty of time, however, to catch up with friends later in the month.

LUCKY DATES 4th, 13th, 23rd, 28th.

After a jittery start to the year you can expect the dust to settle as a more harmonious trend comes into effect. The really good news is that Mars finally takes leave of your opposite sign on the 17th, promising an end to what may have been a rather tough-going experience over the past six months. Relations on all levels will improve, and no doubt you will have learned valuable lessons due to various confrontations that have taken place during this potentially stressful phase.

Jupiter continues to shed a favourable light on your personal affairs, enabling you to make the best of opportunities and bring about desirable changes. All attempts to enrich your life, either materially or intellectually, will meet with success and satisfaction while this planet holds sway.

A journey that had to be postponed earlier last month or in December can be brought back onto the agenda soon after the 3rd. This is sure to delight you because it probably will involve a reunion with an old friend, or a special celebration concerning a relative.

Changes in your usual routines are forecast in the latter half of the month, allowing you a change of scenery and a chance to mix in congenial company. Messages you receive between the 20th and 25th are likely to contain welcome news and perhaps a surprise invitation that has equally surprising consequences. It looks like you'll meet up with an old friend of acquaintance that you haven't seen for some while.

Interestingly, there is a link between travel and romance later in the month, and it could be that the surprise invite provides you with a key to your heart's desires. One thing is for sure: now that Mars leaves you House of Partners, you can hope to find greater contentment through intimate attachments.

Obstacles in the way of matrimony, for instance, are likely to disappear. And where there has been a fairly long-standing difference of opinion or clash of egos, greater harmony and understanding will prevail.

It is likely that work pressures and your determination to succeed at a professional level have clashed with intimate and personal affairs over the past year. This trend gives way to a more relaxed attitude from February onwards, and this is sure to have beneficial effects on your love life. If you've been in a long-standing disagreement with your nearest and dearest this should finally get resolved.

Career interests continue to have a very high profile in your life and ambitions, and your determination to establish a solid material and financial base in your lifestyle will continue to be a major preoccupation. However, you should begin to feel a bit less obsessive about these matters now that you are seeing your past hard work pay off finally. Lunar trends on the 13th suggest completion of a special task and a feeling of being in greater control of your special aims and ambitions.

LUCKY DATES 5th, 10th, 20th, 28th.

A process of rethinking and restructuring seems to be going ahead during these weeks. There may be times when you feel that the foundations - or the goalposts - are shifting, obliging you to draw upon your inner resourcefulness in order to keep things on course. If you do feel that it's time to take stock due to the pressure of events, you can make the most of prevailing trends by taking an honest look at those areas of your life where things might not be going according to your best laid plans.

The Lunar eclipse mid-month suggests a need to change or upgrade your current aims and objectives, or to abandon a certain course of action if it is not delivering the goods. Group activities that have engaged your creative skill in the past may be falling foul of a clash of interests and of egos, so take this as a cue to gracefully bow out!

 You'll need to make allowances for a disruptive pattern in social arrangements for most of the month. Try to keep to a flexible policy and don't expect other people to be completely reliable if you plan a special meeting or an evening's entertainment. An element of absent-mindedness will be the main culprit if a social event falls flat on its face. However, better results in your business and social arrangements can be expected once Mercury turns direct on the 25th.

Spare time or educational interests may suffer a minor setback during these weeks, but perhaps this is because you are expecting too much of others and over-rating your own performance.

 Matters closer to home come under the harmonious influence of Venus throughout the month, making this a source of great satisfaction. Indeed, there will be times when you'll be relieved to spend time at home, to escape from outside pressures for a while and concentrate on those things that give you a feeling of stability and contentment in your life.

Splendid aspects of Venus later in the month suggest congenial company in your home and something good connected with a member of your family circle. It is likely also that you'll be inspired to tidy up your immediate surroundings, get rid of unwanted clutter, and make everything more beautiful. Venus does much to enhance your tastes when it comes to choosing a colour scheme, so it's an ideal time to take action if you feel that your living space has become rather jaded.

Jointly held resources come under the progressive energy of Mars, making this a good month for taking fresh initiatives and dealing with soundly-based financial interests. However, tread carefully when Mars is at odds with Uranus on the 11th. Avoid get-rich-quick schemes and anything of a risky nature - no matter how tempting. Later in the month it looks like an added bonus is winging its way to you, or perhaps a surprise promotion. Some unexpectedly good news is certainly on the cards.

LUCKY DATES 9th, 16th, 19th, 25th.

The presence of Saturn in the topmost sector of your solar chart during 2006 gives a very high profile to your need to further an ambition and establish a definite status in the world. Your attitude to occupational and vocational interests will become more focused, inclining you to shun frivolities and buckle down to the serious business of life in this material world.

This does not imply that it's going to be all work and no play, but you will become more choosy about the company you keep and impatient with people or situations that you feel are simply wasting your valuable time. As Saturn becomes more active from early April, it looks as if you'll be shouldering some added responsibilities and perhaps attaining a more authoritative status in your chosen field of work.

 Mars continues to throw a progressive light on both personal and joint financial interests in the first half of the month. Although an old problem may rear its ugly head around the 8th, this will at least give you a chance to clarify the issues and get things sorted out to everyone's satisfaction. Legacies and legal payments are highlighted, so be prepared to give serious attention to these matters and get a second opinion if in doubt.

The prospect brightens considerably around the 20th, when an element of luck enters the picture. You may find that a spare time interest could be steered into a more profitable channel, thanks to the suggestions of a friend or acquaintance. Don't be afraid to explore different avenues if you're aiming to boost your income.

 Romantic affairs will be blessed with an element of luck during the latter half of the month, with an unexpected twist of events on the 18th putting you in a mood of pleasant anticipation.

Take note also of the 20th and 24th, when it looks as if you'll be drawn into a more varied social circle. Not only will this encourage the development of interesting new friendships, it will certainly enhance the potential for meeting a genuine soulmate.

From a different angle, the prevailing trend favours interests you do for love rather than money. This is good news for those who are intent on developing creative talents and have artistic ability in fields such as music, drama and writing. If you wish to move from amateur pursuits towards a more professional status, now is the time to take yourself more seriously.

 Be prepared for a rather hectic agenda around the 18th, when important and perhaps lengthy journeys are indicated. Business interests may necessitate more travel than usual, and routines will have to be disrupted to take advantage of a situation that could prove highly beneficial. Something will demand initiative and enterprise, so be ready to act quickly if an opportunity crops up. It might be a good idea to prepare to be scrutinised by others in a position to help you out financially.

LUCKY DATES 4th, 5th, 15th, 20th.

This is the month when it all begins to happen for Scorpio individuals! The powerful triple aspect involving Mars, Uranus and Jupiter in the first week sets the scene for an unusual and perhaps quite unexpected train of events. If you get the feeling that the Fates or your guiding angel is taking a hand in your affairs, it would certainly not be surprising.

To add a little fine detail to this intriguing picture, the accent is on creative energy, your sense of adventure and the need to break out of a mould that has felt like an increasing restriction over the past twelve months or so. There's magic woven into this kind of astrological configuration, in the sense that you have it in your power to make the changes you have been longing for and then land firmly on your feet. The basic message is that it is an unusually lucky month, a time when you can and should follow the beckoning finger of chance and opportunity.

 The urge to break loose from confining routines is likely to take you travelling far and wide. It's an ideal month for indulging your need for adventure if the mood takes you in that direction. Wider and distant horizons are beckoning more insistently at this time, so if you have planned a vacation you'll not be disappointed. Even if you have not made such plans, it is likely that long range travel will be a major focus of your thinking and planning.

From a different angle, there is a powerful learning curve woven into the prevailing trends; inspiring and encouraging you to embark on a quest for knowledge, to research a subject that grabs your interest, and to seek out individuals who are able to enlighten and stimulate your mental energies. Incidentally, the outlook is extremely promising for those involved in publishing and the more up-front aspects of the media.

 The cosmic pattern lends positive support to those who are intent on improving their stamina and achieving a vibrant physical condition. You're likely to become more conscious and conscientious about diet and how it influences your self-image. It would certainly be in your interests to explore more deeply into the realms of alternative health methods - particularly if you wish to become a practitioner in this area. Scorpio people often have an inborn instinct for the healing arts, so if this is what takes your interest, now is the time to commit yourself more fully to the development of your latent skills.

 What takes shape during the final ten days of the month is almost certain to raise your spirits in regard to personal or joint financial affairs. A fundraising venture will gain momentum, thanks to a little help from friends or via the lateral thinking of your partner. Imagination and creativity are the essential ingredients in the sphere of money-making later in the month. Ideas you've previously had to shelve will be brought back to life and become viable once again.

LUCKY DATES 2nd, 5th, 7th, 12th, 21st, 26th.

The events of June will demand a fairly high energy input and there will be times when your ability to keep to schedules and obligations will be pushed to the edge. The most stressful phase occurs toward the end of the third week, when Mars joins with Saturn in the top sector of your solar chart and throws a challenging aspect to Jupiter. Indeed, what happens around this time will definitely challenge your abilities.

Where problems do arise, these are likely to be related to career interests or other aims that are important to you at present. There appears to be an element of doubt woven into the situation and you may be obliged to alter and realign your strategies if things are to continue moving on a steady course. Heavier responsibilities may have to be taken on for a short while, but by the end of the month you should begin to see your way clear and know what decisions need to be taken.

A conflict of duties is likely to be experienced during the third week, with a danger of upsetting the emotional climate closer to home. The main culprit will be pressure of work and a sense of urgency that diverts all your attention away from home and family affairs. If someone - your partner for instance - accuses you of being ruthless, it may be the case that you should take this to heart and analyse your own deeper motivations.

On a more practical level, the trend is generally helpful for dealing with important property matters, particularly if you are considering a change of residence in the future or wish to rent premises either for commercial or domestic use. If possible, however, avoid employing builders or tackling DIY jobs beyond your level of skill and competence later in the month. Things could get expensive!

The tricky aspects of Venus on the 4th and 15th warn you to exercise tact and sensitivity towards your intimate partner. Once again it is your involvement in work or other external activities that may bring on bad vibes and make you out to be neglectful or self-centred.

Prospects improve from mid-month, when you have greater scope for cultivating quality time devoted to more intimate and personal affections. If you're single and hoping for romance to enter your life, don't expect miracles, but look out for promising turn of events around the 23rd.

If everything else appears to be going through a rather jittery phase, at least your mind will be clear and you'll be able to make the right decisions if faced with a dilemma. A journey or long-distance message around the 12th is likely to have unexpected repercussions on how you plan your life over the next few months. Take special notice of dreams and hunches at this time as your imagination and your subconscious will provide you with some of your best ideas this month.

LUCKY DATES 8th, 9th, 12th, 26th.

The tide of fortune begins to flow more strongly from early this month as Jupiter turns direct in your own sign. However, as Mercury goes into retrograde phase around the same time, it would be unwise to expect too much too soon, as it will be only too easy to fall foul of misplaced confidence. Your best policy is to steer a steady course while keeping your ear to the ground for ideas that might be useful in future.

Jupiter represents an expansive trend in your affairs, which is something you will become very aware of between now and the end of the year. The direction of your aims and objectives is likely to change and this may entail a phase of intense effort on your part, but you'll get the feeling that the Fates are on your side. This month it seems that, no matter what happens, you'll land firmly on your feet and it will be an auspicious time for going for what you really want.

If possible, aim to finalise plans and tie up loose ends before the 10th - especially if this entails dealing with legal and bureaucratic red tape. Between this date and the end of the month you are advised to double-check travel arrangements and be careful to read the small print if you need to put your signature to any important document or contract.

With Mercury backtracking it is generally hard to avoid a certain level of disruption, particularly in regard to travel. A journey may have to be postponed during the third week, but in some ways this may be a blessing in disguise. By adopting a flexible attitude you will discover that a lot of aggravation can be avoided, so don't be too insistent that everything should go strictly to schedule.

Jupiter's expansive influence is certain to have a very positive impact on your financial interests between now and the end of the year. Events that begin to take shape in July will give a hint of the better things to come, and it may well be that a wonderful career opportunity presents itself soon after the new Moon on the 25th.

The Venus-Jupiter aspect late in the month produces a lucky link between money and travel, making this a prime time for business journeys and making efforts to spread your interests over a wider field. If your work is connected with travel and transport, the prevailing trend could not be much better.

Feelings and emotions are intensified as Venus transits your Eighth Solar House in the first half of the month. This is not necessarily a bad thing, for if an emotional problem does emerge at least it will give you a chance to confront and clarify the issue, clearing the air.

The forces of attraction will come at high pitch around the middle of the month, which could be rather a mixed blessing. At best it might be genuine love at first sight, but equally a mad infatuation that quickly burns out and leaves you exhausted. Whatever happens, it's not going to be boring!

LUCKY DATES 6th, 15th, 23rd, 27th.

Although this is traditionally the month for taking a holiday, it seems that your mind will be largely focused on matters of a very practical nature. Developments that began to take shape in July will gather momentum and may lead to a quantum leap forward in regard to your worldly status. Something you have been working towards for several years is about to enter a transition period the results of which will put you in a more influential position and enable you to break new ground.

If it's co-operation you need, now is the time to rally the troops and get your act together. All activities that engage you in teamwork or where there is a need for dynamic social interaction will be highly rewarding, not only in terms of profitability but, more importantly, in the personal satisfaction it brings you.

As far as career and commercial interests are concerned, you'll have reason to feel confident and optimistic. The key to greater success lies firmly in your own hands now that you are clearer about the goals you are striving to achieve. Increased luck will come through your ability to act boldly and to have faith in your own creative power. Your talents will be in demand if only will have the confidence to let people know what you're capable of.

As Saturn is the moving force in all to do with material aims and ambitions throughout the year, the events of August will be decisive in determining the direction you take in the future. For those considering a career change or who wish to improve their credentials, this is the time to take the initiative.

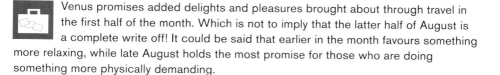

Venus promises added delights and pleasures brought about through travel in the first half of the month. Which is not to imply that the latter half of August is a complete write off! It could be said that earlier in the month favours something more relaxing, while late August holds the most promise for those who are doing something more physically demanding.

It's the first two weeks that also favour the romantically inclined, because it is then that love and long distance journeys are fatefully interwoven. If you have suffered disappointments in your love life closer to home over the past year, there is a chance that a far-flung pleasure trip will work the right kind of magic.

Not only intimate relationships but also friendship will be an important feature in your life throughout the month. A relative stranger, perhaps someone who appears on the scene momentarily, will fire your imagination and set your thoughts spinning in a new and perhaps unconventional direction.

Take extra special care not to injure yourself if you are engaging in sporting activity around the 13th. Better still, try to involvement in anything too strenuous at this time.

LUCKY DATES 2nd, 6th, 11th, 20th, 29th.

An unexpected turn of events towards the end of August could mean that you are faced with a major decision during the month ahead. Much depends on your circumstances of course, but if you are not totally committed to a current project or work situation it could be that a road to greater freedom of self-expression can be opened up.

The prevailing cosmic pattern suggests a break with the past, due to a timely offer or opportunity that has been virtually handed you on a plate. If you are aiming to base your lifestyle on a more independent and creative pattern, now is the time to set things in motion.

Don't be afraid to experiment, for you have Uranus, the planet of originality and freedom activating a highly creative area of your solar chart. Plus the fact that Jupiter in your own sign gives you the necessary confidence and resourcefulness to realise your aims.

Don't go all the way to admitting defeat if a recent romantic promise appears to fade from view. Once Venus shifts into a more congenial area on the 6th you may experience a surprising turnaround in this rather sensitive matter. Love cannot be expected to run an entirely smooth course, particularly with Venus being at odds with Uranus and Pluto on the 16th and 25th, but the situation is far from hopeless.

A likely scenario is that either you or the other person is finding it hard to get untangled from a previous emotional attachment. This is a situation that may change from day to day, giving you a sense of suspense and perhaps a feeling of despair. Although this could signal a rather emotionally draining time if you hang on in there, for it looks as if the tide will turn later in the month, and by October you'll be riding the crest of a wave!

Those engaged in group activities or the affairs of a club are advised to keep a fairly low profile if questions of policy are up for discussion. Certain boats may be set rocking rather wildly early month, when a breakdown in communication may bring on a crisis. If you feel that the whole thing is getting out of hand, perhaps you should take this as a hint and take your leave.

Matters of a private or confidential nature are likely to need careful attention between the 15th and 23rd. There is no dire problem here, but it might help to seek professional advice if something or someone (most likely a young person) is causing you to feel anxious.

An unsettled feeling is indicated late month, but this may be due to the fact that you are moving ahead with domestic changes. An effect of Jupiter in your sign will be to make you feel the need for increased living space. This is given further weight by an aspect to Neptune, inclining you to consider the prospects of a change of residence or an extension of your existing home. You'll be feeling inspired to create more beautiful surroundings. Here's the good news: what seemed a mere dream earlier in the year will begin to appear as a realistic option!

LUCKY DATES 4th, 7th, 16th, 27th.

You may get the feeling that your efforts don't justify the results, or that you are running to stand still. Accept the fact that you cannot always be going forward and that there are times when you need to stand back, take a more reflective stance, and perhaps realise that you are neglecting and missing out on certain valuable aspects of life.

For those who are mystically inclined and trying their hardest to swim against the materialistic pressures of modern life, the prevailing trend is extremely supportive. But looking at the picture realistically, it would be a good therapy to ease the pace and cultivate a simpler lifestyle, especially if you have begun to feel that your time is not your own or that you have lost touch with your real creative centre.

The presence of Mercury in your sign make this a time when new ideas are likely to grab your attention and you'll be more inclined to seek answers to certain questions that have been nagging at the back of your mind recently. You'll feel bored and impatient with people whose conversation does not rise beyond the realm of trivia, preferring instead to seek out personalities with whom you can develop a more meaningful or in-depth dialogue.

Times when meetings and talks are more likely to provide you with fresh insights and inspiration are the 10th, 15th and 22nd. Altogether it could be said that the prevailing astrological trend favours efforts to deepen your understanding and intensify your quest for knowledge.

Until late October you may experience a fall in your usual energy levels and be obliged to ease the pace a little. You're be all the better if you can organise a short break and cultivate some space to simply chill out for a while. Choose the week of the full Moon on the 7th if possible, because this is when your health will be at its most vulnerable. If you're under pressure at work or home this month, it would certainly help enormously if you could get a couple of days to get your strength back.

Once Mars pushes into your sign on the 24th you will quickly regain your usual dynamism and begin to feel that you can access a deeper source of sustaining energy.

Events taking shape later in the month focus your attention on matters closer to home. A property matter that has hung in a state of limbo for several months will at last begin to move forward. Perhaps also a lengthy delay in regard to a home improvement project will come to an end and you'll be in a better position financially to make the changes you desire.

The relations between Scorpio parents and their offspring - and vice versa - are likely to reach a more mature and understanding level later on in the month. It may well be that an issue that has been a source of underlying worries and stress will finally begin to fade into the background.

LUCKY DATES 4th, 10th, 25th, 28th.

After a lull in activity, the pace will gather a lively and at times quite frenetic momentum in the coming weeks. With no less that four planets in your own sign it will be a month of many facets and plenty of incentive to spread your wings. The energising planet Mars increases your motivation to take the initiative, push ahead with vital interests, and manoeuvre yourself into a more influential and leading position.

As Mercury remains retrograde in your sign until the 18th, you need to keep your main priorities clear and avoid allowing yourself to become overloaded with all kind of extraneous obligations and distractions. A positive and perhaps unexpected turn of events later on in the month will allow you to realign certain interests, make fuller use of your creative and technical skills, and enrich your social life into the bargain.

The first half of November is likely to mark a decisive transition in personal relationships. Having both Mars and Venus in your sign describes an action-packed scenario, with new romance liable to come on like a hurricane and passions reaching a dizzying level of intensity. This may be truly blissful while it lasts, but usually with these two planets the situation soon burns itself out.

Much depends on your own attitude and level of maturity. Provided you are clear about what you truly value in a relationship - what would make you feel happy - then you're likely to realise your hopes and wishes. But if your motives are basically egocentric, don't blame the other person if things quickly cool off after what seemed a promising start.

Don't take anything for granted when it comes to attending meetings, arranging interviews or seeking vital information during the first half of the month. Other people may prove unreliable, schedules will be disrupted, and the advice you are given is likely to lead you round in circles. Such hassles can be minimised by double-checking or, better still, putting the whole thing off until after the 18th. A more positive transit of Mercury then ensures that the goods are delivered.

Both Venus and Jupiter shed a fortunate light on financial interests later in the month, making this a prime time for splashing out on luxury items, gifts, and anything that adds to the enhancement and comfort of your lifestyle.

Jupiter will remain in the money area of your solar chart for about twelve months, in which time you can expect to see a vast improvement in your fortunes, with an element of luck playing a large part in this promising state of affairs.

Be very careful not to allow work pressures or other demands to push you beyond your level of endurance late in the month. Things won't go to pieces if you take a day off, and besides, you'll come back feeling more able and willing to tackle any challenges you face head on.

LUCKY DATES 2nd, 10th, 21st, 22nd.

During this final month of 2006 and well into the New Year you will be inclined to focus on consolidating what you have achieved rather than continuing to drive ahead - and risk taking on more than you can competently handle. Saturn swings retrograde in the top sector of your solar chart, advising you to take a more cautious approach to worldly ambitions and make a realistic assessment of what is within your particular capacity.

If you attempt to go beyond certain limits, experience is liable to pull you up short. The wisdom of Saturn is saying that, for the time being, learn to appreciate the true value of what you have already achieved.

A powerful planetary grouping in a very practical area of your chart suggests that your attitude to material needs and possessions is undergoing a subtle shift. Things you previously set a high value on are likely to become less important, and experience will make it glaringly obvious to you that while money is indeed necessary, it is certainly not a sufficient condition for happiness.

Staying with this theme, there is much to suggest that your material fortunes are on course for a steady expansion over the next twelve months. You will certainly have reason to feel easier and more confident about financial affairs.

Now that the beneficial planet Jupiter occupies the money area of your solar chart, you can expect a run of success in all to do with business and commercial activities. If a lack of funds has been an obstacle in the past, what takes place either in December or over the ensuing months will put an end to such restrictions.

A positive trend during the second week greatly favours the spirit of enterprise, so don't hesitate to grasp any opportunities that present themselves and take the initiative if you wish to boost your earning potential.

It's not until late in the month that amorous stirrings are likely to be felt, so if you are hoping to find a romantic partner don't expect any instant miracles. Don't be surprised, however, to hear that a relative or friend is planning to marry early in the New Year. Although you might feel a twinge of disapproval or even jealousy, this will certainly not prevent you from indulging in some added celebrations later in the month.

Although there may be a few more ups and downs that you'd like, you can expect to be surrounded by an aura of affection over the festive season. You'll be feeling a little oversensitive about a couple of relationships, so don't blow it by throwing one of your epic moods when Mars and Uranus are under stress on the 22nd!

Mercury combines with both Pluto and Saturn on the 24th and 25th, signalling a somewhat nostalgic atmosphere. However, someone you believed to have gone from your life for good is likely to get in touch. This person may be an ex-workmate with some interesting suggestions connected with a commercial venture. There may also be talk of a lengthy journey in the near future.

LUCKY DATES 8th, 18th, 25th, 29th.

sagittarius

november 23 to december 22

Planetary Ruler:	Jupiter	**Wood:**	Oak
Quality & Element:	Mutable Fire	**Flower:**	Hydrangea
Colours:	Purple,	**Animal:**	horse
	Autumn Tints	**Gem:**	Amethyst
Metal:	Tin	**Fabric:**	Velvet

Everything of importance appears to be taking shape behind the scenes in the early stages of the New Year. In other words, you may get the feeling that not much is happening and that you efforts are falling flat. This is likely to be a misrepresentation, because with Jupiter (your ruler) generating a strong undercurrent of rising fortunes, you may find that you are more highly thought of than you had previously imagined.

If you were hoping to push ahead with a new project in January, it would be a good policy to keep your ideas under wraps, adopt a stealthy approach and avoid giving too much away at this stage. The aims and objectives connected with your current work situation may need to be re-adjusted in view of certain helpful developments, but make sure you know your own ground before taking initiatives, especially around the middle of the month.

 Business and commercial activity gathers a lively momentum during the second and third weeks of the month, when you'll have increased scope and new incentives to diversify your interests and establish useful contacts. Now is a good time to develop and try out new ideas if you are intent on improving your earning potentials in the coming months. Make your best efforts when favourable trends are at their peak between the 9th and 14th, for it is then that your initiatives are most likely to pay dividends and that your creative inspiration will be at its strongest.

Think carefully before splashing out on apparent bargains and luxury items in the third week and around the 27th. The chances are you'll end up lumbering yourself with an impulse buy that you will quickly lose interest in and might not even be able to sell. Think twice before you shell out any of your hard-earned cash!

 There will be added demands on your time and energy in the first half of January, with a danger you could burn out around the middle of the month. Forewarned is forearmed, so make it a strict policy to pace things out and don't allow yourself to be exploited. If people tell you that urgent tasks have to be completed if targets are to be met, a critical and rational view of the situation will tell you that this is largely a myth. Don't get bullied or pressured if you can help it.

There is a need to stick to usual routines and to forego certain options if you are not to end in a state of confusion. It is not until after the 22nd that the feeling of being programmed like a robot by everyday pressures will begin to loosen its grip. In the meantime, concentrate on what is of immediate significance, rather than letting your mind wander to future plans and projects.

An unusual turn of events at the end of the month will help to rescue you from a situation that has perhaps cramped your style over the past months. Travel comes into the picture and wider horizons begin to beckon. This is an ideal time to explore the various options if you are planning a special trip or vacation for later in the year.

LUCKY DATES 9th, 13th, 19th, 26th.

Since the beginning of the year you have probably not had much of a chance to relax and take time out. Work pressures or a whole host of other chores have seemed to crowd in on you all at once, leaving you with a feeling of being completely tied up. It is not until the third week of February that this trend really begins to ease, but until then you can expect to make tremendous progress in the goals you are aiming to achieve.

The extra effort you make now is sure to stand you in good stead in regard to what looks like very positive developments in your practical affairs in the coming months. Take this as a time of preparation and set out to get your act together. This might mean hard a period of extra hard work, but the end result is sure to meet with your satisfaction.

After a slow start, your financial affairs begin to stir into life from the 3rd onwards. Venus then comes to the end of a retrograde phase in the money area of your solar chart, promising a healthier cashflow, the end of money worries, and more ready cash in your pocket to spend on fun and frivolity.

Venus is of course the planet of beauty and the good things of life, so if you feel inclined to splash out on luxuries and things to enhance your own image. This month it is likely you'll have the necessary funds to indulge your tastes.

Although relatives or neighbours may insist on taking up your valuable time earlier in the month, you can expect the domestic scene to take on a more congenial trend from the 9th onwards. Whether or not you have made any special arrangements, it is likely that your home will become the centre of lively gatherings around the middle of the month and between the 23rd and 25th.

Youngsters will be much in evidence, probably because you are called upon to mind other people's kids for a few days. Alternatively, you may be end up throwing a lavish party later in the month which involves have a lot of young people around. Whatever happens, this will turn out to be a delightful state of affairs.

With fiery Mars pushing into your House of Partners on the 17th, you may be entering a transition phase with regard to love affairs and your personal relationships. This is not necessarily bad news, but it does mean there are a number of matters that need to be confronted. This is particularly the case if a relationship is fairly new, because this is a time when underlying tensions and personality differences are likely to loom large.

The impulsive nature of Mars can incline you to make mistakes through misjudgement and impatience. This is something you'll need to watch out for in the coming weeks. It is not the best of times to plunge into matrimony or to make any hasty decisions on the strength of what seems like the ultimate romance. Plans to set up home together should be looked on as practically as possible to avoid disappointments at a later date.

LUCKY DATES 3rd, 14th, 15th, 20th.

This is one of those months when you will feel you are struggling upstream, or taking one step forward and two back. In other words, you will need to exercise a certain level of patience and avoid being led off course by irrelevancies and distractions. This is not to say that there are no helpful trends in force, but it would be unwise to take too much for granted and expect everything to go exactly to plan.

The transit of Mars through your opposite sign suggests a challenging month ahead, a time when obstacles will prevent you from making the progress you had hoped for. Be prepared to take more of a back seat and cultivate a detached attitude to the world. If you are involved in a fairly competitive field of activity, be it business or sports, this is definitely going to be a testing time.

 Closer to home it is likely you'll be tied by a host of smaller duties and chores and will have resign yourself to the fact that this is a time when certain personal interests have to be shelved temporarily. Sagittarian parents may be feeling a bit anxious about a younger member of the household and a problem relating to education and schooling may need extra attention.

The outlook brightens later in the month. Minor anxieties fade into the background, and you'll have more time and freedom to entertain congenial company at home. Unexpected news concerning a property matter will free you from certain heavy responsibilities that you were obliged to shoulder over the past year or so.

 If everything else is threatening to spin out of control, at least you'll have some escape routes via pleasant journeys and convivial contacts at various time during the month. Events taking shape in the affairs of a relative or friend will give rise to celebration or allow you to take a break from your usual routines for a day or two around mid-month.

 Although Mars in your opposite sign means there is greater potential for conflict and confrontation, a helpful transit of Venus ensures that harmony ultimately prevails. At best this is a time when a certain element of confrontation can act as a therapy in regard to personal relationships. Emotional ambiguities can be brought out into the open and clarified, bringing a deeper level of understanding.

The passionate combination of Venus and Mars later in the month promises a fulfilment of your heart's desires via a chance encounter while travelling. Even a short trip is likely to develop a certain romantic flavour, just when you least expect it.

 In view of the potential stress factors woven into the events throughout March, it would be in your best interests to keep things as low key as possible and go out of your way to avoid unnecessary confrontations. This would be an ideal time to work from behind the scenes and perfect your plans for future.

LUCKY DATES 1st, 9th, 19th, 30th.

Saturn's constructive influence brings a more settling trend into effect from early in the month onwards. After a rather uncertain phase over the past month or two, you will finally begin to feel that you are gaining a firmer handle on your destiny.

Long range plans are likely to occupy your mind at a more serious level. Obstacles start to fade away and a clearer picture begins to emerge regarding the changes you hope to make in the near future.

A greater sense of continuity in your lifestyle will help you to feel more in tune with your inner self and confident that your goals are coming within your reach. If you find that your outlook on life is undergoing a shift of emphasis, this reflects a maturing process that has been going forward within you for the past year or so.

The workings of the mind are very much in focus under the rule of Saturn. This is good news for those involved in serious studies or working in fields such as education and publishing. The experience you gain during April will prove invaluable in the future, and it could be quite by chance that you encounter ideas that set you off on a special quest for knowledge.

Travel is likely to connect with the wish to gain new knowledge and wider experience, particularly during the third week, when a discussion with an older person could do much to enlighten your mind and give you answers to soul-searching questions.

Property interests are favourably highlighted early in the month, with good news promised for those who are in process of seeking a suitable abode either to rent or buy. The accent on long-term issues makes this one of the best months in 2006 for giving attention to security issues, family planning, and the need to establish a firm foundation on which to base your lifestyle.

Although this might seem a rather foreign concept to your happy-go-lucky, freedom-loving Sagittarian nature, you would be undermining your own best interests by neglecting these matters while Saturn has a favourable placement during 2006. But on a somewhat lighter note, the presence of Venus in the home area of your solar chart should inspire you to give your home a much-needed face-lift. It also brings the promise of a pleasant twist of events relating to your family affairs and perhaps a surprise visit or two from an old friend later in the month.

Aim to consolidate your assets rather than attempting to make too many changes or embark on a new venture that calls for a large up-front investment. In the latter half of the month, jointly-held resources come in for consideration. If you are not entirely happy about your arrangements and wish to release certain funds, this will be the month in which to seek advice and talk things over with your partner. A small windfall later in the month will arrive at just the right time to pay for a short trip.

LUCKY DATES 4th, 15th, 20th, 26th.

There is a kind of occult theme in your affairs during these weeks. It is almost as if hidden influences are offering guidance and making sure you are in the right place at the right time.

If you believe in a guardian angel or divine providence, the events taking shape during the second week will do much to convince you that something like this is going on.

Looking at the situation from a more rationalistic angle, it could be that a phase of inner psychological growth is coming to fruition, giving you a certain poise and wisdom in the way you deal with life. At a practical level it could be that a lengthy period of study or preparation has been completed and an opportunity arises that enables you to express yourself more creatively.

Destiny smiles on those who are hoping to find a meaningful relationship this month. What take place on the 8th and around the 25th will put you on the road to recovery if you have suffered an emotional disappointment in the past. By nature you are not the easiest person to please when it comes to love, simply because you like to leave your options open. Your fear of being too tied down or of losing your independence is what often stands in the way.

However, there is much to suggest that you will make the acquaintance of someone who has an uncanny affinity with you and who is unlikely to bind you in chains of possessiveness. If this has been a problem in the past, the situation will take a pleasing change for the better before the month is out.

If you're married or working in partnership, it is likely that initiatives taken by your partner will have an unexpectedly favourable impact on your income. A very positive trend between the 5th and 8th gives an added impetus to any ongoing business projects and fundraising ventures. There may be also extra cash heading in your direction around this time. This could arrive in the shape of a surprise bonus, a rebate or a good return on an investment.

Make the most of this favourable trend for dealing with all soundly-based financial affairs - investments, insurance, pension schemes and property interests. Don't waste time, either, if a job opportunity arises and you see your way to upgrading your earnings.

Be prepared for a lively exchange of ideas later in the month and be ready to consider new ideas and suggestions if you are seeking to broaden your range of interests. Information that comes to light on the 29th brings you fresh inspiration and an opportunity to develop a creative dialogue with someone on your own mental wavelength. If you've been looking for a partnership for a creative venture, you're likely to meet someone who will spur you on to get a treasured project up and running.

Tread carefully with other people's sensitivities on the 26th, when your usual directness of speech may be interpreted as a personal criticism.

LUCKY DATES 5th, 7th, 24th, 26th.

may ♐ sagittarius

Recent developments may have been unusually favourable to your interests, but it could be that a changing situation has given rise to the need to commit yourself more fully to a certain course of action. The effort to do a double act in recent months may have left you with the feeling that you are walking on a high wire. This is likely to reach a rather stressful and critical phase in the third week of June.

However, the undercurrents of good fortune in your life continue to gather force, and just when you feel the situation is about to run aground something will happen to present you with a much needed solution. In other words, you're likely to be pulled out of a seemingly hopeless dilemma by an eleventh-hour miracle. If you are willing to break with old habits and move into a new field of experience, now is the time to act!

The critical events of the third week of June are likely to have a major focus on domestic affairs, with much to suggest that changes are looming on the horizon. This is unlikely to cause anxiety, because this is something you have been mulling over in the back of your mind since the beginning of the year.

It is as if the cosmic pattern is about to open a new window on the world, allowing you to expand your horizons, gain fresh experience, and break free of a situation that has been threatening to confine your natural spirit of adventure. If this means pulling up roots and settling elsewhere, you can be sure of a satisfying outcome. Changes to your domestic scene will go well and give you a much needed fresh perspective.

As Uranus is the moving force in this pattern, good luck will be with those who are willing to experiment with alternatives and look towards adopting a relatively unconventional lifestyle.

Speaking of adventure, there will be ample scope for breaking out of monotony in the month ahead. With Mars pushing into a positive area of your solar chart, the accent is on far-flung excursions and the need to broaden your horizons. It's therefore an ideal month for globe trotting, embarking on a cruise and seeking wide open spaces.

A journey contains a more serious element around the 18th. Maybe you'll visit a place that was important to you in the past or has some kind of sacred significance. Indeed, if you are on a quest for spiritual and mystical knowledge, travel could bring unusual inspiration. Ideally, this is a time to go on a retreat in order to regain contact with the deeper energies of your soul.

Taking a look at more material matters, you can expect favourable developments in personal and joint financial affairs in the second week. A legal matter is likely to be resolved, giving you the green light for a project that has been in a state of limbo, perhaps since the start of the year.

LUCKY DATES 9th, 10th, 19th, 28th.

Jupiter, your ruling planet, pulls out of a retrograde cycle from the 6th onwards, signalling the end of a relatively uneventful or perhaps rather stagnant phase. It is as if everything went into a state of suspension about three months ago and that you have been obliged to plod along a fairly routine track. However, it is likely that you have benefited from this quieter trend, as it has meant you've had time to reflect and get in tune with your deeper self.

Indeed, this Jupiter factor does have an inner psychological significance, indicating the emergence of a wiser and more intuitive attitude to life. In July this is likely to manifest itself as new ideas come to the surface and fragmented thoughts begin to pull together into something meaningful and creative. It could be said that thoughts that have been floating around in the back of your mind for several months will take a clear shape, and lead you to begin a new chapter in your life.

The transit of Venus through your opposite sign until the 19th promises greater harmony and understanding in all close ties of affection and friendship. This could turn out to be something of a bumper month for engagements and weddings. If this is what you have decided, then you have chosen well, because the long-term prospect is particularly bright at this time.

Venus will certainly help to pull you out of the doldrums if your love life has been either disappointing or nonexistent over the past year. An unexpected twist of events in the early part of the month may not seem very romantic at the time, but the consequences will be pleasantly surprising. However, it would be unwise to attempt the revival of an old affair, which is something you may be tempted to do around the 14th.

If your work has to do with travel, the media, information technology or education, be prepared for hassles between the 4th and 10th. A minor problem or dispute due to misinformation is liable to throw everything into chaos and create delays. If possible, wait until the latter half of the month if you wish to implement change or arrange a special conference.

There may be a sense of urgency connected with a journey on the 5th. Immediate plans will have to be sacrificed for the sake of something that appeals to your higher sense of duty - all of which should make you feel extremely virtuous.

Don't overlook the fine details if you have to deal with legal and official matters during the third week of the month. Attempts to cut corners or overlook minor ambiguities may cost you dear. Make the best of the prevailing trend by overhauling personal and joint financial interests, for you may now find that you are not making optimum use of your assets. If in doubt seek professional advice, and then get a second opinion. It looks like if you make a small adjustment to your finances you will gain large rewards, but it will need a fresh pair of eyes to identify the problem.

LUCKY DATES 6th, 9th, 18th, 27th.

Whether you are planning a leisurely break, flying off to an exotic destination or sticking to business as usual, everything will meet your expectations during the coming month. Jupiter continues to generate a powerful undercurrent of good fortune, giving you a kind of cosmic support system if you wish to launch a new venture or make desirable changes in your life.

A high point in your astrological year is the 29th, when your ruling planet Jupiter forms a powerful aspect with Uranus. This points strongly to the quite sudden emergence of new interests, perhaps entailing a break with the past. Whatever transpires, the feeling is that you are breaking out of confinement and acquiring a new sense of freedom

Travel is going to be a key feature in your life throughout the month, for there appears to be a certain life-changing element woven into a far-flung journey. With Venus and Mercury much in evidence you'll be in the mood for fun and frolics and have plenty of opportunity to indulge your pleasure-loving instincts. A good month for getting together with friends you might not have seen for a long time. You'll be welcomed with open arms by friends that need to hear your cheery voice and optimistic outlook.

However, there does seem to be a rather serious element associated with long distance excursions. If your main purpose in travelling has to do with education or a historical interest, then you are certainly on the right wavelength. But even if this is not your prime purpose, chances are you will meet with experiences that put you in a thoughtful frame of mind. A journey in search of fun may spark off a spiritual quest.

From the 12th onwards there is a fateful link between travel and romance. A honeymoon atmosphere prevails around the 22nd, and this applies whether you are recently married or not. An escape from familiar territory with your loved one will work wonders for your relationship at this time, especially as it may be that circumstances have tended to come between you since the start of the year.

Sagittarians of more mature years are more likely to reap the benefits of favourable trends later in the month. If you are a divorcee or otherwise single, the chances of meeting a genuine soulmate will be increased over the coming weeks. Here, too, it will be a journey that provides the key.

Mars is pushing through the topmost sector of your solar chart, which lends added dynamism to your worldly aims and most deeply-held ambitions. At this time you have the power to create your own opportunities, so don't be afraid to stick your neck out if you see a way to improving your status. You are particularly favoured if you work at a managerial level, or are self-employed and aiming to push things towards a more profitable situation. Exercise discretion around the 13th, when you may inadvertently encroach upon someone else's territory.

LUCKY DATES 2nd, 12th, 17th, 23rd, 29th.

Events taking shape in the early days of September will bring greater scope for furthering your current aims and achieving a new level of empowerment. It also means that your sense of purpose is becoming more intensely focused now that you are getting your major aims and objectives into a clearer perspective. It's a time when your best progress can be made by working co-operatively rather than trying to cut a path of your own.

Between late August and the first week of this month several unusual planetary configurations suggest a time when the Fates are more likely to intervene. At least this is how it will feel under the impact of changing events. What previously occupied a central place in your plans for the year is likely to be pushed off to the side due to the appearance of new interests on your horizon. These changes could end up leading to an important career shift before too long, giving your confidence an extra boost.

A lunar eclipse on the 7th stirs up the winds of change in the domestic sphere, making this an apt time for those who are considering a move in the near future. The underlying theme of transformation that seems to be gaining force throughout the month is likely to be felt in the home and family circle. It could be that a new job offer or a decision affecting your career has important repercussions in regard to domestic affairs and family life.

If you do experience an element of disruption in this area, this is unlikely to come in the shape of a crisis. On the contrary, it will be for a definite purpose and very much part of a positive pattern of changes that is beginning to gain momentum.

The workaholic tendencies of previous weeks may have left you feeling somewhat exhausted, but over the coming weeks it looks as if your dedication and effort will be getting the results you had hoped for. This is bound to cast a positive light on financial affairs, enabling you to upgrade your budget and look further ahead in planning how you wish to use your assets and resources.

For job seekers and those aiming to find a more definite direction in regard to their career path, the outlook is good. Venus in a pivotal area of your solar horoscope smoothes your path to success and helps you to keep cool if attending important interviews or meetings.

Heated arguments are liable to break out if you are engaged in group activities or community affairs around mid-month. This may not be a bad thing if it allows you to sort out underlying grievances or a dispute over policy and leadership. But don't be too insistent on imposing your own views if the situation does threaten to go into meltdown. Around the 23rd, communication with imaginative individuals will bring fresh inspiration to those who are working to realise an ideal or involved in global and humanitarian issues.

LUCKY DATES 1st, 7th, 13th, 28th.

There is a continuing accent on your higher aims and ideals during the first half of October. This could mean either that you are being drawn into a more creative role in group endeavours or social affairs, or perhaps that you are about to make a real breakthrough with regard to an activity that has up until now been little more than a hobby. The upshot of all this is a huge enrichment of your social life and a very fruitful dialogue with like-minded souls.

Prevailing trends suggest the positive influence of certain persons and an opportunity to get on closer terms with someone who is in a position to support your aims and give guidance. All activities that focus on wider social, political and humanitarian issues are given powerful backing by a progressive cosmic pattern, so if you are aiming to drum up support for a campaign and get a message across, now is the time to get out there and make a noise!

There is a fairytale quality surrounding romantic developments around the middle of the month. Venus forms a magical link with Neptune, which should produce a rather dreamy atmosphere. However, the whole thing is unlikely to dissolve in a fog of wishful thinking and sentimentality. On the contrary, if your relationship has a solid footing it could also be a genuine case of a dream come true.

It looks quite likely it will be someone you've been on friendly terms with for several months who will begin to appear in a more attractive and amorous light. On the other hand, you should try not be totally surprised if a secret admirer makes a dramatic declaration of love later in the month!

It's a good month for those involved in special studies or research projects. Information that suddenly comes to light on the 10th will enable you to solve a puzzle and will give you an intuitive insight into the deeper implications of what you already know. It's a time when discoveries will be made, secrets unearthed, and theory can be put into practice.

A potentially tricky date is the 15th, when you are advised to double-check information and not rely too closely on hearsay and verbal agreements. If you don't wish to undermine your integrity and reputation, steer well clear of gossip and petty bitching at this time. Take note of favourable trends on the 21st if you need advice on a personal and confidential matter.

There may be anxiety over the health of an older person later in the month, probably a relative or in-law. You may be called upon to play the part of a protecting angel, so be prepared to sacrifice some of your time if someone you know needs assistance due to poor health.

The good news is that your own resilience and vitality are gaining in strength, giving you the feeling that you are beginning to tap into a deeper level of creative energy. Your energy levels will be high and you'll be ready to face any obstacles in your path.

LUCKY DATES 7th, 11th, 16th, 24th.

If you get the feeling of being on the edge of a breakthrough, or that something good is about to happen, chances are that this will turn out to be a correct intuition. Whatever happens, it looks as if you will have reason to feel optimistic and confident. Indeed, this does have all the makings of a very special month for those born under the sign of the Archer, for on the 24th your ruling planet Jupiter enters your sign.

An enhancement of luck is indicated, with developments in your life taking a decidedly expansive turn over the following twelve months. Not only will Jupiter bring greater scope for material enrichment; you'll also feel more together as an individual and more in tune with your real potential. Basically, throughout November you'll feel that the Fates are on your side and that things are definitely on the up-and-up.

 Although you have fortunate trends coming into force later in the month, there is no excuse to take things for granted or let your self confidence run away with you. There may be loose ends to be tied up earlier in the month, or a need to sort out a long-standing financial conundrum. By focusing on the problem areas now, you will be doing yourself a very big favour. Neglect may cause you to miss out on a prime opportunity very late in the year.

Lunar trends on the 5th signal the completion of a task and the fruition of your efforts. This could mean that you are now ready to take a step forward in your career, or move into a new field of work that allows you to make more productive use of your skills and experience. Luck is on your side if you are seeking employment, but don't be over-modest about your capabilities if you are looking for greater job satisfaction.

 Negative aspects involving Neptune on the 9th and 17th warn you to slow down if you have been working intensively lately. The indications are that your energy and vitality will take a plunge, forcing you to switch to a lower gear or take some time out to recuperate.

After a lengthy wait, you can expect domestic changes to move ahead soon after the 20th. What takes place then is sure to please those who have been longing to move out of cramped conditions into something more spacious. As Jupiter is moving into your sign around this time, you can look forward to a phase of increased contentment and enrichment over the next twelve months.

It is extremely significant that Venus joins forces with Jupiter late in the month, so this is where luck is likely to intervene in the realisation of your most cherished hopes and wishes. This is a time when many Sagittarians are likely to meet a future marriage partner or certainly a special person who could figure in your romantic life for many years to come.

LUCKY DATES 11th, 15th, 21st, 24th.

There is a kind of grand finale theme to the final month of 2006, which could turn out to be the most eventful month of the year. An extraordinary concentration of planets - plus the Sun - in your own sign at this time marks the start of a highly progressive trend in your affairs. It is as if several strands of experience are being pulled together to give you a completely new and very exciting direction.

The key feature is of course the position of Jupiter in your sign, signalling a phase of opportunity and enrichment in all the important areas of your life. At a material level you can expect rising fortunes in the coming year; and at a psychological and emotional level you will feel confident and very much more secure within yourself.

Your own energy and initiative will play a vital part in what you achieve in terms of financial success in the coming month. A combination of Mars and Jupiter during the second week suggests a progressive time, with greater demands on your energy and a need to act decisively if changes and innovation are called for. The prevailing trend favours the entrepreneurial spirit, so don't be afraid to aim high if you are hoping to expand a business venture or embark on something entirely new.

The presence of Venus in the money area of your solar chart from the 11th ensures that you have the necessary funds for gifts and festive goodies. You'll be in a generous mood and inclined to entertain on a lavish scale later in the month, and this is not likely to leave you with a depleted bank balance!

The unusually eventful trend is likely to have a positive impact on your amorous hopes and needs, helped greatly by a marked expansion in your range of social contacts in the coming weeks. An invitation on the 8th or an impromptu get-together during the third week might give you the opportunity you've been looking for to make a much closer acquaintance with someone you have admired from a distance for several months. You'll be encouraged by the response you'll receive when you get the confidence to take things a stage further

In view of the electrifying cocktail of planets in your own sign, surprising and quite dramatic encounters are forecast, for this is a time when a chance encounter could change your life.

As already hinted, it looks as if your home will be the focus of much activity later in the month, so it would be a good policy to plan things well in advance. Other people are liable to expect a lot from you in the way of effort and energy, and there may be times when you feel as if you're dancing on hot coals. However, it is more likely you will thrive on this scenario and have much a great deal of fun into the bargain. But don't allow gatecrashers over your threshold on the 22nd, otherwise you'll be inviting disaster into your home!

LUCKY DATES 1st, 10th, 18th, 20th, 31st.

capricorn
december 22 to january 21

Planetary Ruler:	Saturn	**Wood:**	Yew
Quality & Element:	Cardnal Earth	**Flower:**	Fushcia
Colours:	Brown, black,	**Animal:**	Goat
	grey	**Gem:**	Jet
Metal:	Lead, pewter	**Fabric:**	Hessian

You begin the year with a feeling that things are moving forward and giving you greater scope for expressing your creative energies. A phase of preparation seems to be coming to an end and confinement to a rather restricted routine is opening out into something more in keeping with your inborn practical talents.

The prevailing astrological pattern is particularly favourable in placing the main accent on practical affairs and the need to create a sense of continuity and efficiency in your life. The Mars-Jupiter opposition mid month may mean readjustments in certain corporate endeavours, perhaps a clash of temperaments over aims and objectives, but this is a good time to sort out differences and decide on what is and is not a genuine priority.

Mercury's presence in your sign between the 3rd and 22nd weaves a variety of threads into the fabric of your life. You'll be drawn into congenial company during the second week, meeting people who stimulate your mind and encourage you to make more productive use of your ideas. The accent on practical affairs makes this an excellent time for establishing useful contacts and cultivating a productive dialogue between persons who share your interests.

Travel is likely to have an enriching influence on your circle of significant friendships, particularly if you are involved in social issues or aiming to promote a special campaign. You'll meet like-mined souls that will make you feel as though your opinion really matters and you'll feel excited at he prospect of meeting up with this new group of similarly-minded individuals for future events.

If you feel that romance is following the law of diminishing returns during the early part of the year, perhaps you should take this as a cue that something needs to be decided once and for all. Significantly enough, Venus is backtracking into your sign throughout the month, calling for a more reflective attitude towards your own emotional needs and what you expect from others.

It could be that you are given a second chance, but this will depend very much on what you honestly feel rather than simply being driven by habit or conventional expectation. Remember that there is another person over there, not just a hook on which to hang your fantasies.

Much can be achieved by adopting a more enterprising approach while Mars occupies a highly creative area of your solar chart. But make your best efforts after the 22nd if you are aiming to diversify or incorporate some of your new ideas into an existing project.

There is need for serious consideration regarding jointly held resources later in the month. What seemed like a failsafe policy earlier may not be meeting your expectations, so don't hesitate to get professional advice if you are unsure about investments or other long term financial affairs.

LUCKY DATES 2nd, 9th. 19th. 28th.

As far as practical affairs are concerned you won't have much cause for complaint; but it is likely that you have felt emotionally deprived over the past few months. This unsatisfactory state of affairs is likely to switch into something more positive from early month onwards, when Venus turns direct in your own sign. This gives promise of finding a better integration between practical life and emotional needs.

Those born under Capricorn do have a tendency to sabotage emotional fulfilment by getting too wound up and hidebound in regard to worldly aims. Everything depends on reaching a certain goal before you allow any real emotional commitment. In the meantime opportunities pass you by. However, the prospect brightens and events will prompt you to relax your defences.

♥ The upshot of what's just been said is that affairs of the heart are likely to become a more important feature in your scheme of things. If past experience made you rather cautious about emotional involvement, it is only now that you are beginning to emerge from under the dark clouds. There won't be instant miracles and fairytale romances, but there is much to suggest that sympathetic threads are being woven due to a chance meeting around mid February.

Towards the end of the month a message or short journey could hold the key to romantic developments. A colleague or friend may pass on an interesting bit of gossip that will make your heart soar. Perhaps you'll hear something through the grapevine that helps to thaw the ice

£ You may be obliged to forgo a shopping trip early in the month due to unforeseen expenses arising. A likely scenario is that the car needs a service or essential machinery may need some urgent repairs. All of this could mean a bit of a dent in your bank balance. However, you can expect a shortage of funds to be a temporary blip, for it looks as if an added bonus is heading in your direction soon after mid month. If you've been working hard over the past months don't think your efforts have gone unnoticed. Someone in a position of power has their eye on you.

Work is likely to demand a higher energy input later in the month, but any extra efforts you make are certain to stand you in good stead, especially if you are seeking advancement and better pay.

 Usual routines and carefully laid plans are liable to be disrupted around the 14th. Something unexpected will crop up, entailing a journey at very short notice (or perhaps visit from a relative). This may be felt as a total hassle at the time, but in fact it will turn out to be highly enjoyable - and enlightening.

If you are willing to cultivate an open and flexible attitude during the latter half of the month, you can greatly enrich your experience and perhaps make contact with someone who is destined to play an influential role in your life.

LUCKY DATES 3rd, 5th, 16th, 25th.

You can make best progress (and keep your sanity) by sticking to familiar routines rather than attempting to bring about changes, either in work or in private life. Mercury's retrograde movement brings an element of indecision, but if in a quandary about something it would be better to let things ride until late month. What takes place soon after the 25th will enable you to see things more clearly.

Jupiter's benign influence also drops into a lower key from early month. This does not mean that everything is about to disintegrate, but perhaps it would be a good idea to take a critical look at your aims and expectations. You might not have noticed, but certain changes have been taking shape over the past few months that may call for a revision of your ideas and a re-alignment of objectives.

 Provided you don't attempt to go against Jupiter's thoughtful influence by aiming too high, you can expect finances to take a smooth course throughout the month. After a phase of relatively heavy expenditure, you will soon be able to get a firmer handle on your current earnings and assets. A little practical planning is called for and perhaps an audit of your incomings and outgoings wouldn't be such a bad idea. If you can get some sort of a budget together this month you might even be able to stick to it!

It's the presence of Venus in the money area of your solar chart that brings an easier trend in regard to material interests and the way you spend your money. You're likely to find yourself with cash to spare in the latter half of the month and inclined to splash out on leisurely interests, luxuries and fun.

 Don't allow yourself to be rushed into completing various tasks in the third week. Adopt a steady pace at work early in the month and stick to it. There is an increased danger of accident and injury on the 11th, but this will be due to impatience or attempting to do too much at once.

Apart from such hazards, the prevailing trend helps to boost your energy and keep up your stamina. It is in fact an excellent month to make a conscious effort towards improving your health and fitness.

Minor delays and disruptions are to be allowed for if you are hoping to take a special trip, attend an interview or go in search of special advice and information. Be fairly non-committal if you are called upon to give an opinion or make a decision, and definitely don't attempt to simply bluff your way through just in order to keep up appearances or save face.

Later in the month any hazy situations are likely to take on a clearer outline, and a chance meeting or talk on the 27th could be a real inspiration. An idea you thought to be on the impractical side may get a new lease of life. Be prepared to give serious consideration to unusual, original and unconventional perspectives late month; it'll make you realise that there is more to life than meets the eye.

LUCKY DATES 6th, 16th, 20th, 23rd.

From a small beginning early in the month could come far-reaching developments, focusing generally on material interests and more particularly on domestic affairs. It might no mean that you are about to pull up roots and completely change the direction of our ambitions, but it does give more than just a hint that important transformations are taking shape.

There is also a psychological aspect to this picture, because now that you are reaching a new level of stability and maturity within yourself, you will be more confident about changing the structure of your lifestyle. An urge to get rid of excess baggage and to get real values into the field of your vision will be your main motivation in April.

 Your ruling planet, Saturn, turns direct on the 5th, marking a major turning point in all to do with property and domestic affairs. A long-standing difficulty is likely to be resolved, giving you greater room for manoeuvre and a more encouraging prospect if you are hoping to provide a more stable background for yourself and those who depend on you. Although initially you might have to put up with a less than perfect but temporary situation, you'll soon see it was all worth the extra hassle and effort. In fact you will probably be able to look back and smile at the way things were.

Not only can you expect welcome news on the 19th and 25th concerning these matters; a visit from an old friend at very short notice will put you in a cheerful mood and perhaps give you some deep food for thought.

 Pleasant variations in your usual routines are forecast, allowing you something of a breathing space and a chance to devote some quality time to those areas of your life that have perhaps been neglected since the start of the year. Events taking shape in the affairs of relatives, neighbours and friends will contribute to the convivial atmosphere, especially in the third week, when something totally unexpected may call for celebration.

If you're longing for a break and wish to get away from it all for a few days, choose the final week, when you won't be so encumbered with work pressures or other duties.

 A message, invitation or last minute journey on the 18th may open up romantic possibilities in ways that you would least expect. A very ancient sage once said that if you don't expect the unexpected it won't happen. So maybe you ought to bear this in mind in view of the intriguing planetary trends around this date.

 You certainly will not be lacking energy and drive during April, but you may need to ease the pace when Mars is at odds with Pluto on the 8th. This is where you will be inclined to play the hero, fly too high, and get your wings singed! A little planning or foresight will prove invaluable this month. Remind yourself also that speed is not equivalent to progress.

LUCKY DATES 5th, 13th, 19th, 27th.

There is an intensely purposeful aura surrounding you, especially during the second week when events are likely to open a new window on your world, enabling you to upgrade and streamline your current aims and objectives. The prevailing astrological trend suggests a breakthrough, a quantum leap onto a new level of activity and aspiration.

It is by co-operating with like-minded individuals that substantial advances can be made and hopes realized. There will be fortunate opportunities to broaden your field of expression, to win friend and influence people in ways that are mutually beneficial. It's a time when favours given and received will go down well and your innate sense of loyalty is greatly appreciated.

Venus casts an easy and harmonious light on all things domestic throughout the month. Underlying tensions will be resolved without too much aggravation and a better understanding will be established between Capricorn parents and their offspring (notably the teenage variety).

The influence of Venus in this area makes you more sensitive to your immediate surroundings and put you in the mood for making changes. As this planet also enhances your tastes, this would be an ideal time to give some thought for a makeover. If you're into lucky or therapeutic colour schemes, Venus suggests a deep red, terracotta or dusky pink. However, make sure you have agreement with your partner or other members of your household before going ahead with refurbishment.

The presence of fiery Mars in your opposite sign could stir up tensions or cause underlying irritations to come to the surface. This is not likely to amount to anything traumatic, and in fact the favourable aspect of this planet in the second week suggest a deep strengthening process in regard to personal ties of affection.

As a sensible Capricorn, you can be rather a cool customer emotionally, not inclined to be forthcoming when the more sensitive feelings need to be confronted and sorted out. If an emotional issue were forced on your attention at this time, you'd be doing yourself and your partner a great favour by facing it squarely rather than continuing to skirt around it or pretend it does not exist. If the pair of you can have a frank discussion about your feelings this month it will certainly put a stop to some behaviour that could get out of control if not acknowledged.

What takes place between the 5th and 19th will do much to advance your interests if you are involved in learning and education, either as a student of a teacher. If the welfare of the younger generation is close to your heart, now is the time when you will feel that you are making a very definite contribution.

Later in the month there will be exciting news for those who recently applied for a job or took an exam and the financial implications are sure to please you. A celebration is in order and you'll enjoy planning a party or gathering with friends.

LUCKY DATES 6th, 8th, 17th, 29th.

Existing tensions and skirmishes that you may have experienced in recent weeks will fade into the background, giving way to a feeling of greater co-operation and agreement.

You'll also find that your efforts meet with less resistance as obstacles are finally overcome and problems ironed out. Competitive elements that you have been up against are likely to become less intense, putting you in a position where you can call the shots.

There may be pressure on you to scale down certain activities during the third week and not expect too much of others. Involvement with special groups, clubs and associations is likely to be important, but if you feel that you have to break allegiance and bow out of certain projects, better to do this now than later. This could mean something of a conflict of loyalties, but you can be sure that the persons concerned will understand.

 It's the third week when important financial issues are likely to need careful attention. A joint business venture may need overhauling and you will need to decide whether to go for a complete restructuring or to abandon the whole thing as a drain on your emotional as well as your financial resources.

In one way or another, throughout June there will be a need to gain a greater degree of control over your financial affairs at this time. This is when your instinctive economic good sense will stand you in good stead, particularly if you feel it's time to update your investments or slim down a business venture with a view to greater efficiency. You'll actually enjoy this process and may even discover that there's a money-making opportunity that you weren't making the most of.

 Existing amorous attachments are moving into a more settled phase now that certain emotional quirks are a thing of the past. A feeling of increased contentment descends over your love life, and perhaps many Capricorn persons will be turning their minds to thoughts of marriage.

For the unattached, what takes place mid month may seem blissful, but appearances may prove deceptive. A better prospect appears on the 23rd when developments in your social life will give rise to romantic anticipation.

 The various people you encounter during these weeks will provide you with tremendous mental stimulation and help greatly if you need to discuss and clarify your thoughts and feelings. It's a spellbinding month for those who are engaged in high-powered debate, diplomatic missions, and situations in which there is a need for constructive dialogue.

It looks as if your learning curve is due to take a sharp upswing, which is something you can help greatly by enlarging you network of significant contacts and seeking out persons with whom you can develop a fruitful exchange of knowledge.

LUCKY DATES 3rd, 10th, 13th, 25th.

A project that has been in the planning stage for several months is likely to gather momentum during the first week of the month, and at last you'll begin to feel that your wishes are being realized. There is a highly encouraging accent on efforts that call for team-work and close co-operation. Whether this has to do with sport, business and social interests or spare time activity, your experience in these areas will bring tremendous reward and satisfaction. This is also where you will establish one or more extremely valuable friendships.

Psychologically you will be feeling much stronger within yourself, perhaps regaining your equilibrium after an emotionally stressful phase. Whatever the case, it seems that you are tapping into a deeper source of spiritual energy, the effects of which will to give you a clear sense of direction.

From one angle, you have tremendous support from friends and colleagues, but from another angle you are likely to get at cross-purposes with certain people due to quite trivial disagreements. This is more likely to be experienced between the 10th and 29th, when Mercury is moving retrograde in your opposite sign. If you feel that you are not getting a point across, maybe you should take a closer and more critical look at where your thoughts are coming from. Consider that you may be seeing things from too narrow a vision.

A message, or chance discussion, in the final days of July will help you to clear away ambiguities and put you in a position when an important decision can finally be taken. A Discussion with colleagues or with a person in a position to open your career prospects will go better than you had expected.

Although there continues to be a progressive accent on both personal and joint financial interests, you are strongly advised to tread cautiously around the 5th. It will be only too easy to get tempted by those who promise you a large return on investments or a get rich quick scheme. The problem is that it will indeed appear very tempting! But be warned that appearances will be very deceptive. Don't sign anything too important or life-changing until you have really thought through all the possible connotations. Try to get second-opinions on contracts, if possible.

It might pay you to keep a wary eye on the spending habits of your partner, or someone closely associated with you. If you feel that he or she is not being entirely open and honest, be prepared to confront the issue earlier rather than later in the month.

A certain obstacle that has stood in the way of romance is likely to fade into the background soon after the 19th. Something that previously appeared hopeless will take a sudden turn for the better, and by late month you will be pleasantly surprised how everything seems to be falling into place. This is certainly good news for those who are hoping to take the plunge in to matrimony in the next month or two. Suddenly it will all become very possible!

LUCKY DATES 10th, 11th, 22nd, 30th.

An unusual configuration of Uranus and Saturn at the start of the month shows that the Fates are liable to intervene in your affairs. Something from the dim and distant past will attract your attention, recall certain almost forgotten experiences. Perhaps there will be a feeling of déja vu, an uncanny feeling that somehow you have been this way before.

There is indeed something decidedly occult written into this planetary aspect, so if you are delving into the deeper realms of knowledge and are interested in such things as hypnotism, reincarnation or mystical awareness, you're likely to find yourself on the track of intriguing insights and discoveries.

The theme of looking back to the past may have an interesting focus in the sphere of family connections at this time. If you are researching your family roots, it is almost certain you'll stumble upon something enlightening - though this may take the shape of a skeleton in the cupboard! Whatever it is you discover will certainly change the way you have thought about a relative or friend of the family. These events may bring up some uncomfortable questions and there may be a couple of people who would have preferred to have been kept in the dark.

There are also indications too that an elderly relative will enlighten you on an almost forgotten family matter, or an event that has long been a mystery to you. If you discover that you are heir to a fortune, it would not be surprising in view of your prevailing astrological pattern!

If you are feeling adventurous, this is an excellent month for the kind of holiday that challenges your physical stamina and gives you a sense of achievement. Your sign is closely associated with the proverbial mountaineer - someone who wants to scale the heights. If this, or something similar, is what you're into, so much the better - it's certainly a good month for anyone thinking of planning an adventure holiday or a sporting break of some sort.

For those who are seeking something more relaxing, you are likely to find everything you desire by taking a vacation at this time. The only potentially tricky date is the 13th, when it would be best to avoid travel altogether. If this is impossible, then it would be in your interests to double-check schedules and make sure the car is well serviced before setting out on any lengthy trips.

Promising developments towards the end of last month continue to generate a feeling of euphoria during August. Capricorn people often find it hard to accept the fact that someone else is genuinely fond of them. It is as if you have a deep misgiving about emotional attachment and often express this is a rather cynical manner. However, what takes place during August is likely to get through to you and kindle a brighter flame in your heart. If something has made you feel rejected and dejected in the past, this is where it is all going to change.

LUCKY DATES 6th, 7th, 15th, 21st, 26th.

Eclipses often highlight areas of potential change in life, according to where they fall in one's solar horoscope. During September there is a Lunar eclipse on the 7th then a Solar eclipse on the 22nd, both of which put the main focus on the things of the mind. It is likely that your ideas and your general outlook on life will undergo a shift of emphasis between now and the end of the year. Certain interests will fade into the background, while some ideas that you stuck on the back burner will now take a much higher profile.

The upshot of this will be in terms of a quite radical change of routine and a determination to establish greater freedom in how you run your life at a day-to-day level. You'll be inclined to look at the world with a more critical eye and motivated to play a more active part in efforts to ease the plight your less fortunate fellow beings.

Fortune smiles on those involved in corporate endeavours, social interests and the affairs of the wider world. It's the position of Jupiter in your solar chart that is likely to stir up a deep social conscience within you, so if it is your wish to push for reform or campaign for a good cause, this is a time when your efforts will bring highly productive results.

Long-range travel is highlighted during the first half of the month, with the main accent on practical endeavours and business interests. The people you meet and talk with on your travels are likely to change your ideas in some way. Indeed, if you a travelling on business, it is likely that you'll come away from a meeting with radically changed views. However, don't let this cause you to throw overboard what you already know.

Distant horizons throw a pleasant light on romance during the middle weeks, endowing travel with a satisfying honeymoon atmosphere. Quality time spent with the one you love will act as a deep therapy, bringing a feeling of deeper under-standing and togetherness.

Alternatively, there is a very high chance of meeting your affinity via travel in distant lands or on the seas. Maybe you'll simply fall in love with a place you happen to visit and want to return there again and again. There's certainly a magical feel to foreign shores at this time and it's a particularly favourable month for meeting someone that could blow your socks off - so keep your eyes open to all possibilities!

Turning to more mundane affairs, it looks as if career interests are engaging you at a more dynamic level from mid month onwards. There may be pressure on you to step up the pace or play a more leading role in the work situation. However, this is something you will welcome, because you will now feel that real progress is being made. Be careful about making financial commitments in regard to a group venture or social event later in the month. Watch out for misplaced enthusiasm and idealism, wishful thinking could land you in some hot water financially.

LUCKY DATES 4th, 10th, 19th, 26th.

Your range of social activity and influence continues to increase and will have a direct bearing on practical aims and material fortunes during October. By joining forces with people who are on your own wavelength you'll be able to bring major aims and objectives closer to realization. You stand to gain considerably by giving your range of significant contacts a broader base. The astrological pattern is highly supportive and this will be felt most of all in the way that luck and opportunity come via friendships.

A change for the better is forecast in regard to material aims and interests, particularly in the latter days of the month when you'll find yourself in a better position to re-organise your life at a very practical level. Persons of influence are likely to be favourably disposed towards you, which will ease your path to success if a new project is under consideration.

 The changing pattern of things will have an important bearing on your personal economic situation during the coming weeks. The underlying trend is extremely encouraging, especially to those who work in partnership, work in a team or are aiming to make a career change in the near future. However, there may be a fairly tough decision looming around the 25th, as this is when Jupiter will throw a challenging aspect to your ruling planet, Saturn.

There's a need to overhaul certain financial objectives, particularly if you work with a team and have begun to feel that you are not making best use of your potential. It may simply be a case of getting stuck in a rut when you should be focusing on the need to bring things up to date. Your budget is unlikely to suffer any traumatic setbacks, but it would pay you to get together with others to do some serious thinking about how you are managing your money.

 Events will pull you into a wider and more varied social circle throughout the month. You're likely to be in a more gregarious mood anyway and therefore strongly motivated to cultivate a wider circle of contacts. A decision or invitation to get involved in a new field of activity will add a mentally stimulating aspect to your life, and this is where new friends are likely to gravitate in to your orbit.

Travel is suddenly brought into the centre of the frame around the 10th and may have an important bearing on certain group interests that have recently grabbed your allegiance. Journeys for the purpose of educational efforts or the promotion of special ideas will have a successful outcome - and here too you'll make new friends and very useful contacts.

Although the main emphasis falls on straightforward friendships throughout the month, links of a more intimate nature are not entirely out of the running. Once Venus changes signs on the 24th, there is much to suggest an unusually passionate episode as the result of a chance meeting earlier in the month. It could be that a simple friendship will suddenly blossom into a fully-fledged amour!

LUCKY DATES 1st, 4th, 12th, 28th.

If cherished hopes and wishes are going to materialise, then this is the month when it could all happen! Even a modest assessment of the prevailing cosmic pattern suggests that an important objective is due to take a quantum leap to a more productive and rewarding level. The efforts made and experience gained in the past will enable you to reap a rich harvest in view of certain fresh options and opportunities that emerge between now and the end of the year. Whatever happens during these weeks, it is bout to make you feel confident that you are on the right track.

Suddenly you'll find yourself in a more authoritative position where you can call all the shots and influence a situation in a way that does not antagonise others. The intensification of your sense of purpose will have the effect of winning the respect of others and allowing you to do make full use of your very practical talents.

A meeting that took place in the latter half of October may have stirred up deeper emotions and made you realize that an element of the unpredictable can often work like magic. Amorous attachments continue to engage your feelings at a rather intense level, but this is not necessarily a bad thing. Being a Capricorn, you are inclined to get out of touch with your deeper emotional nature. This is felt by others as a kind of unapproachable aura around you and may act as a self-sabotage mechanism in regard to your own ability to experience fulfilment via intimate attachments.

Even if a romantic affair is not destined to last, its effect will be wholly beneficial in melting that icy surface that can so easily block your way to love. You might feel a little vulnerable at first but slowly you'll begin to trust your feelings and feel less frightened of opening up to another person.

Mercury remains retrograde until the 18th and throws a tricky aspect to Neptune on the 8th. Unforeseen events are liable to disrupt your plans and allowances will need to made for unreliability and absent-mindedness in those you co-operate with. The Neptune factor brings a deceptive element in to the situation and people you are in dialogue with are likely to misinterpret your message.

Best advice is to avoid making any major decisions and commitments until after the 18th, particularly if group interests are involved or you are not sure of the motivations of certain individuals.

You're advised to switch into a lower gear when Mars is at odds with Saturn at the end of the month. This is where the stresses and strains of the past few months are liable to catch up on you, so watch out for the warning signals and be prepared to take time out if you feel the need to recoup your flagging energies.

Alternatively, it could be that a project you're working on is held up due to the poor health of a friend or colleague. Patience seems to be called for at this time.

LUCKY DATES 5th, 9th, 15th, 24th

Someone once said that those who don't learn from the past are condemned to repeat it. If you now begin to realize that perhaps a decision you made somewhere back in the past has been leading you in the wrong direction, you'll have to face up to the fact that something will need to be done about it.

A fairly radical change in the pattern of the zodiac as the year comes to a close suggests a time for deeper reflection and a need to clarify those areas of your life that may be creating stress or causing you to have misgivings about certain aims and interests. There are indications that you are about to enter a transition phase in which you are more inclined to call into question what you have previously taken for granted. Out of this is bound to emerge something very positive, but perhaps some deeper soul searching will be needed in the next few months.

The things that give you a feeling of inner and outer security are very much at the centre of your attention as the end of the year approaches. Saturn turns retrograde, inclining you to reflect more deeply on the material and emotional needs of those closest to you. You may begin to see that dependence on certain material things can sometimes put you out of touch with your real inner needs, as well as causing you to lose sight of the deeper sensitivities of other people. You might have lost sight of what it is that makes you really happy and vital or forgotten that you can change things. But an overhaul of your scale of values might be something to consider now that the festive season is upon us once more!

Something that has been kept on a rather secretive level and made you feel rather uneasy will take a turn for the better soon after the 11th. You then have Venus in your own sign, signalling the end to any doubts and anxieties connected with romantic affairs.

This planet will greatly enhance your personal appeal and incline you to pay more attention to the image you present to the world. An upswing in your social popularity is indicated during the latter half of the month, and this may not be entirely due to the party atmosphere around the 25th and 31st. Whatever happens, there is much to suggest that you will not be short of new admirers. For lonely-hearts and single Capricorns looking for someone special this is very welcome news indeed!

Everything of significance appears to be taking shape behind the scenes from the second week onwards. Something that is as yet only indirectly linked with your own interests will give rise to unusual opportunities very soon. This could amount to the opening of a completely new chapter in your life, almost as if you are at last finding your true path after a lengthy phase of experiment and exploration.

Trust your own deeper instincts and intuitions if you are faced with a decision in the third week, when the formula for success is an indirect approach.

LUCKY DATES 1st, 11th, 19th, 24th, 30th.

aquarius

january 21 to february 19

Planetary Ruler:	Uranus	**Wood:**	Pine
Quality & Element:	Fixed Air	**Flower:**	Pansy
Colours:	Electric blue,	**Animal:**	Fox
	bright pink	**Gem:**	Garnet
Metal:	Lead, pewter	**Fabric:**	Crepe

2006 is likely to go down in your personal history as a year of destiny! This is nothing to feel alarmed about, because it looks as if various threads are being pulled together, giving you a clearer sense of direction and a feeling that at last you are in sight of realising an ambition. There will be times when the pace of events will carry you along at a dizzying rate, but it is unlikely you'll lose sight of what is most important and will know instinctively when and when not to act.

Four major planets forming what is known as a grand cross in your solar chart indicate this very 'fateful' scenario. Neptune in your sign enhances your imaginative and creative powers, while Mars in the lower angle gives you the initiative to open a new chapter in your life. Saturn in your opposite sign brings wise guidance from others and perhaps a meeting with a guru figure. Finally, Jupiter oversees the whole show and ensures that you are in the right place at the right time when the big opportunities arise.

Your ruling planet, Uranus, continues to track through the money sector of your solar chart. As an Aquarian, you have a natural flair for originality and taking the unconventional approach to life. It is in regard to financial and business affairs that these qualities will stand you in good stead throughout the year. Your inventive ideas will come at the right time and serve to liven up a somewhat staid state of affairs at work or in your business affairs.

The unusual link between Uranus and Saturn on the 19th enables you to combine the old with the new for the purpose of promoting a money-making venture. However, if your partner is not too happy about what you have in mind, listen carefully to what he or she has to say. Make sure your alternative schemes are not totally off the wall and have at least some semblance of practicality.

A romantic attachment may appear to be losing momentum throughout January. The flame goes dim and feelings will suddenly begin to resemble the seasonal weather. Looked at realistically this could be a hint that the whole thing is due to fizzle out completely, and if you are honest with yourself you will see that perhaps you have been labouring under a misapprehension -tat you're in love with the idea of love, rather than with another person.

However, this is a time when you are going through a phase of inner emotional growth and transformation. Maybe it is simply a case of seeing that you have outgrown a situation and not it is time to move on.

You're unlikely to be moving far out of your familiar circle during these weeks, and perhaps there will be times when you feel confined by circumstances. But this is no bad thing if it allows you to cultivate the necessary inner space for serious reflection and meditation. It's an excellent time for turning ideas over in your mind and taking more notice of insights and intuitions that seem to emerge from nowhere.

LUCKY DATES 3rd, 11th, 21st, 29th.

Events taking shape behind the scenes are concocting something very pleasant, though you might not become fully aware of this until later in the month. Alternatively, it could be something that has been incubating in the deeper level of your mind that will emerge into a clearer light as the month progresses, opening up interesting creative possibilities for those of a more artistic inclination.

Mars finally takes leave of the lower sector of your solar chart on the 17th, after an unusually lengthy sojourn in this area. This too suggests an upsurge of creative energy and a feeling that you are finally breaking free of a situation that has increasingly cramped your style over the past six months.

 The movement of Mars puts special focus on matters closer to home, with every indication that a stressful phase is coming to an end. Upheaval may have been caused by a removal, or more likely because of renovations and alterations to your current abode. Whatever the case, the trend is towards a feeling of greater stability and contentment within the home and family circle.

If you experience a conflict of duties earlier in the month, it would be better not to neglect a domestic matter for the sake of some quite trivial outside engagement. Someone may feel a bit miffed that you can't always be at their beck and call, but really that is their problem, not yours. This will be a great month for asserting your point of view and making your feelings on particular issues crystal clear to your family. There's also the possibility that someone you've had an on-going argument with will finally decide to call it quits, feeling that the relationship is more important than the reason that may have caused the rift in the first place.

 Sooner or later the tide reaches its lowest ebb. For a while nothing seems to happen, but slowly you realise that it has turned. This gives a fairly accurate picture of your experience of intimate relationships over the past months and how things are likely to shape up from early February onwards.

As Venus finally begins to gather a more positive momentum on the 3rd, any lingering sadness over the past will fade into the background, and before the month is out you may begin to see a new light rising over your horizon. It is no good expecting any instant miracles, but there is much to suggest that someone you got to know recently thinks very fondly of you. Something you hear through the grapevine on the 23rd or 25th will make you realise that the time has indeed begun to flow!

 From the second week onwards commercially minded Aquarians may find it hard to keep up with the pace of things, but if you are not fazed by new ideas and varying your schedules, the rewards could be great. The 14th is a key date if you a looking for a sideline or wish to promote an unusual fund-raising venture. Diversification is the name of the game, and this is where your natural inventiveness could put you ahead of the game!

LUCKY DATES 6th, 8th, 14th, 25th.

Whatever goals you are aiming to achieve over the long term, the pattern of events during the month ahead will incline you to see things in a different light. A change of direction may be called for if you feel that somehow the goalposts are shifting, but this is not a recipe for panic measures.

After a phase of successful activity and a feeling of moving forward, you may have to accept the fact that there are times when the situation reaches a plateau and you might even begin to think that things are taking a backward turn. With Jupiter and Mercury turning retrograde early in March a project you have been working on may suffer a temporary setback, but this may turn out to be a blessing in disguise.

Financial and business interests may come under stress during March and perhaps there will be a phase of uncertainty concerning current employment or career interests. It is not a good time to make hasty decisions that might affect your long range aims and aspirations, but if you do feel that finances need a radical restructuring, now is the time to seek advice.

Whatever happens, it would be a good policy to keep a tighter rein on your budget and to look carefully at ways and means of improving your assets. Instead of attempting to make a fortune overnight, it would be in your best interests to stick to the familiar route and spend some time getting your priorities in order.

If material affairs are causing you some aggravations, the same cannot be said for the emotional side of the equation. The presence of Venus in your own sign most of the month brings a promise of desires fulfilled. This encouraging prospect is given further support by a favourable transit of Mars, which adds a certain intensity and passion to the romantic climate.

March promises to be the most significant month in ages as far as new amorous encounters are concerned. So if you have not had much joy in your love life since you cannot remember when, it looks as if you'll be riding the crest of a wave before the month is over. Just when you decided to give up on your love life, there will be unexpected romantic possibilities to explore. Even if you don't get together with the love of your life, you're sure to be very flattered by the attentions of someone rather special.

You're likely to be moving in a larger social circle throughout March, probably as a direct result of certain interests that are beginning to gather greater momentum. The accent will be on creative activity and spare time occupations. Whether this has to do with the arts, the world of entertainment, or a desire to prove skills on the field of sports, you can expect that these things will do much to enrich your life and raise your self-esteem. But sports fanatics be warned: there is danger of doing yourself an injury on the 11th due to over-aggressive tactics, so make sure you play fair, and watch you don't get overly enthusiastic.

LUCKY DATES 6th, 16th, 21st, 25th.

Although you may not be entirely out of the woods in regard to worldly aims and material interests, at least you will know that a crisis has been avoided and that you are in a better position to judge the right course of action to take. Jupiter continues to ride high in your solar chart, promising expansion and scope for improving your status. But while this planet is in retrograde mode it would be better to consolidate (and appreciate) what you have already achieved, rather than attempting to scale the heights.

Of great importance is Saturn, which begins to take a more positive direction from the 5th onwards. This date could mark a significant turning point having its main focus in the sphere of close personal relationships. This planet indicates benefits through contact with older and wiser persons, or a greater motivation on you part to seek a more integrated relationship with the world at large.

 Of course, Saturn does occupy your House of Partners, indicating a more serious attitude towards personal relationships and perhaps a certain reluctance to take the step into matrimony. Saturn inclines you to be more selective about potential partners, but once a relationship is established you can be certain that it will last.

New romantic attachments may need to be given more time to emerge and develop. There is no forcing of issues when Saturn takes charge, but the chances of meeting the right person for you are greatly enhanced. You might find yourself drawn to an older person or to someone in a position of authority.

 Matters of a very practical nature are likely to engage your mental energies at a fairly intense level early in the month. This is the best time for seeking advice and information if you wish to improve your qualifications or want to discuss a project with your bank manager or other financial advisor.

You're likely to be on the move during the latter half of the month - perhaps not going far from home base, but certainly clocking up the miles via shorter trips. Much of this will focus on various practical duties and chores, but towards the end of the month an outing or visit will bring delight and mental stimulation.

 The Saturn factor throws a more favourable light on property interests and is particularly helpful for newlyweds who are in the process of setting up home for the first time. The new Moon at the end of the month signals a phase of increasing emotional contentment within the domestic circle, as well as a bright prospect for those who are involved in transactions on the property market. Home improvements and DIY projects are favoured and you'll be keen to have a clear for a fresh start. This month a litle organisation will go a long way.

Keep your arrangements on a flexible basis between the 18th and 26th, for this is when relatives are liable to make demands, or when several visitors will be in the habit of landing on your doorstep at short notice.

LUCKY DATES 4th, 9th, 21st, 24th.

Though you may find that life demands a high-energy output from you throughout the month, there will also be plenty of scope for varying your routines and cultivating small oases in the busy schedules for relaxation and the pursuit of leisurely interests. You will certainly have reason to feel more confident in regard to practical aims and objectives, which have probably been in a state of limbo over the past couple of months.

Events taking shape towards the end of the first week may contain unexpected possibilities, and if you play your cards right there will be a chance to pull strings in your favour. Much will depend on a combination of initiative and faith in your own capabilities. If an opportunity to boost your status arises, go for it - even if you feel out of your depth, you'll be glad you tried.

 At last you will begin to feel that things are gathering a more productive momentum, and after several months of having your nose firmly to the grindstone, you will begin to see some tangible returns on your efforts. As already hinted, an unexpected opportunity during the first half of the month could take you a very long way towards realising your ambitions - or at least making a substantial advance in regard to career and status.

The progressive trend is particularly favourable for the self-employed, or those who are hoping to strike out in a more independent direction in regard to earning a living. The best advice is to take the tide while it is at the flood. Initiatives geared towards greater freedom of expression are sure to bring rewards both materially and personally. Have a re-think about whether your current aims and objectives are carrying you in the right direction.

 Shorter journeys, outings and visits, will provide a special source of delight and entertainment throughout the month. If you can see your way to taking a short break from the usual round, so much the better, for this is a time when a breathing space will have a deeply settling and therapeutic influence on your inner being. Even a day spent sitting in the park will have a therapeutic affect on your psyche.

Later in the month, notably between the 24th and 27th, a message you receive or a visit from an old friend will put you in a cheerful moon. There may be some cause for celebration, for it's likely that someone will announce a wedding, engagement, or birth of a child. Whatever transpires, it looks as if an old link will be renewed as a result of a short message or brief visit.

There is a pleasant and affectionate aura around you during the final week of the month. Nor only are old friendships likely to be renewed, but there is much to suggest that a certain friendly attachment will begin to take on a deeper meaning for you. A powerful aspect between Venus and Pluto indicates a possible revival of an old affair due to a chance meeting, and maybe you'll take to heart that you don't know what you've got till its gone!

LUCKY DATES 2nd, 8th, 12th, 27th.

If you feel that a confrontation is brewing, a situation is liable to reach a crisis during the third week. An old bone of contention may be forced upon your unwilling attention, but provided you can overcome certain prejudices and look at a situation in a detached manner, this may be the ideal chance to sort out a long standing problem once and for all. You may come to the realisation that the main obstacle is not always completely outside yourself; more often than not, it is a case of being unable to admit one's own inner limitations.

Neptune in your own sign receives a tremendous boost of solar energy on the 10th, highlighting the urge to express yourself more creatively and to be more imaginative in the way you pursue spare time interests and social activities. Don't be surprised if you find yourself in the spotlight around this date.

If harmony threatens to break down at home, you'll probably have only yourself to blame - especially when adverse trends are in force on the 4th and 15th. Like all persons born under 'fixed signs' you do have an awkward and stubborn element in your character. Once you make up your mind to go your own way, there will be no persuading you otherwise. However, you're asking for trouble if you refuse to make some compromise where family duties are concerned. Be prepared to make some sacrifice of your own time and interest in the service of good relations and peace of mind. This might be difficult to come to terms with at first but in a couple of weeks time you'll wonder why you were being so stubborn over an issue you actually don't care that much about.

A clash of egos is liable to cause stress within marriage or other close relationships during the third week. If your partner seems intent on going ahead with a project that you disagree with, be prepared for a showdown at this time. Here, too, it is the element of stubbornness that is likely to get in the way of a rational solution, but forewarned is forearmed.

It's not all storm and stress by any means. Once Venus moves into a congenial area of your solar chart on the 24th, not only will romance flourish but you will begin to feel that a new and more mature level of understanding is growing up between you and your partner. By the month end you'll fell like you're both going from strength to strength.

In view of the stressful planetary configuration in the third week, it could be that a bout of poor health or lack of energy proves to be the main obstacle to your progress. However, don't feel that you have to put up a huge fight. It would be better to accept certain limits and take things in your stride.

You can expect to receive encouraging news concerning employment or career around the 9th or 12th. This may entail a journey or an important interview at short notice. However, a helpful transit of Mercury ensures that you have the necessary presence of mind and all the answers at your fingertips.

LUCKY DATES 10th, 11th, 24th, 27th.

An intense concentration of planetary activity in the first week of the month marks this out as perhaps once of the most eventful times in the year for those born under Aquarius. There are stress factors woven into this pattern, but Jupiter resuming a forward momentum on the 6th acts as a saving grace.

It's a time when you may feel that you are growing away from certain persons or situations and will have to come to terms with the fact that your attitudes and your goals do occasionally undergo a subtle shift of emphasis. There is potential for disagreement and perhaps heated arguments early in the month, but provided you don't completely lose your cool and let emotional reactions take over, you have an excellent opportunity to settle a question that has nagged at the back of your mind for several months.

 Best progress can be made by keeping a relatively low profile until later in the month. Being over competitive or too up-front is sure to create antagonisms and sabotage your own best interests. If you do wish to take fresh initiatives with a view to boosting your earning potential, a strategic moment will arrive soon after the 22nd. In the meantime do your homework and be prepared to bide your time.

What takes place in the final days of the month will come as a welcome bonus to those who have been working at full tilt since the start of the year. The ideal job offer may come your way, so be on the alert for the lucky break! Everything points to a sudden upswing in your status and perhaps a change in your work pattern that allows you to take a more relaxed angle on your financial affairs.

 Recent stress levels have been high, putting your usual resilient health in jeopardy. However, once Mars takes leave of your opposite sign on the 22nd you'll soon be able to re-charge your batteries. An easier pace of life begins to prevail from late month and any worries concerning your own or someone else's health and wellbeing will fade into the background.

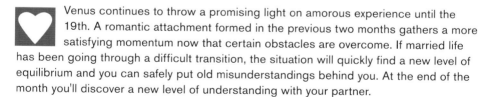 Venus continues to throw a promising light on amorous experience until the 19th. A romantic attachment formed in the previous two months gathers a more satisfying momentum now that certain obstacles are overcome. If married life has been going through a difficult transition, the situation will quickly find a new level of equilibrium and you can safely put old misunderstandings behind you. At the end of the month you'll discover a new level of understanding with your partner.

 Work routines are liable to get disrupted due to misinformation or overlooking details. A colleague or perhaps a boss will think it's to their advantage if they can manipulate you into taking on extra responsibilities - but they haven't told you the whole story. Make sure you're being properly compensated for any extra work and don't take anything for granted between the 10th and the end of the month.

LUCKY DATES 6th, 10th, 13th, 31st.

Once again you will get the uncanny feeling that the Fates are moving in mysterious ways during the first half of August. As Saturn is the dominant force, it is likely that an older person will play an important part in your life, inclining you to reflect more deeply on the past and to call in question what you have learned to take for granted. In fact the prevailing cosmic pattern can be read as the urge to seek deeper wisdom and to establish contact with a guide or guru.

Even if this is not a priority with you at present, nevertheless it looks as if someone you meet and talk to early in the month will profoundly influence your way of thinking. You will be made to realise how easy it is to get locked into negative habits that tend to shut you off from your deeper potential and dull your senses.

Personal relationships are very much in the centre of the picture throughout the month. At best, the powerful Saturn influence contributes to the feeling of greater strength and stability in established ties of affection. This planet does of course have a rather negative reputation, but this will only be felt where a relationship has been built on a flimsy foundation. In other words, if you have been viewing a situation through rose-tinted spectacles, this is a time when you may have to face up to reality. You'll find it particularly difficult not to nit-pick or criticise when you feel you're being challenged for no good reason.

This certainly does not take away from the fact that this is perhaps the most auspicious month in the whole year for those who are taking the plunge into matrimony, or planning to do so in the near future. The proviso for success in this sphere is that your love is deep rooted and coming from a fairly mature level. Marriage is an issue not to be taken lightly while Saturn holds sway in your House of Partners!

You are advised to put something aside in case of emergencies. Around the 13th you may be faced with unexpected expenses, probably due to urgent repairs that need to be carried out on the car or other essential machinery. It's the very mundane things such as central heating, plumbing and technical gadgetry that need attention and oblige you to dig deeply into your reserve funds.

However, the underlying trend is one of steady progress, particularly if you work in tandem with another person. Alternatively, your marriage partner is likely to receive welcome news regarding finance and career later in the month. An unexpected twist of events focusing on career interests will throw an optimistic aura over financial prospects as the month comes to a close.

As Saturn closes in on the opposition of Neptune at the end of the month you are warned not to neglect health issues if you are planning a far-flung journey. Give your immune system all the support you can muster, get some exercise and make sure you're getting all the nutrients you need from your diet.

LUCKY DATES 2nd, 11th, 17th, 29th.

You may be under the impression that things have been changing quite radically over the previous few months, but really it is more to do with a change in your own attitudes and perspectives that has been the key feature. What happens early in September will make your realise the truth of this. Something you had previously felt was beyond your capability will have come well within the bounds of possibility.

It's a time when key aims and objectives are likely to undergo a process of re-alignment. This may entail cutting out what is no longer essential and perhaps abandoning one course of action in favour of something much more in tune with your current way of thinking.

 From the 12th onwards Mercury throws a lively accent on far-flung journeys and long distance contacts. A change of scenery is something you are likely to crave now that various mundane duties and pressures have eased. Trends in the latter half of the month rouse your adventurous spirit and make this an ideal time for exploring the wider world.

A star date for long range excursions and exotic holidays is the 23rd. Not only will the people you meet stimulate your mind; you will be deeply impressed by certain places you happen to visit. Whatever happens, it seems that experience that comes to you via travel will fire your imagination and give you a fresh perspective on some long-held beliefs and attitudes. Don't turn down the opportunity to travel overseas if you get it, whether for business or for pleasure it's sure to turn out well.

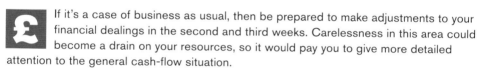 If it's a case of business as usual, then be prepared to make adjustments to your financial dealings in the second and third weeks. Carelessness in this area could become a drain on your resources, so it would pay you to give more detailed attention to the general cash-flow situation.

While this might not the best of months to make any important new commitments, it would certainly be in your best interests to get priorities clarified, even if this means foregoing a tempting investment or business venture. Better to take a long view rather than kid yourself that a fortune can be made overnight. It's a case of making haste slowly and taking a sceptical view of those who are always urging you to go forward whatever the cost. Trust your instincts in business matters this month.

The forces of attraction are intensified early in the month as Venus links up with the mysterious Pluto. The keyword here is transformation, and what this means for the romantically inclined is that a relationship is about to take a quantum leap into the realms of pure passion. It could be that someone you have been on nodding terms with for several months suddenly grabs you at a deeper emotional level. The surprise factor will be that the feeling turns out to be mutual. Although you might be feeling more shy than usual, the other person won't be backwards in coming forwards!

LUCKY DATES 2nd, 7th, 13th, 23rd.

The urge to broaden your horizons is likely to reach a new level of intensity throughout the month. The dynamic pattern of influences favours those who are intent on breaking with routine and exploring a wider field of self-expression and development. Whether your ultimate aim is material enrichment, worldly success, or spiritual enlightenment, your imagination and insight will allow you to take a giant step forward.

Symbolically, the astrological picture conjures up an image of rugged individualism! This translates into ordinary life as an intense desire to cut your own path, to assert yourself with greater independence and to create a wider margin of creative freedom in your lifestyle. So, if you are aiming to make desirable changes, now is the time to take the initiative and realise your dreams.

The need to break free and to widen your horizons is likely to involve you in much travel throughout October. If a journey involves an element of sport or physical stamina, this will be a source of tremendous satisfaction. Journeys with a more relaxing goal in view may nevertheless contain an element of surprise or challenge, because it is likely that you'll encounter someone who ignites new ideas in your mind and becomes a lifelong friend.

An unexpected twist of events, perhaps a new job offer, will throw career interests into different perspective around the 10th. Keep your wits about you if you wish to take advantage of what could be a chance in a lifetime! Whatever happens, it looks as if your financial affairs will take a sudden turn for the better soon after this date.

Make your best efforts to sort out any existing legal and official matters in the first half of the month. A combination of forcefulness and diplomacy will get the right results if your are negotiating a new deal or wish to turn around a situation that threatened to get bogged down in red tape.

With travel high on the agenda, romance is likely to blossom amidst unfamiliar scenery. But whether you are travelling far and wide or remaining on home ground, if you find yourself attracted to someone from a different cultural background, take this as a good omen!

Saturn continues to favour those who take a more serious attitude towards close personal relationships and are hoping that love will last. It's not the most passionate planet around and it can be a little calculating at times. Saturn does not take too kindly to casual flirtations and hasty decisions, but at the same time you do need to be wary that you are not being used simply to bolster up someone else's insecure ego. This is where your proverbial detachment will enable you to steer clear of Saturn's negative potential. But remember that all long-lasting, solid relationships need a good, solid base - and that's where Saturn can really shine.

LUCKY DATES 4th, 10th, 21st, 29th.

Just when you felt that everything was on course, some quite trivial matter will throw a spanner in the works early in the month. While this is not likely to cause a complete meltdown, it will put you in a rather tense mood and incline you to get at loggerheads with the people around you. The good news is that what seemed impossible earlier in the month will be well within your powers by later.

There are times when circumstances give you more than just a hint that perhaps you are getting a bit out of your depth, and now that you can see another wave approaching there will be tendency to panic. Be prepared to beat a retreat when Neptune is under stress on the 8th and 17th, and admit that perhaps you are not quite ready for the challenge.

Provided you keep to a relatively modest target, the path to success will present you with few real hurdles in the coming month. Occupational and vocational interests are highlighted, with plenty of scope and incentive for constructive effort. If you are planning a fresh initiative or wish to manoeuvre yourself into a more influential position, make your best efforts after the 18th.

It is not only Mercury but also your ruling planet Uranus that turns direct around this date. With the main accent on finance and professional activity, it seems that an unexpected turn of events will work magic as far as your personal fortunes are concerned.

Lunar trends on the 5th bring a feeling of increased contentment to the domestic circle. Any lingering aftershocks of upheavals that took place earlier in the year will finally fade into the background, leaving you with a feeling more at one with yourself and your immediate surroundings.

Although the demands of work and career may be occupying a larger slice of your time and energy throughout the month, this is unlikely to create ructions at home. However, be prepared to compromise if tensions do threaten to build around the 17th. The end of the month will be a particularly good time to organise a family gathering, or it may that a celebration is in order.

A similar pattern prevails in regard to intimate affairs, where emotional tensions will result from your workaholic inclinations. External demands may be heavy, but there is no reason why this should sabotage your love life. All it needs is a sense of proportion and a refusal to sacrifice your soul to the rat race.

Romantic hopes and wishes come under the amorous rays of Venus during the latter half of the month. Your social life will gather momentum, bringing you a better chance of making new friends and perhaps finding your affinity. You'll certainly prove especially attractive to the opposite sex this month. However, keep flirtatious impulses in check when Venus is at odd with Uranus on the 25th. What seems quite innocent to your quirky and unconventional nature may not appear so to a friend.

LUCKY DATES 2nd, 3rd, 20th, 22nd.

The field of action has changes considerably over the past month or so, but it is only now that you will begin to see the advantages that such changes are opening up for you. With Jupiter beginning to activate a significant area of your solar chart, your main aims and objectives are due for a tremendous uplift, and no longer will you feel that you have to accept second best.

The planetary configuration has a deep resonance with the Aquarian personality as the year draws to a close. A positive accent falls on wider social interests, friendships, and all activities that engage you in group effort and teamwork. Between now and about the same time next year you are likely to be moving in very congenial social circles and have the benefit of influential and highly supportive friendships.

There is not doubt that this is a time when you have it in your power to win friends and influence people in ways that can greatly enhance your life in many directions. If it's knowledge you're seeking, it is the people you make close contact with who will inspire you and help you to clarify both your higher ideals and the more tangible objectives.

Aquarians who take a serious interest in larger humanitarian concerns are very much in their natural element at this time. Again there is emphasis on the need to establish a wider network, to assert your influence in order to win the support you need. All interests that contain a political factor are greatly favoured from December onwards. The coming year could bring you tremendous success and acclaim.

A dreamy and glamorous aura surrounds romantic experience early in the month, with passions likely to reach a pitch of great intensity around the 8th. Love is liable to become the great intoxicant at this time, to the extent that friends are likely to think that you have completely flipped! However, trust your own feelings, even if these do carry you above cloud nine. It is not often that Aquarians let themselves be carried away by emotions, but occasionally it can be deeply fulfilling as well as uncannily liberating. It looks like you'll also be drawn to art and music at this time which will also have an inspiring influence on your thinking.

Provided an emotional trance does not cause you to neglect more mundane matters, the prospect is entirely favourable when it comes to buying, selling and making money. It is by joining forces with like-minded individuals or groups that you stand to enhance your fortunes. Initiatives taken now are sure to have positive repercussions over the coming year.

It is unlikely you'll be short of funds for the festivities, but think practically when buying gifts, for it seems that other people will be more inclined to appreciate something useful rather than purely ornamental. You could take advantage of this month's creative energies and add a personal touch to any gifts or presents you send out this year.

LUCKY DATES 1st, 8th, 14th, 20th, 31st.

pisces

february 19 to march 21

Planetary Ruler:	Neptune	**Wood:**	Cedar
Quality & Element:	Mutable Water	**Flower:**	Lupin
Colours:	Silvery blues,	**Animal:**	Fish
	grey, green	**Gem:**	Carnelian
Metal:	Platinum/Tin	**Fabric:**	Chiffon

Although you may agree that there areas in your life that are far from ideal, you can take encouragement from the fact that you are blessed with a very benign sky in the year ahead. You begin the year on a friendly note, with a positive Solar-Mars aspect giving an added zest to life and ensuring that your enthusiasm will carry you a long way towards realising current aims and objectives.

Jupiter occupies a highly expansive area of your solar chart, inspiring you to broaden your horizons either through travel or by devoting yourself to the pursuit of knowledge and the development of your creative potential. It a year when you have it in your power to enhance your luck and enrich your life by breaking old habits and telling yourself that you are not obliged to always stick to what convention dictates.

As the urge to travel and see the world is strongly highlighted most of the year, it is likely that you will be preoccupied with plans and preparations in the early stages of the year. Take note of suggestions put to you by certain friends, particularly if you are uncertain about how to get the best out of travel. It is likely that a chance discussion or something you discover on the Internet will give you the inspiration you need if a future excursion is under consideration.

Friends will be particularly helpful if you are aiming to promote a group venture or wish to drum up support for a social event or campaign that is dear to your heart. Don't be afraid to ask favours or to pick people's brains if you a stuck for ideas a simply need a helping hand. There's also a good chance of being able to get yourself a real travel bargain at this time; a one-off chance at something petty special or the opportunity to stay with friends, or friends of friends who have some property abroad.

If a promising romance appears to cool off as the month progresses, there is probably not much you will be able to do about it. You may have to accept the fact that the situation is going precisely nowhere and that perhaps you have been a victim of your own wishful thinking.

The good news is that if a parting does take place, it will be by mutual agreement and you will probably remain on friendly terms with each other. Perhaps it will be a case of certain lessons needing to be learned so that the same mistakes are not made again. Whatever you discover about each other, you will certainly learn a valuable psychological lesson about how you handle your emotions.

There may not be any spectacular financial gains being made early in the year, but a feeling of stability in your work situation will give you much reassurance and enable you to plan finance on a sound basis. If you work for yourself or are hoping to take a more independent line in the near future, this is an excellent month for getting things in order, dealing with the legal side of things, and focusing on establishing a secure foundation for future efforts and enterprise.

LUCKY DATES 9th, 13th, 14th, 31st.

Relationships on all levels come under the harmonising influence of Venus throughout the month. Activities that depend on co-operation and teamwork will go smoothly, and if a difference of opinion does arise your sympathetic approach will help to prevent the whole thing degenerating into an impossible clash of egos.

Someone you meet soon after the 3rd, or perhaps later in the month, may have helpful suggestions to make if you are feeling unsure about embarking on a new project. You will begin to feel more confident about reviving an interest that you were obliged to put on the back-burner several months (even years) ago. Maybe you have been hiding your talents under a stone and now gain the necessary confidence to express yourself more openly.

 Mercury's presence in your sign from the 9th will introduce an element of variety and motivate you to widen your range of significant contacts. If you have been feeling confined and cramped by all-too-familiar routines for too long, this is the month to do something about it. February will prove to be a particularly interesting month for spending some time re-evaluating whatever it is that makes you happiest. Are you working towards a concrete goal or feeling a bit lost?

Mercury helps greatly if you are cultivating a new field of interest or wish to improve existing skills and knowledge. What takes place mid month gives you the necessary incentive to get where the action is, make a quick decision and create the right impression if you need to justify your credentials. An interview at this time is sure to deliver the goods, so don't be over-modest about your capabilities.

 At last things are beginning to show signs of promise after what has probably been a phase of disappointed hopes. Recovering from an emotional crunch is not always easy and can take time, but it certainly looks as if you are beginning to regain your inner equilibrium.

With Venus turning direct early month there are indications of a promising turn of events for the romantically inclined. Just when you were beginning to give up hope of ever meeting a genuine soulmate, something will happen that raises your expectations and makes you realise that perhaps it is your own negative feelings that have been the main obstacle to your heart's desires. What takes place towards the end of the month is sure to swing you into a more positive frame of mind.

 For one reason or another you will be focusing more energy on matters closer to home later in the month. This may be due to a spate of visitors and the impromptu entertaining you may be called upon to do. More likely is that you will be motivated to push ahead with something very practical geared towards improving your current abode. It is more likely that you'll get a good service if you need to employ a workforce to carry out major jobs.

LUCKY DATES 1st, 6th, 19th, 28th.

This is a month when you are advised not to leave anything to chance. With Mercury apparently back-pedalling in your own sign you may be obliged to rethink certain ideas and strategies, so it is essential that you keep a clear mind and stick to what you know best. There will be many people around who try to persuade you to do this, that and the other, all with a promise of greater ease and efficiency. Know that this is a con!

Jupiter also swings into reverse, warning you not to look too far ahead or get carried away by big ideas. There is need for a sense of realism, particularly in regard to the central interests and aims of your life. If doubt and questions begin to haunt your mind, maybe your guardian angel is trying to put you back on a path that is more in tune with your real creative potential.

The dynamic influence of Mars continues to ensure good progress in all to do with property interests and home improvements. The only exception is the 11th, when a disruptive aspect to Uranus could signal a sudden emergency due to malfunctions in electrical systems or plumbing. It would be in your best interests to have on hand the contact numbers of various services around this date! Above all, don't rake risks with anything that might present a fire hazard.

At the emotional level, a minor difference of opinion within the family circle could develop into a slanging match. Forewarned is forearmed, so do your best to defuse the situation as soon as you feel the vibes getting tense.

The negative Mercury factor heightens the potential for communication breakdown during the second and third weeks. Plans are liable to be disrupted and seemingly trivial matters may throw carefully laid plans completely off course. You can do much to minimise aggravations by double-checking arrangements, getting your fact straight and making allowances for simple human error.

It would be better to put off any important longer journeys until later in the month, but if this is not possible choose the 9th and 14th if a business trip is on the cards. Apart from these external hassles, the prevailing trend is helpful if you are involved in studying Eastern philosophies or are interested in methods of inner development such as yoga, psychology and meditation.

A lunar eclipse in your opposite sign on the 14th suggests a need for emotional readjustments if a relationship is to remain a source of personal and mutual enrichment. By nature you are a sensitive and sympathetic soul, but there are times when feelings can cloud issues and you lose touch with the real needs of your partner or lover. If you notice a some tension creeping into your partnership, take this as a cue to talk things over and establish a more open dialogue between yourself and your love one. By bringing out something uncomfortable into the open, you'll eventually feel a whole lot less worried and burdened.

LUCKY DATES 9th, 17th, 19th, 26th.

After a rather nebulous phase, you can expect to see the mists clearing and a new light beginning to dawn. Ideas that have been floating rather incoherently in the back of your mind will be pulled into shape, giving you the necessary confidence make important decisions and impose a greater sense of purpose on your scheme of things.

Saturn begin to gather momentum from the 5th, indicating a constructive and steadying trend in regard to the practical affairs of life. If it's a case of finding greater satisfaction in your work, the events of April are likely to open new doors. But don't be tempted to rush at the first thing that grabs your fancy. Time is of the essence with Saturn and therefore best results will be achieved by adopting a thoughtful approach.

£ While commercial interests are due for an upswing from mid month onwards, it would be in your best interests to overhaul your financial resources earlier in the month. By making the right inquiries you may find that existing assets can be turned to more efficient use. In fact you may have to face the fact that you have become rather careless in your attitude to money over the past few months, and what happens during the second week will give you a signal to change tack in order to avoid a crisis.

A more positive force kicks in around the 19th, bringing success to those who are seeking suitable employment and involved in fund-raising ventures. This is where your creative flair and imagination will stand you in good stead, for you may discover that a spare-time interest can be steered into a more lucrative channel. You'll also be re-thinking how you spend your money - are you really making the most of it? Or are you using it to plug up other financial holes? Once you've found out where you're going wrong you'll be able to enjoy the fruits of your success.

♥ A month of pleasant surprises lies ahead for romantically inclined Pisceans! Dramatic and quite unexpected encounters are forecast when Venus joins Uranus in your sign on the 18th, the only drawback being that affairs begun then are not likely to stand the test of time. If you're hoping for something more lasting, you're more likely to realise your wishes if you meet someone special in the final ten days of the month.

Not only does Venus guarantee increased harmony in close ties of love and affection; it also enhances your personal magnetism and enables you to attract the right kind of friends (or lover) into your orbit.

 Elements of stress and disruption that have plagued domestic life over the past couple of months will give place to a more settled state of affairs from mid month onwards. If you have been feeling restless and dissatisfied with your current domestic surroundings, it looks as if you'll be taking more seriously the prospect of pulling up roots and moving to somewhere more in tune with your current lifestyle. Initiatives taken around the 8th are likely to spark of a train of events that could transform your life.

LUCKY DATES 4th, 15th, 20th, 30th.

A series of spectacular planetary aspects during the first half of the month shows that creative influences are entering your life and that a new chapter is about to open. Though you may feel that the forces of chaos are threatening to take over in the first few days, it is unlikely that this will amount to a complete disaster. In fact it may contain the seeds of new ideas and potentials out of which emerge a greater happiness.

The key feature is Jupiter's aspect to Uranus on the 5th, promising a lucky break and increased motivation to broaden and enrich your range of experience. This is given a very creative emphasis by powerful aspects of Mars on the 7th and 8th. This signifies a break-through to a new level of self-expression and initiatives almost guaranteed to transform the quality of your life.

If the main obstacle to desirable change has been of a purely financial nature, the events of May steer the whole situation onto a smoother path. Luck is linked with your own creative energy and your ability to turn situations to your advantage. By adopting a more forceful and enterprising approach, you could do much to improve your earning powers and boost your status.

The presence of Venus in the money area of your solar chart ensures a healthy cash flow, helped greatly by an added bonus that may arrive on the 11th. All of which should put you in a spending mood! Indeed, this is an excellent time to splash out on luxuries and to indulge your pleasure-loving instincts - without feeling too guilty about it. Money spent on holidays for the future will also be well spent.

You certainly won't be short of vital energy during these weeks, and there is no doubt that the positive developments taking shape at this time will contribute to a general feeling of well-being. Mars in favourable angle to your sign motivates you to get yourself in good shape both physically and mentally. Sport and physical exercise will bring more pleasure than usual and any efforts to get in better physical shape will not go wasted. Extra attention to these matters will have a very positive spin-off if you happen to be actively involved in a sporting event later in the month.

Your mental energies shift into a higher gear as Mercury zips through your 3rd solar house between the 5th and 19th. The pace of life will gather a breath-taking momentum at times, but this is something you are likely to welcome if it means a break in the usual routines.

There is, however, just one proviso: take care if dealing with legal or official matters between the 12th and 15th. Don't be tempted to cut corners and be prepared to double check information you receive. If a certain matter seems ambiguous, don't let it pass until you are absolutely sure of how you stand. There is a danger of having the wool pulled over your eyes, so keep your critical faculties on the alert and don't be fobbed off. If you can employ the help of a professional at this time, so much the better.

LUCKY DATES 2nd, 5th, 12th, 29th.

Powerful solar trends in the first half of the month illuminate the deeper levels of your being and bring a feeling of finer attunement to the spiritual energies of the universe. What this means in practical terms is that you can trust your intuitions, which are likely to give rise to illuminating insights at this time. If you have artistic interests or are genuinely drawn towards mystical teachings, then you can expect to find plenty of inspiration and perhaps a real guiding light in the month ahead.

These subtle astrological influences signify changes taking shape below the threshold of your conscious mind. This will emerge as a feeling of restlessness and a tendency to call into question things that are usually taken for granted. It is as if a learning curve is taking place on a subtle level, leading ultimately to a more insightful and mature attitude to life.

 The solar force sheds an unusual light on domestic affairs, and maybe it is in this area that a feeling of restlessness will be most apparent. With both Uranus and Neptune strongly activated, you are likely to experience a feeling of confinement and an urge to escape into something more spacious.

While a complete change of residence may be impractical at present, you could do much to improve the situation by giving your current abode a makeover and, more importantly, getting rid of accumulated clutter. This in itself will have a spiritually liberating effect and you'll be able to think more clearly.

 Your social life will gather a satisfying momentum throughout the month, with special highlights on the 9th, 12th and 27th. Business and pleasure mix well on these dates, and the people you meet are likely to be on your mental wavelength. There is an element of serendipity woven into a journey on these dates. A surprise combination of luck and inspiration will put you in a cheerful frame of mind.

Be prepared to take seriously any unusual ideas and suggestions that crop up during the course of conversation. This could give you the necessary impetus to develop further a spare time interest or revive a little-used talent. The prevailing trend makes this a prime time for pursuing educational activities on a part time basis. You'll also be inspired by news from afar, when someone overseas will decide to pay you a visit.

 Important tasks are likely to reach completion soon after the 11th and you'll begin to see a more substantial reward for past efforts. Work pressures will continue heavy through the third week when you may be asked to shoulder added responsibility. Provided you are not just playing the martyr and letting people take advantage of your pliable nature, you may find that strings can be pulled in your favour.

Money is not likely to run short, but you will certainly feel that you have earned it. It's important that you make sure you appreciate the value of the work you do this month and that you don't let anyone take you for granted at his time.

LUCKY DATES 9th, 10th, 17th, 24th.

Since the beginning of the year you may have felt a vague feeling of disappointment in regard to the progress of certain plans. What you thought were brilliant ideas and schemes were probably met with a rather half-hearted response from others. You felt thrown back on your own resources and felt that maybe your imagination had led you to the realms of impractical dreams.

This rather negative state of affairs will give way to something more encouraging from early July onwards. Jupiter, the planet of luck and opportunity, then begins to gather force and helps you to recover faith in your own creative powers. Events will contrive to favour your efforts and enable you to salvage something useful from a project abandoned earlier.

 A feeling of restlessness that is likely to be with your for most of the year will have the positive effect of motivating you to explore wider horizons, both mentally and in a purely geographical sense. What takes place at the end of July is likely to involve preparations for a far-flung excursion, perhaps a holiday in some far off and romantic place that you have long wished to visit.

The powerful Jupiter factor will throw an inspiring light on the things of the mind, which is very good news for those involved in educational and academic pursuits. Anything to do with publishing, the media, broadcasting or getting a message across, is sure to meet with a great deal of success between now and the end of the year.

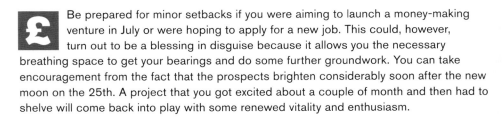 Be prepared for minor setbacks if you were aiming to launch a money-making venture in July or were hoping to apply for a new job. This could, however, turn out to be a blessing in disguise because it allows you the necessary breathing space to get your bearings and do some further groundwork. You can take encouragement from the fact that the prospects brighten considerably soon after the new moon on the 25th. A project that you got excited about a couple of month and then had to shelve will come back into play with some renewed vitality and enthusiasm.

It is not until Venus shifts into a congenial area of your solar chart that amorous experience is likely to gather momentum. Don't get despondent if a romantic attachment hangs rather loosely and uncertainly during the first half of the month. This situation will take a turn for the better soon after the 19th when Venus begins to hold sway. Later in the month a long journey or vacation has a romantic flavour, so perhaps this will provide you with a key to your heart's desires and perhaps even indicates the possibility of a holiday romance.

 Take notice of warning signals around the 5th, when your energy level is liable to plummet. The heavy work pressures of recent weeks may take a toll at this time, so if you can see your way to taking time out, this would be an ideal therapy. Don't play the martyr and let other overload you with chores early month!

LUCKY DATES 6th, 10th, 14th, 27th.

At the start of the month Uranus in your own sign receives an unusual aspect from Saturn. The effects of this provide a keynote to the whole year, but it is at this time that events are likely to converge to create a feeling that you are being guided by destiny. The combination of these two important planets suggests a link between the old and the new, past and present. Some astrologers would read this as a 'karmic' pattern, which means that certain unfinished business from a previous life now needs attending to.

Whatever happens, an unusual twist of events could have a profound influence on your life and personality at this time. The key feature is Uranus, which inclines you to develop a style of life that is more in tune with the real you.

If you feel a certain lack of vitality and motivation during the first week of the month, be prepared to go along with this rather than force yourself to keep to a business as usual schedule. Even if you're feeling OK, the chances are that someone close to you will need your care and attention. Be prepared to play the ministering angel or Good Samaritan, and don't worry if certain practical chores need to be put in parenthesis for a day or two.

A feeling of euphoria continues to accompany amorous experience in the first half of August. Far-flung journeys continue to have a romantic aura and will be a pure delight, and it could be that you simply fall in love with the place at which you are staying. If a relationship does emerge via travel, there is much to suggest that this will develop into something more than a fleeting holiday romance.

A potentially tricky date is the 13th when you something quite trivial might spark of an epic confrontation between you and your partner. Feelings are liable to be sensitive, including your own, so don't let minor irritations get the better of you.

Although you are not the kind of person who prefers to be up front or over-competitive, you are nevertheless advised to exercise a certain diplomacy in dealing with other people throughout the month - and more particularly around the 13th! It could be that your actions are misinterpreted by someone and seen as threatening their self-esteem.

Alternatively, if someone seems aggressive and critical towards you, try not to take it too personally, for it is more likely that this person is simply feeling stressed out and you are the nearest target. Once Mercury enters your opposite sign late month, communications will become easier and existing differences of opinion will be easily ironed out. You might even find that expressing your heartfelt opinion will be less frightening than you thought it would be.

A long-range journey, either for business or pleasure, will contain an unexpected element of good fortune at the very end of the month. Horizons could suddenly broaden for you in more ways than one!

LUCKY DATES 11th, 12th, 19th, 30th.

Pluto turns direct in the topmost sector of your solar chart early in the month, signalling a phase of increasing empowerment and a rise in status. Events taking shape throughout the month will make you realise that certain activities central to your sense of purpose are undergoing an important transformation. The upshot of this will be to give you a feeling of increased self-confidence and inner security.

If you have felt pulled in two opposing directions over the past year, it is likely that your interests will become more focused, thanks to the influence of helpful persons you encounter during these weeks. The lunar eclipse in your sign on the 7th suggests that you are breaking away from certain restriction as gaining a sense of increased freedom.

Venus takes the place of fiery Mars in your opposite sign on the 6th, bringing a feeling of peace and reconciliation where there may have been ructions lately. You'll get the feeling that you are now emerging from a rather sensitive transition in your emotional life and finding a new level of intimacy and rapport with the one you love.

This promises to be a special month for romantic encounters and amorous interludes, with a bumper crop of engagements and weddings indicated during the second and third weeks. After a lengthy phase of searching and broken promises single Pisceans are now on the way to finding something truly fulfilling. You'll also be able to share in a creative or artistic venture with your loved one as music, art and even cooking will appeal this month.

The Mercury-Uranus opposition early in the month warns you to steer away from controversial issues and areas that might be politically sensitive. The presence of Uranus in your sign inclines you to take radical views in regard to wider social and world issues. But what you have to realise is that not everyone has your insight and imagination in these matters.

Information that comes to light around the 9th may reveal to you that someone has not been completely straightforward with you. If you feel that a younger person is being secretive and cagey, this would be the time to lend a sympathetic ear and offer guidance. Although it might not feel like it, your thoughts and ideas will be taken to heart.

An urgent matter calls for immediate attention around mid month when you or your partner will need to make a firm decision concerning a financial or business matter. This may entail quick re-alignment of a current project, but if you play your cards right and don't waste time dithering, there could be a chance to boost your income and carry through a one-off commercial transaction with great success.

Be prepared to trust your hunches and intuitions around the 23rd, and keep your ear to the ground if you are looking for ways to expand your field of activity. Something taking shape in the background could ultimately benefit you financially, but you'll need to keep your wits about you if you're not to miss an opportunity.

LUCKY DATES 7th, 15th, 23rd, 27th.

Your ruling planet, Neptune, receives an energisng aspect from Mars early in the month, enabling you to draw upon a source of inner strength and bring your ideals closer to reality. The combination of these two planets conjures up the picture of a spiritual warrior, someone who through sheer will power is able to bring about creative transformation both within and without.

This may sound a bit high-flown to some, but what it means is that you have it in your power to bring about desirable changes by breaking free of old habits and breaking through to a new level of creativity. So, if you wish to change your life, give yourself more room to manoeuvre and make optimum use of your special abilities, now is the time to take action!

 All efforts to widen your mental horizons and improve your technical skills are given added momentum throughout the month. It is a fine time for embarking on a course of study and thinking seriously about improving your credentials and qualifications. Ideas and information you chance upon around the 10th could make a profound difference to your aims and aspirations, and for many Pisceans this could be a time when your life-path gains a clearer sense of direction. You'll suddenly remember what it is that you love doing and will gain a new found sense of direction and optimism.

Travel and long-range contacts are a key feature in your scheme of things during the latter half of the month. The astrological pattern has the aura of a voyage of discovery, so maybe you will learn something of great value through someone you meet at your destination - or perhaps a contact made via the Internet. Generally speaking this is a time when your learning curve takes a sharp upswing!

 Until the third week you are advised to keep a fairly tight rein on your budget and be prepared for added expenses due to unforeseen circumstances. The underlying trend is decidedly progressive, but it would be in your best interest to take the long view in regard to finance rather than aiming for a quick profit. A little patience and careful planning will certainly pay off this month.

Favourable aspects on the 4th, 10th, 12th and 22nd encourage you to make sound investments and seek advice on insurance, pensions, loans and mortgages. It could be that a fairly long standing problem involving jointly held resources will finally get sorted out, opening up fresh possibilities for improving your financial status over the next few months.

 An invigorating trend ensures that you have the stamina to cope the extra demands that you may need to deal with throughout the month. The only exception to this rule is around mid month, when you may find yourself feeling over-anxious about keeping up with the pace of things. In view of this hazard, make a conscious effort to give yourself a breathing space, otherwise you may fall into a state of total exhaustion. Make sure you have a proper think as to whatever it is that's stressing you out is really worth all the mental anguish.

LUCKY DATES 4th, 10th, 14th, 29th.

It would not be at all surprising if you felt an intense desire to escape from usual routines and familiar scenery in November. The need to broaden your experience, to seek new fields of knowledge and self-expression, is stronger than ever. Whether your aim is to take off on an epic world tour or to explore the higher reaches of the mind, the prevailing cosmic pattern lends you tremendous support and inspiration.

If this seems an unrealistic option for you in your present circumstances, it would certainly not be out of the question to think more seriously about taking a special vacation or even a spiritual retreat in the near future. If you feel you have missed out on something essential and have sacrificed part of yourself for the sake of mundane aims and ambitions, now is the time to set the balance straight.

 Distant horizons beckon very strongly during the first half of the month. This is excellent if you have planned a special journey for these weeks, for you can be sure that everything will meet your expectations whether your journey is for business or purely for the fun of it. If you are planning a journey for the future, this is an excellent time to get things finalised.

At a more mundane level, you are advised not to overlook the small print if you are negotiation or signing a contract or legal agreement. If in doubt, seek specialist advice. Better still, wait until after the 18th if you need to cut through red tape or get a definite decision on an important matter.

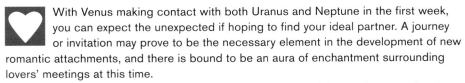 With Venus making contact with both Uranus and Neptune in the first week, you can expect the unexpected if hoping to find your ideal partner. A journey or invitation may prove to be the necessary element in the development of new romantic attachments, and there is bound to be an aura of enchantment surrounding lovers' meetings at this time.

Whatever happens, there will be something that has special appeal to your deeply romantic and idealistic soul. Even if you discover later that you were seeing things through rose-tinted spectacles (always a possibility with Neptune), the experience will enrich you and make you appreciate the true power of love. Music, film and fiction will also appeal to your imagination this month and your artistic sensibilities will be finely tuned. If you've been thinking about taking up a craft, this is a good month to get stuck in.

 The very positive planetary configuration ensures a feeling of well being both physically and psychologically. However, if you feel you could benefit through certain dietary measures or therapies, now is the time to explore the possibilities and take more seriously the need for personal and spiritual enhancement.

For those who are involved in the healing arts and wish to develop their special skills, this is a prime month for engaging in further studies or seeking out a genuine teacher to put you on the right path.

LUCKY DATES 3rd, 10th, 20th, 29th.

The year ends on a high note, with an unusual planetary grouping in the topmost sector of your solar chart. As Jupiter has recently moved into this area, you are likely to experience an unusual run of success and advancement between now and about the same time next year. And it is not only material aims and interests that will benefit under the sway of this fortunate planet. More importantly you own attitude to life will be marked by a very positive and optimistic quality, and this in itself will carry you far.

Events taking shape around December 11th are likely to give a tremendous boost to an ongoing project. The best case scenario is that you will realise an ambition or at least receive an offer that puts you on the road to success. Whatever you are aiming to achieve, the prospect looks good, so don't be afraid to aim high!

 A boost to your fortunes and your status is forecast as the festive season approaches. There will be increased scope and incentive to enlarge your earning powers, for you now have it in your power to create your own opportunities and write your own ticket. Opportunities for advancement are likely to arise, so if you are hoping for a promotion or wish to upgrade your career prospects, be ready to take positive action around during the second week.

 Although matters of a very practical nature are likely to occupy a large slice of your time and attention, this does not mean that the more personal and intimate affairs are reduced to a side-show. Once Venus moves into a very friendly area of your solar chart on the 11th an intriguing turn of events will put you in a mood of pleasant anticipation.

Someone with whom you have long hoped to form a more familiar acquaintance will gravitate into a closer orbit, perhaps with surprising and heart-warming results. Venus highlights your cherished hopes and wishes, so it would not be totally beyond the realms of possibility that you happen to meet a very special and kindred spirit around this time. You'll certainly prove more attractive to the opposite sex than usual, so make the most of this particularly romantic time!

A journey early in the month will be more a duty than a pleasure, and though you may feel that you are wasting your time or being led on a wild goose chase, you may learn something that proves invaluable. An elderly person may give you some very wise and timely advice that prevents you having to learn from your own mistakes.

A significant link between Mars and your ruling planet on the very last day of the year is a good omen for what could turn out to be a highly successful chapter in your life. At the same time a favourable aspect between the Moon and Venus give a friendly atmosphere and points to a phase of increasing emotional and material contentment as you launch out into the New Year.

LUCKY DATES 1st, 10th, 18th, 26th, 31st.

prediction phone line

Astro-LIVElink

If you need guidance in your relationships, direction in your career or advice on money matters, get a live personal reading on your unique birthchart by one the Astrological Association of Great Britain's approved Astro-LIVElink astrologers.

For a one-to-one astrology reading with a professional astrologer call 0906 1111 346. Make sure you have your date, time (if you know it) and place of birth ready for the astrologer to examine your chart. By examining the current planetary line-up and looking at themes in your personal birth horoscope you will receive astrologically-customised information and advice on any matter.

call our astro-LIVElink on
0906 1111 346

Our live astrology line is open from 8am-midnight.
Calls cost £1.50 per minute with a maximum length of 20 minutes
Callers have to be 18 or over.
Calls are for guidance only

The tarot year ahead: 2006

By drawing three cards for each month of the coming year, I have taken 12 snapshots of the possible trends of 2006. More cards appear from the suit of Wands than the other suits of the Minor Arcana, suggesting that it will be a year of great energy and power. Enjoy it!

by Xanna Eve Chown

January 2006

Knight of Cups
The Sun
Five of Wands

At the start of the year, as resolutions are made - and broken – the **Knight of Cups** asks what it is that attracts us to certain things and not others. Are we guilty of accepting things on face value? Do we dismiss things out of hand without even trying them first? This Knight is sometimes described as 'the essence of water behaving as fire' – for example a fast-flowing river. The appearance of this card in January's draw suggests that 2006 will start with a rush!

Emotions take precedence over considered actions. An unlikely person assumes centre stage this month and wins people's hearts. The Knight causing a stir is an eager young man, intense and emotional. **The Sun** card reversed can suggest nostalgia, looking back to an idealised time when the world seemed less complicated: perhaps a longing for more traditional values. There may be a return to a 1950s style mood, with a harking back to the values of that more simple - if repressed - era. This message could be key to the Knight's success.

The **Five of Wands** suggests that this is a time when teamwork is needed. However, it is reversed to show that quarrelling and in-fighting are more likely to occur. This card may be a warning that someone who seems to be acting in the public interest is more interested in the pursuit of their own fame and fortune. However, this person's claims will be challenged by those who can see through it all.

February 2006

The Fool
Seven of Wands
Two of Cups

Don't believe everything you read in the gossip columns this month! **The Fool** is a card that shows a heady combination

of fearlessness, imagination, and open-mindedness. Someone in the public eye may be throwing caution to the wind in February, displaying an adventurous spirit that is likely to win them equal admiration and disapproval. **The Fool** is not the most trustworthy of people. He displays a nonchalant attitude towards being on the threshold of losing or gaining everything. It is easy to feel envious of the carefree way in which others seem to be able to live their lives, but things are not always so straight-forward. The **Two of Cups** suggests that this display may be connected with a high-profile relationship, possibly even a marriage. The union will bring a lot of happiness to the people involved, and create much interest for those not involved. However, people are likely to question whether or not this connection is the deep and harmonious one presented. Gossip will be that it is a marriage of convenience. The **Seven of Wands** reflects the struggle that the couple have been through to reach the place they are now. Great obstacles have been met with surprising amounts of determination and inner strength behind the scenes.

March 2006

Five of Swords ®
Hanged Man
Judgement

Spring is in the air, and a general change in people's point of view is happening this month. **The Hanged Man** is all about pausing to reflect on things and seeing them from a fresh angle – upside down if needs be! This is a stepping stone towards greater enlightenment, as people adjust to new ideas. The draw suggests that this month will see a move towards a long-awaited balance of karma, one that is long overdue. **Judgement** is a card of transformation, noted for the strength of the changes it heralds. The trick to coping with these kinds of changes is to move with them, rather than resisting. It is a time to draw on the energies present, rather than trying to fight them off. The card appears to show that a swift and conclusive decision is going to be made. This will be in the political arena, with an emphasis on legal proceedings. The reversed **Five of Swords** suggests that an idea or plan will be abandoned as someone backs down to maintain the equilibrium. This is a good thing, as the gain involved would have been dishonourable, and friendships are salvaged. A tricky situation is narrowly avoided.

April 2006

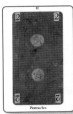

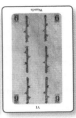

Two of Pentacles
Wheel of Fortune
Six of Wands ®

Like many of the cards in the Tarot deck, the **Two of Pentacles** is a card of change. But here, it signifies imbalance and disharmony, possibly as a result of the upheaval and transformation of the previous month. After big steps have been taken, the smaller ones that follow can seem to be insignificant and tiny in comparison. At worst, it can feel like two backward steps are being made for every one taken forward. Projects and priorities seem to be drifting, and actions give negligible results. This is all the more apparent in April as things are directly under scrutiny from a media that wants instant results. The **Six of Wands** backs this up, suggesting frustration over delays. It is reversed to show that someone's overconfidence may lead to a false sense of pride in their achievements. However, the **Wheel of Fortune** sheds light on events. Karma is being played out on a grand scale here. It is in an upright position, suggesting that good fortune is on its way. Events are just a link in a chain that is leading to a better place.

May 2006

The Tower ®
Ten of Pentacles
The Devil

The Tower makes its first appearance in the month of May. It is reversed, which suggests that unexpected upheavals will lead to positive changes. This card might represent a shock divorce or separation for someone very much in the public eye. This news is sudden, like the bolt of lightning on the card, and the **Ten of Pentacles**

suggests that gambling or family problems may be involved in the case. This card also raises issues about inheritances. It could refer to a lost inheritance or a will playing an important role in the proceedings. **The Devil** card also hints at the material nature of events. The people involved may have too much of a taste for money, power, or luxury, which has tipped the balance over into scandal. Important political decisions made at this time demand co-operation from all parties, which may not be forthcoming. A challenge to the government from members inside the party is possible. Any sudden changes are sure to make way for a smoother, more co-operative few months. Financial decisions come under the auspices of the **Ten of Pentacles**, and investments by major companies may come under scrutiny.

June 2006

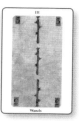

The Wheel of Fortune ®
Five of Wands
Three of Wands

The **Wheel of Fortune** that appeared in April is now reversed for June. This could show an unexpected turn of bad luck, possibly in the same area that was under discussion two months ago. Two cards from the suit of Wands show that there is a lot of buzz around this month. Wands are governed by the element of fire, and reflect energy and power. The preponderance of Wands over these 12 months suggests a desire to get things done and a strong sense of vitality.

Fire is creative and life-giving, but fiery

energy can be destructive if not channelled correctly. The **Three of Wands** describes someone with a strong character taking command of the situation, isolating themselves by taking on responsibility, possibly leading to a fall from power. Most leaders know that mutinies are fostered when restrictive controls are applied by the leader in question. This could well be the case here.

The **Five of Wands** appeared first in January. It reappears here to suggest competition, struggle and a lack of agreement. Too many people with ideas are trying to get heard (and not able to hear each other above the noise they are creating.) A stressful situation is suggested, but one that brings out the best in its participants. The chances are looking good for a great sporting victory this month in a hotly contested race or match.

July 2006

 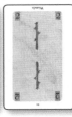 

Eight of Swords ®
Two of Wands ®
Hanged Man

As the summer continues, the reversed **Eight of Swords** shows someone in a position of power learning a valuable lesson from the consequences of previous decisions. Frustration is often a key word for this card, which in many decks depicts someone blindfolded and surrounded by swords. Swords in the Minor Arcana often represent conflict, but also symbolise the use of the intellect in dealing with matters.

The suit of Swords is associated with the element of air. The **Two of Wands** is also reversed for this month, demonstrating the erosion of power and influence for someone who has been discovered making bad decisions. Possibly, they have been caught off-guard, and are regarded as lying to the public. This is an impossible position to be in with the glare of the media turned on them. This card suggests irresponsible leadership. The **Hanged Man** appears here for the second time, to suggest situations being turned on their heads again. Facts come to light that would have been unthinkable before now. The key to surviving these investigations for those involved is not to struggle against events.

August 2006

King of Wands
Seven of Pentacles
Queen of Cups ®

'Fire behaving as air' is the essence of the **King of Wands**. Lightning is often used as a good example of this. Someone keen to present themselves as a great and daring leader will be in the spotlight this month. This person will be someone who can inspire others, with a magnetic personality and an authoritative air.

Difficult financial decisions are suggested at this time, however, and industrial disputes and strikes can be linked to the **Seven of Pentacles**, which shows a pause in work as people evaluate their future options. In some decks this card shows a farmer who is about to harvest his crop, but is gazing into the distance, wondering why he doesn't have as much to show for his hard work as he thought he would have when he began! However, hard work always pays off in the long run, and sometimes in unexpected ways. The **Queen of Cups** is reversed here to show that spiritual matters come to a head – and make the headlines. The Church may show itself unduly susceptible to outside influences, backing up the opinions that have been expressed in the news.

September 2006

King of Pentacles ®
The Moon ®
Knight of Pentacles ®

Three reversed cards suggest that this may be a frustrating month for many people. This King shows the prominence of a businessman with a role to play in current affairs. This person is seen to be exploiting a situation for his own personal gain, without interest in new ideas, so long as he gets the right results. The **Knight of Pentacles** also appears here, backing up the King. This is someone who is on his side, but maybe less cautious in his approach. The suit of Pentacles is connected with money and financial dealings and is associated with the element earth. Both people concerned are likely to be very 'down to earth' in their dealings. **The Moon** card also shows up here, reversed, which hints that some darker spiritual matters are coming to light. **The Moon** often deals with illusions and secrets. At this time, a major story will

hit the headlines, one that has been kept hidden for a while, and may be concerned with a high profile murder.

October 2006

Hanged Man
The Sun
Tower

All three of the cards for October have appeared in draws for previous months. This month is a time of reflection. People mull over what has been going on, taking stock as the **Hanged Man** describes another pause. The **Hanged Man** appears more times than any other card in this yearly reading. The card is associated with Neptune, a watery, fluid planet connected with emotion, intuition and psychic power. It can also speak of sacrifices. It can be hard for people to accept another world-view, especially if it is the direct opposite of their own. Looking at things from a different angle can be one of the hardest things to do – as proved by the 18th Century Tarotist Antoine Court de Gebelin. He was so entrenched in his own world-view that he decided the upside-down man on the card was a printer's error, and reversed it, renaming the card Prudence! **The Sun** card also reappears this month, but it is not reversed as it was in January. Things have moved on in the last few months. However, the reappearance of the **Tower** suggests a sudden shocking piece of news that will take over the papers, causing a great deal of stress and possible heartbreak.

November 2006

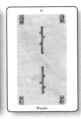

Nine of Cups
The Empress
Two of Wands

Another love affair hits the headlines in November, with the **Nine of Cups**. A famous woman will reveal that she is pregnant, or maybe even have a much-talked about child this month. **The Empress** is a card of fertility and creativity and the event will be a joyful one. This card, numbered three in the Major Arcana, is ruled by Venus the goddess of love. Many decks show a woman wearing loose robes that are gathered to suggest a pregnancy. She is usually shown out of doors, surrounded by ears of corn to represent the fertility of the Earth.

The **Two of Wands** suggests a lot of energy flowing around someone this month. Here, this card suggests that he or she will be an influential person with a lot to say and many ideas. It is also a card of future ideas and planning, of travel and communication. All this suggests that the person who is in the headlines is connected to these areas through their work.

December 2006

The Chariot
The Star
Seven of Pentacles

The end of the year promises an important decision that is central to people's lives. **The Chariot** card, which often refers to difficult choices that must be made, signifies advancements being made through bold actions. Opposing forces must be mastered, and the influence of this card suggests progress being made by the meeting of forces that have previously seemed irreconcilable.

The Star appears too, shining a ray of hope for the coming year. This is a good card to end the year, as it suggests that there is still hope for a postive outcome to most problems experienced throughout the year. Ruled by Aquarius, the water carrier, she promises the calm after the storm, the quiet settling down and the promise of a time of stability. Aquarius is the sign that is said to dream of a Utopian society where there is no inequality. It is a card that looks to the future with hope.

However, the **Seven of Pentacles** suggests that many people do not think a situation has gone far enough, and

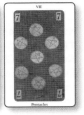

that there is need for more action. While **the Star** has indicated a positive turn of events, this card reminds us not to count our chickens before they hatch. The card creates another pause at the end of this year, but it also asks for patience and perseverance – there is still a way to go before **the Star**'s hope is fully realised.

The tarot deck we use for all our readings is *The Destiny Tarot Book & Card Pack* **by Jane Struthers (Collins & Brown, £14.99). It is available from all good bookshops.**

180 annual 2006 • www.predictionmagazine.co.uk

prediction

UK's original mind, body, spirit magazine £2.95

Reincarnation
amazing true life stories

Get
**star
appeal**
tips to boost
your confidence

**Haunted
Venice**

prediction
UK's first mind, body, spirit magazine
only £2.95
september 2005

THIS MONTH Boost your psychic energy • Tarot • Dreams • Chinese signs

**Become
lucky**
follow our weekly plan

EXCLUSIVE
'There will be a

THIS MONTH beat stress • tarot • dreams • Chinese signs

prediction
UK's first mind, body, spirit magazine
only £2.95
october 2005

**'Stonehenge
cured my depression'**
how the stones can heal you

WIN!
a psychic
reading

**Tried and tested
reflexology**

York: the world's
most haunted city

FREE INSIDE!
accredited
astrology
course

TRO MONTH **AHEAD**
ORK AND HOME

OCTOBER'S ESSENTIAL HOROSCOPES
YOUR MONTH AHEAD REVEALED

**Find ULTIMATE
HAPPINESS**
rune magic for love and money

Prediction, the UK's original mind, body, spirit
magazine, has a monthly in-depth
18-page astrology section, regular Tarot, psychic
and dreams columns plus the most amazing fea-
tures covering everything from fairies to feng shui.

If you want to have a window into the future as
well as learning about your mind, body and spirit,
don't miss out on this great offer!

Direct Debit Guarantee This guarantee is offered by all Banks and Building Societies that
take part in the Direct Debit Scheme. The efficiency and security of the Scheme is monitored
by your own Bank or Building Society. If the amounts to be paid or the payment dates change
IPC Media Ltd. Will notify you at least ten days in advance of your account being debited or as
otherwise agreed. If an error is made by IPC Media Ltd. Or your bank or Building Society you are
guaranteed a full and immediate refund from your branch of the amount paid. You can cancel a
Direct Debit at any time by writing to your bank or Building Society. Please also send a copy of
the letter to us. Direct Debits can only be paid through a Bank or Building Society. Your Direct
Debit price will stay the same for 1 year from start date.

Chinese *love* Signs

Was your romance written in the stars? Discover how Chinese astrology can help you along the path to true love

By Charles Graham

*i*s your boyfriend a Snake? Is your girlfriend a Dragon? Each of the 12 Chinese zodiac signs is symbolised by an animal and embodies that creature's characteristics. In the West we find that some of these choices sound a little insulting. The Rat, for example, is commonly thought of in the West as a dirty scavenger, and the pig as slovenly and greedy. In Eastern cultures, however, both animals are greatly respected: The Rat for its ability to acquire valuables and the Pig for its intelligence and tenacity.

Right or just right now?

Is compatibility related to lasting love? Love can be ecstatic or a curse depending on how the people involved get along with each other; not all romantic relationships remain sweet forever. Something you initially found attractive about your partner might be the very thing that drives you mad in future. But Chinese astrology can help you find a truly compatible mate. Discover your own and your partner's Chinese sign from the table below, then locate the signs in the following pages to discover your perfect match.

what's your animal love sign?

Locate your year of birth to discover your Chinese animal sign.
Were you born in January or February? The Chinese signs are based on the movements of the Moon, and change every year in either January or February. To check your sign visit:www.chinese.astrology.com
Born before 1940? The signs repeat every 12 years so just add 12 to your birth year, e.g. if born in 1932: 1932 + 12 = 1944 (Monkey).

1940	Dragon	1950	Tiger	1960	Rat	1970	Dog	1980	Monkey
1941	Snake	1951	Rabbit	1961	Ox	1971	Pig	1981	Rooster
1942	Horse	1952	Dragon	1962	Tiger	1972	Rat	1982	Dog
1943	Goat	1953	Snake	1963	Rabbit	1973	Ox	1983	Pig
1944	Monkey	1954	Horse	1964	Dragon	1974	Tiger	1984	Rat
1945	Rooster	1955	Goat	1965	Snake	1975	Rabbit	1985	Ox
1946	Dog	1956	Monkey	1966	Horse	1976	Dragon	1986	Tiger
1947	Pig	1957	Rooster	1967	Goat	1977	Snake	1987	Rabbit
1948	Rat	1958	Dog	1968	Monkey	1978	Horse	1988	Dragon
1949	Ox	1959	Pig	1969	Rooster	1979	Goat	1989	Snake

Rats are energetic, meticulous, persistent and generous. You need a patient but clever partner that can help you relax and curb your tendency to be so harsh on yourself.

Rat

Best love matches
Rat: this is an extremely lively and competitive relationship where the pair of you will support each other's ambitions and dreams.
Dragon: together your courage and determination make for an unbeatable team. You give each other enough freedom to allow the partnership to grow and have enormous respect for each other.
Monkey: this is a lovely combination of charm and quick wits. The two of you are sociable and friendly and enjoy each other's quirks. You're proud of your modern, albeit slightly eccentric, partnership.

Ox are tenacious, hard-working, stubborn and loyal. You need a reliable partner with whom you can trust and build a rock steady partnership.

Best love matches
Rooster: you're both conscientious and work very hard for what you believe in. You both love analysing and organising and therefore enjoy discussing the psychology of your relationship.
Rabbit: sensitive Rabbits tune into your moods easily and know how to soothe your nerves. You love the Rabbit's sympathetic nature.
Snake: the pair of you share strong family values and your idea of what makes a happy home is very similar. This is a trustworthy, stable and happy combination.

Ox

If you're a tempestuous Tiger, passion and courage are more important to you than stability and routine. You need someone to fire your imagination and inspire your emotions!

Best love matches
Horse: this is an honest, if volatile relationship. You appreciate and defend each other's views and respect that you both need space too.
Dog: Dogs are happy to live a little in the Tiger's shadow but Tigers will want to fight for the Dog's causes and bring them out of their shell.
Dragon: Dragons bring wisdom to the Tiger, who will not usually listen to anyone, but will always take the Dragon's advice. Mutual admiration and attraction keep you together.

Tiger

You're a peace-loving, kind and diplomatic soul. Your home and family are of utmost importance. Rabbits need a warm, gentle and affectionate partner.

Rabbit

Best love matches
Dog: The Dog and the Rabbit form a lasting and emotionally fulfilling romantic partnership. This couple cheer up each other up and are sensitive enough to understand each other's erratic moods.
Dragon: On the surface, this relationship may seem challenging: the Dragon is dynamic while the Rabbit conservative. But the Rabbit can teach the Dragon diplomacy and the Dragon will keep the Rabbit from getting into a rut.
Pig: This is an auspicious, peaceful match. The Pig loves the Rabbit for being so patient and the Rabbit feels tranquil and less nervous around the Pig.

As a dragon you're a vital and independent person and in a romantic partner you look for someone who is self-sufficient and larger than life.

Best love matches
Monkey: these two love performing and admire each other's creative and artistic flair. This partnership promises much adventure and challenges to enjoy conquering together.
Rat: both signs are enterprising and ambitious. Dragons learn from the Rat's flair for organisation and the Dragon manages to persuade the Rat to be more focused.
Rooster: both signs are strong-willed, ambitious and clever and there will be plenty of excitement and attraction in this electric mix of personalities.

Dragon

Snake
Snakes are wise, elegant, compassionate and philosophical. Your emotions run deep and you seek a partner that can tolerate your extremes.

Best love matches
Rooster: you have similar tastes and are ambitious, methodical and demanding. Roosters enjoy the Snake's eye for detail.
Ox: this is a fairly balanced match. The Ox is stable and industrious while the Snake is ambitious and intelligent. This is a prosperous and satisfying partnership for both parties.
Snake: two snakes together create a very sensuous love match as both instinctively know what the other needs and wishes for. However, they should watch they don't get too stuck in their ways.

Horses are charming, entertaining, rebellious and sometimes tactless. If you are a Horse, you are attracted to jovial types that don't take life too seriously, but you do need someone to bring you back to Earth sometimes.

Horse
Best love matches
Tiger: initially this could be a rocky ride but eventually it can lead to an enduring partnership. There is excitement and enthusiasm here. Both are temperamental but are on the same wavelength.
Goat: The Horse is supportive and encourages the Goat while the Goat is able to provide the Horse with sensible advice.
Dog: the Horse is impressed with Dog's ability to see life in a nutshell while the Dog happily lets the more aggressive Horse take the lead.

Goat
As a Goat you'll be very sensitive to your immediate environment. You need someone imaginative, understanding and not afraid to express their feelings.

Best love matches
Rabbit: both characters are gentle and caring, the Goat can learn to be less passive and more open from the Rabbit and the Rabbit will learn the true meaning of compassion from the Goat.
Horse: the Horse is supportive and encourages the Goat to be more adventurous. The Goat has a positive, steadying influence on the Horse.
Pig: Pigs and Goats are both loyal and they need stability in their relationships. They're psychically tuned in to each other's needs and feel compelled to stand up for one another's causes.

Monkeys are clever, flexible and spontaneous. If you're a Monkey, you need someone to bounce your many ideas and plans against.

Monkey

Best love matches

Dragon: when the Dragon and the Monkey join forces sparks fly and the energy level is high. These two occasionally rub each other up the wrong way but this usually just increases the attraction.
Rat: Rats know how to keep restless Monkeys amused and entertained and the Monkey is drawn to the Rat's sense of humour.
Monkey: no problem is too great for the Monkey/Monkey couple and they never tire of each other's behaviour. If this pair can learn to deal with jealousy, they usually last a lifetime.

Rooster

Roosters are very observant, critical creatures. If you're a Rooster you're efficient, good with detail and a born organiser. However, you also have a flamboyant side and like a stylish partner with similar taste to your own.

Best love matches

Snake: both are methodical, ambitious and clever. It takes a while for you to 'heat up' emotionally, but once you do, your feelings remain strong and constant.
Ox: the Rooster's perfectionism complements the ambitious but down-to-earth Ox. Both are conservative, faithful and honest.
Dragon: the analytical Rooster is drawn to the bold, bright Dragon personality and together they're an intellectual force to be reckoned with.

If you're a Dog, you're courageous, noble, loyal and discreet. You're not naturally optimistic so you appreciate a partner that will bolster your confidence and believe in you.

Dog

Best love matches

Rabbit: this can be a long-lasting, comfortable, if a little lacklustre combination. There's a high level of trust and loyalty in this pairing.
Tiger: the Dog is able to make the Tiger's crazy dreams come true. Both are rebellious but the Tiger's optimism will bring out the Dog's more experimental ideas.
Horse: Horse people admire Dog's ideas and bring the Dog their enthusiasm and optimistic outlook on life. The Dog encourages the Horse to be more realistic and practical.

Pig

Pigs are sincere, indulgent, loving and sensual. If you're a Pig you want a partner that's peaceful, devoted and able to enjoy all the good things in life with you.

Best love matches

Rabbit: this partnership is enriching and loving. Both signs are generous and wish to pamper each other. There's a tendency towards laziness but generally there's a very contented lifestyle indicated by this partnership.
Goat: the Pig person is sturdy and emotionally strong, able to protect and nurture the Goat person, who needs to be with a strong person.
Rooster: there will be areas of disagreement between this couple but there's also a willingness to sort out any differences. This is a very capable, honest relationship that's worth the occasional argument.

World's *weekly* predictions

Our astrologer Peter West predicts what the main astrological trends for all of us will be in 2006. Take advantage of the week at a glance format to see how your year will shape up

by Peter West

Jan 1 - 8

A sense of eager anticipation and then an anti-climax - nothing quite seems to fit. Glamour and crime may be in the news for the first few days. Gamblers are likely to take huge risks although failure means very heavy losses. Education, travel and special merit for those involved. Personal ability may be outweighed by appearance.

Jan 9 - 15

Ideas may be good but can they be translated into workable projects? Military and police work could be in the news. Health and physical fitness regimes may be prominent - a tad early for most perhaps. "Might does not make right" so those with an inflated sense of self-importance may well come unstuck.

Jan 16 - 22

What you see is not what you are likely to get! Intrigues and behind the scenes planning and activities affect health and safety. Insurances, taxes and corporate monies may be under investigation. Hold back from planning new ventures in savings or trying to get a mortgage organised. Not a good time to ask the boss for a raise.

Jan 23 - 29

Quite a lot of dark emotional overtones with bickering and disagreements between lovers and partners at most levels. Attitudes to young folk likely to be restrictive and that can lead to problems between parents and siblings. Beware potential incidents involving the skin and bones or use the time to have a regular dental check-up.

Jan 30 - Feb 5

Go with your instincts but don't daydream too much. It could be a fascinating short period for those with an artistic streak but there will be extremes of temperament as well as some backbiting that might spoil it for a few. Travel problems likely. If you don't feel well, forget the aspirin - see a doctor.

Feb 6 - 12

If at first you don't succeed - try again! The odds are in your favour to achieve aims or even assume a leadership role in one of your undertakings. Make sure you follow the rules, obey instructions and read the small print. A very healthy attitude to love, sex and romance is in the air.

Feb 13 - 19

One of those weeks! Not everything will go to plan but even if things do go awry you might just as easily benefit because of the way matters do turn out. Concentrate on one issue at a time but be prepared for change - even total disruption in some instances. Aim high but hang loose.

Feb 20 - 26

Travel for both business and pleasure is highlighted along with starting new projects with more than a fair chance of success. Educational, social and show business pursuits all benefit along with an excellent background that favours practical and intellectual work. For some, there may be a chance of wedding bells for later.

Feb 27 - Mar 5

Quite promising for freedom of expression and for dealing with people from the scientific and humanitarian fields. However, Mercury goes Stationary Direct on the 2nd. This marks a time for pausing plans or halting some activities altogether. People drag their feet because they cannot help or simply because they do not want to become involved. Remember that this is their right and is not maliciousness on their part.

Mar 6 - 12

A favoured few can expect a jump from relative obscurity to some fame, either locally or nationally in a few cases so they should seize opportunity and benefit as it arises. Later, there may be danger through travel, machinery or conflict of some kind. People may become increasingly selfish or just plain self-centred.

Mar 13 - 19

All that glisters is not gold. Check details carefully, don't accept too much at face value. Somehow things might not be quite as they seem. It will be easy to be talked into, or become self-deluded into activities that just won't work. Avoid people who say one thing but who may mean something else.

Mar 20 - 26

Not an auspicious start especially if dealing with the older generation but by sticking to the rules you should put up a good fight for what you want. A partner from a previous relationship may re-surface but dreams taken into reality might create more problems than you appreciate. From the 25th communications become much easier.

Mar 27 - Apr 2

This eclipse signifies many changes, some brought about by your own efforts while others will be forced upon you by other people or events that occur. Those who have cried off marriage may do an about turn. People in high places can fall from power. Unusual or unnecessary violence may be in the news.

Apr 3 - 9

Sportsmen and women will come into prominence and there may be great strides forward made in this or the entertainment worlds generally. Money should become more readily available and what might have been seemed to be a heavy load could lift suddenly. Watch out for those who would work secretly against you.

Apr 10 - 16

A short period when no one wants to trust anyone else or even themselves in some circumstances. People act out of character. The strong seem to lose their forcefulness while weaker folk gain an inner strength to get their own way. Not a good time to gamble or to give the impression of prudishness.

Apr 17 - 23

Social life gets a boost and there will be a general upswing with new friendships, love and meaningful relationships happening almost everywhere. The acting profession may see the rise of a new star - an understudy who gets the chance to shine perhaps? The computer world may also receive a boost with new technology.

Apr 24 - 30

Try not to ignore the needs of young folk who approach you for advice and guidance. Curb your ambition a little and don't be too rigid in your approach. Possible emotional blackmail or a sudden break-up of relationships is also possible. The criminal element may be involved in financial coercion or underhand dealings.

May 1 - 7

Try not to over-play your hand or take too much for granted. You could so easily walk into a trap of your own making. Money luck for some, a chance of new friends and, possibly, a completely new interest may capture your imagination. Historians could also find this a rather fascinating time as well.

May 8 - 14

The electronics industry, computers, inventions and innovations within these parameters may be gripped by the announcement of new advances. Make a promise - then keep it! There may be some absentmindedness but do your homework if you are going to convince others of your abilities. Slap-dash preparation creates black marks when you least want them.

May 15 - 21

A case of "open mouth, place foot in" is likely. One of those times when little seems to go or wants to go right for anyone - almost anything from inefficiency to letting slip secrets. Changes may be about to take place. Money matters may need another look. If travelling, be ready for alternatives.

May 22 - 28

Love, sex and romance are high on the list. Much will go well but a few will have some extremely awkward moments - especially those who enjoy secret or illicit liaisons. Business wheeling and dealing will be much in evidence. Take-overs and mergers could threaten job stability. Keep your sights aimed high.

May 29 - Jun 4

Not the best of times to start a new job or apply for promotion; don't enter into any new written agreement and be reasonable when dealing with any partnership matter. You or someone around you may be too outspoken or impulsive and others will be offended.

Some may receive or make "the" proposal. A happy conclusion to a romance for some.

Jun 5 - 11

Events may overtake you and changes occur that did not see coming or you could not stop. It would be best to move along with the times and adjust as and when. Favourable for students and teachers to apply for positions of their choice. Travel for business.

Jun 12 - 18

Take the time to think before you take any action. Some may try to take advantage of your good nature or even try a "con" trick. It wouldn't hurt to harden-up your responses. Police and or other forms of keeping order may be in the news. An element of the free spirit could surface.

Jun 19 - 25

Reputations held for account do measure up and there may be red faces in some places. So, don't believe all you hear, read or see. Someone in a high military position could fall from grace. If you can't see your way clear don't move on - wait for better times. Not a good time to change jobs.

Jun 26 - Jul 2

Stay with what and whom you know. New ideas or changes implemented now may not work as originally conceived. People engaged in the building trade and design work should prosper. Partnerships created now have a good chance of succeeding. Politics and "spin" may not be all they seem. Somebody somewhere has to take the blame.

Jul 3 - 9

For a couple of days social life, hobbies and anything to with rest and relaxation may have to be put on hold. Self-employed people may feel vulnerable. Then, as things begin to lighten up somewhat there will be a lot of flirting which be fine as long as those involved don't take it too seriously.

Jul 10 - 16

A new association started now will not last for long for neither party will truly want it that way. This relationship is for the excitement of the present and has little future. Monetary matters look brighter than they have for some time. Nevertheless, don't fritter anything away and take care with new investments.

Jul 17 - 23

One way or the other your sixth sense is working well - perhaps too well at times. Make the most of it and use your hunches to advantage. You can look forward to a fair share of excitement but your emotional life could go up and down like a yo-yo. Relationships might break up permanently.

Jul 24 - 30

Good time to start a holiday and just mooch about under the sun - if you can find it. If this is so then pursue things different for a change. If not away, make the most of any opportunity to become involved with anything new and untried. New love affairs can start under these auspices.

Jul 31 - Aug 6

Changes can come about with a devastating swiftness and be totally unexpected. Money and health matters are the most likely issues to need special attention. Relationships might suffer for a while otherwise keep a check on everything else very carefully

indeed. If you can't deal with what is happening seek someone who can.

Aug 7 - 13

Legal affairs must be treated with respect. Athletics and most sporting arenas should do very well. The rebel streak or feelings of resentment could cause you to take impulsive actions possibly against the wrong people. Elsewhere, precipitate actions might lead to accidents which in extreme cases could lead to a period of hospitalisation.

Aug 14 - 20

Many will feel quite forceful and will want to strike out to better themselves. To impress the people who matter attention to detail will be important. This is not the time to produce sloppy workmanship. Ensure that what you do is one hundred percent. This is the only way to climb up the ladder.

Aug 21- 27

Some folk have all the luck and waltz in and out of love affairs without any harmful scarring. Well, this week, so can you. The only thing that will spoil it is to know (in advance now) that whatever begins it won't last long - but you won't forget it either whatever your personal status might be.

Aug 28 - Sept 3

The feel-good factor should be quite strong possibly enhanced by an improved emotional life or your social position. Career wise and quite out of the blue a chance may come to make a real difference for yourself - an opportunity that doesn't happen very often. Your choice is to decide what you really, really want! Once that's decided you'll find the rest comes very easily.

Sept 4 - 10

Medical practitioners could be over-worked and many silly accidents and incidents may happen all of which might have been easily avoided with just a little fore-thought. Elsewhere, the tax man is lurking just around the corner. On a more personal level close emotional partners could disagree over purely private issues.

Sep 11 - 17

People will employ deception and play tricks to get their own way. Secrets will out. There will be a few red faces as news of indiscretions, possible promiscuity and foolish antics come to light. View all get-rich-quick schemes with suspicion. If you don't like what you see then don't get involved.

Sept 18 - 24

This eclipse covers many possibilities. Some may move house, others could experience change in the working place. People may want to change their image or seek out new or different "alternative" health matters or other interests. An air of impracticality may be about. Check warranties still have life left for repairmen may be needed.

Sept 25 - Oct 1

Discretion is called for so keep a civil tongue in your head. If things are bad don't make them worse. If all is going well, don't crow. Relationship changes are possible. The temptation will be to hang on to what you have whereas the practical solution is to let all go and, eventually, start again.

Oct 2 - 8

Here is a chance to really shine by taking the lead or setting a good example with what you do. Your natural abilities will inspire others to observe and even follow. Your inner strengths will keep you going until what has to be done has been done or is well on the way.

Oct 9 - 15

Others may turn to you for help and, if so moved, you will expend a lot of energy to be a Good Samaritan. Listen to your sixth sense and back your hunches. This is a time to push ahead with your own ambitions. Don't step on any toes and this should be a rewarding time.

Oct 16 - 22

A constructive period that should encourage and educate both adults and young folk. This may be carried out in business through work orientated courses. Travel to learn, not to stay for any length of time, just for a day or so to complete the project(s). This should open up opportunities for further long-term study courses.

Oct 23 - 29

Take a break from work and concentrate on your social life but don't give up your job because of managerial attitudes. Outdoor pursuits, sport, gardening, or wild life activities help clear the mind and let you mull things over while you are away from the hustle and bustle of the workplace.

Oct 30 - Nov 5

People in authority or "officialdom" and red tape requirements could drive you up the wall. Try to contain your feelings and postpone issues if you can. A new sense of freedom of expression may occur. Some may find new areas of interest to capture their imagination.

A chance of extra cash is possible. This will be particularly welcome at this time.

Nov 6 - 12

Feelings and emotions rule. Short, but happy affairs may start and end. New interests take you into hitherto unknown areas. Some will thrive, others will hold back. This rather favours the creative soul more than the practical sort. Relax, experiment and give yourself a chance to learn something new - but terribly fascinating as well.

Nov 13 - 19

Take proper care of business, legal and financial matters. Young folk should take the opportunity to keep out of the way so that adults do what they must. Health and diet may be affected. Be sure you have the right remedies and do see the right people if you are feeling unwell.

Nov 20 - 26

Make the most of everything because really ambitious folk should attain that next important step. Socially good, health and general well-being are top-notch. There will be romantic opportunities but take care you do not become embroiled in an eternal triangle situation. They have a habit of becoming public knowledge at all the wrong times.

Nov 27 - Dec 3

Rather serious start to the week. Legal battles, military or police actions are likely and, perhaps, a danger of injury indoors or out. There could be a new "beauty" for the press to feature. The rest of the week will be favourable to those in the arts, cinema, photography and the entertainment world.

Dec 4 - 10

A pleasing if somewhat traditional atmosphere should be in the air. People tend to do things properly but should anyone step out of line they will be dealt with! An ideal period in which to renew old ties. People from abroad or news from overseas could help shape your first few months of 2007.

Dec 11 - 17

Good for business and most commercial organisations. A few may go over the top as they try to quell some of the younger element who will naturally want to ease back and enjoy the coming festivities. Creative ideas can be translated into good practical projects. More senior folk should appreciate that "might does not (always) make right".

Dec 18 - 24

Could be a rather more serious approach to the holiday with increased crime and/or violence toward people. There is a danger of incidents and or accidents that become blown up out of all proportion. News may come of changes that will be put into place as the New Year gets under way.

Dec 25 - 31

Could be a tendency to over-worry about things that might seem important now but probably won't be later. Society may be called upon to more than observe ecological matters. World wildlife sites could be under siege from developers and demonstrations staged against them. Many will be horrified at the suggestion that economics should govern what we do to the planet and conflict is definitely on the cards. Luckily, a positive emotional outlook will be in place as the year closes.